Lex Fullarton

Heat, Dust, and Taxes

A Story of Tax Schemes in Australia's Outback

Lex Fullarton

HEAT, DUST, AND TAXES

A Story of Tax Schemes in Australia's Outback

ibidem-Verlag
Stuttgart

Bibliografische Information der Deutschen Nationalbibliothek
Die Deutsche Nationalbibliothek verzeichnet diese Publikation in der Deutschen Nationalbibliografie; detaillierte bibliografische Daten sind im Internet über http://dnb.d-nb.de abrufbar.

Bibliographic information published by the Deutsche Nationalbibliothek
Die Deutsche Nationalbibliothek lists this publication in the Deutsche Nationalbibliografie; detailed bibliographic data are available in the Internet at http://dnb.d-nb.de.

Cover picture: Wikimedia Commons. Photo: Brian Voon Yee Yap, licensed under CC BY-SA 3.0 (https://creativecommons.org/licenses/by-sa/3.0/deed.en)

∞

Gedruckt auf alterungsbeständigem, säurefreien Papier
Printed on acid-free paper

ISBN-13: 978-3-8382-0705-6

Printed in Germany

ACKNOWLEDGEMENTS

One person has been my constant companion throughout decades of study and research. It has sometimes been fun and sometimes boring, but always challenging. She has never faulted in support of my ramblings on my quest to find the perfect taxation system—my wife Julie. She has been the wind beneath my wings for nearly forty years.

I have special thanks to Chris Evans for accepting the challenge to be my supervisor for the final stages of my quest, without him the end would not be possible. Chris has seen fit to include me in his unbelievable workload. I am humbled that he took the time to include me in his Herculean burden. Also to Dale Pinto, his co-supervisor, who has put up with me and my unusual circumstances and approach since the late 1990s.

To the staff of Curtin University in particular Doug Yorke. We started together many years ago when I was a first year student in 1974 and he a junior lecturer. Thanks also to the staff of Australian School of Business, School of Taxation and Business Law of the University of New South Wales who have supported me despite the tyranny of distance across Australia—from 'Sydney to the Bush'.

Finally to all those people who took part in the research—a very special thanks. Of course they cannot be named but they know who they are. I hope in some small way I have given them a voice which will be heard by higher authority. These interviews were not easy. At times they were emotionally challenging. I appreciate the honesty and sincerity of all those who took part in compiling this historic story.

TABLE OF CONTENTS

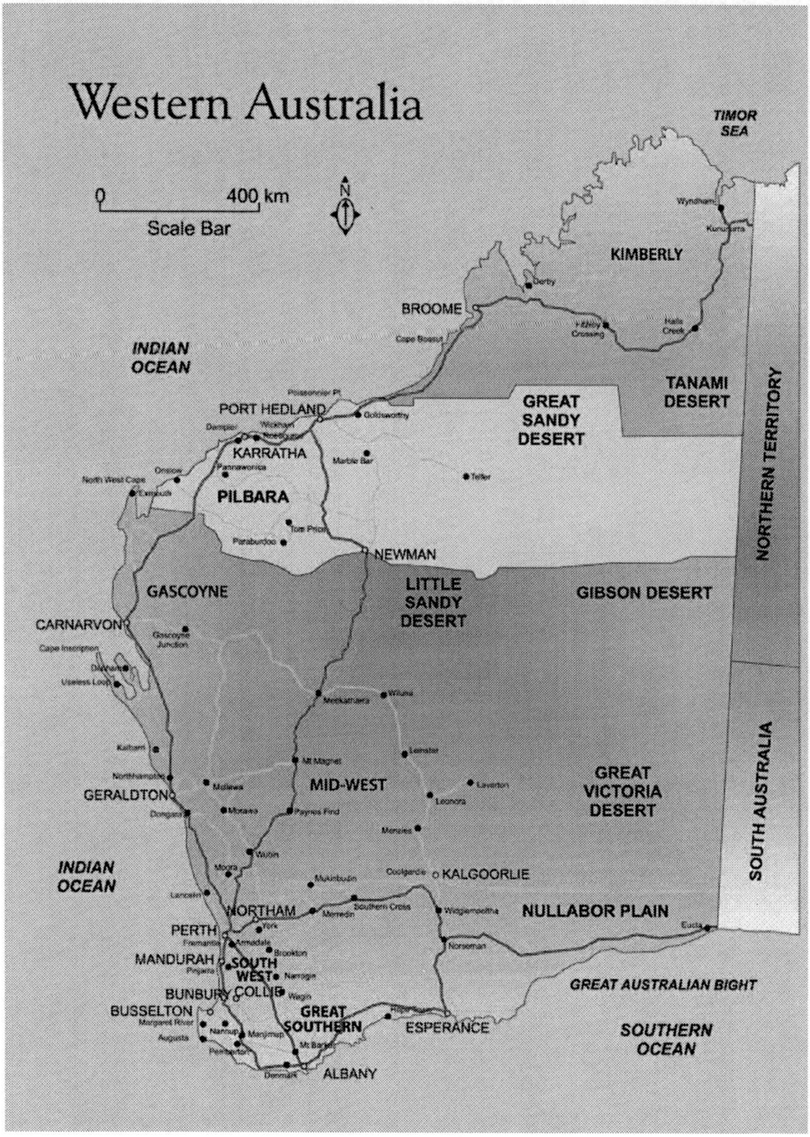

Figure 1 The Pilbara Region Western Australia.

LIST OF FIGURES

LIST OF TABLES

ABBREVIATIONS

ABC	Australian Broadcasting Commission
ABS	Australian Bureau of Statistics
ACT	Australian Capital Territory
ALP	Australian Labor Party
ASIC	Australian Securities & Investments Commission
Atax	Australian School of Taxation
ATO	Australian Taxation Office
BISEPS	Business Industry Sociology Economy Psychology Systems
BPS	Budplan Company Syndicate
CSIRO	Commonwealth Scientific and Industrial Research Organisation
CTSI	Centre for Tax System Integrity
DCS	Deputy Crown Solicitor
ELS	Electronic Lodgement System
FBT	Fringe Benefits Tax
FCA	Federal Court of Australia (Single Judge)
FCAFC	Federal Court of Australia Full Court (3 or more Judges)
FSDU	Federated Ship Painters and Dockers Union
GAARs	General Anti-avoidance Rules
GST	Goods and Services Tax, see also VAT
HWIs	High Wealth Individuals
IRS	Internal Revenue Service (USA)
ITAA 1936	*Income Tax Assessment Act 1936* (Cth)
LP	Liberal Party of Australia
MMTAS	Mass marketed tax avoidance scheme
OECD	Organisation for Economic Co-operation and Development
PAYE	Pay-as-you-earn (later part of PAYG below)
PAYG	Pay-as-you-go
QC	Queens Counsel
TAFE	Colleges of Technical and Further Education
USA	United States of America
VAT	Value Added Tax, see also GST
WA	Western Australia

1. CHAPTER ONE: INTRODUCTION

'I call a spade a bloody shovel'
Frederick Sidney Cotton, Australian aviator, inventor and spy (1894–1969)

Set in the picturesque, but treacherous landscape in the Outback of North-western Australia, this book portrays the story of one of the greatest series of tax avoidance schemes in Australia's history.

Prior to the 1970s, the North-west was, by European standards, largely uninhabited. A few inland towns, not much more than settlements, served the pastoral industry. The ranches, or stations as they are known in Australia, were owned and managed by European-Australians. They relied heavily on the labour services of local Aboriginals, who had occupied the land for thousands of years prior to settlement by the British in the 19th Century.

Fortunes had been made, and lost, by large family pastoral holdings since 'colonisation'. However by the late 1960s much of the pastoral industry was in decline. This book describes the two critical events that influenced the Pilbara region in the early 1970s and led to the development of one of the World's, and certainly Australia's, largest mining industries.

As with the hordes of 'booms' in human history, the mining boom in Australia was little different to the 'gold fevers' that struck California and Eastern Australia in the 19th Century. Towns sprang up where, only a few short years before sheep and cattle had meandered seeking sustenance. Sleepy colonial seaports became major international ports for the World's giant bulk carriers seeking iron ore.

Record after record was broken, as immense railway trains, laden with seemingly endless tonnages of ore, were dragged down the rivers of railway line, rapidly laid from the ranges to the sea for that one single purpose. Exports to Japan turned from nothing to negligible to enormous volumes almost overnight. Industry had arrived in the Pilbara.

As with earlier booms in history, workers of all kinds 'headed north' to make their fortunes in 'the mining game'. This book focuses on the tradespeople and labourers who chased the 'big money' in one of the World's last frontiers.

They certainly found the high incomes that the mining industry promised. They also found the isolation and harsh physical environment that had kept the region unpopulated for so long. They also encountered something they had never previously experienced—Australia's high marginal income tax rates, reserved for the high income earners at 'the high end of town'.

Suddenly 'Joe the Worker' was making as much money, or even more, as accountants, lawyers and medical practitioners. He was also paying the rates of tax that they had been subject to for years. 'Joe', however, was engaged at work for as much as 80 hours a week, as well as living and working in extreme temperatures. All in what the Australians call 'the bulldust-out-the-back.' The all pervading talc-like dust bonds with everything it touches—and it touches everything.

It is small wonder, that in this land of heat, dust and taxes, that the silk-tongued salesmen of the 'white-shoe brigade' found very willing audiences to the promises of avoiding tax, with ever increasingly complex and mind boggling schemes, to alleviate at least one of the plagues of the Pilbara blue-collar worker.

History says 'show me the miner, and I'll show you the gambler who preys on him'—read on.

From the beginning of the 1970s, almost the entire population of taxpayers of the Pilbara region of Western Australia have been engaged in the mining industry. Apart from a very small minority of indigenous Australians in remote communities and a handful of Europeans engaged in the waning pastoral industry, almost every worker is directly, or indirectly, connected to the mining industry. Seamen engaged in the ports of Dampier, Port Walcott, and Port Hedland are focussed on bulk ore and salt carriers. Railway workers and maintenance crews are exclusively engaged in the carriage of bulk ore. Service industries such as educational and medical and health services exist almost exclusively to provide for the mining industry.

In the context of the research covered in this book, it is instructive to develop an understanding of what it is like to live and work in the Pilbara, and this section explores the physical and social environment of the mining communities of the region. This examination takes the form of an ethnographic study and is provided to establish a clear understanding of the physically harsh living environment and heavy working conditions endured by taxpayers of the Pilbara region during the 1990s.

1.1. The Pilbara: landscape and climate

In terms of overall size, the Pilbara is approximately 300,000 square kilometres, roughly the size of Poland. It consists of the local authority Shires of Port Hedland, Roebourne, West Pilbara, and East Pilbara.

The map of Western Australia shows that the Pilbara region is bordered in the north by Port Hedland, in the east by Marble Bar and Newman, and to the west by the coastline from the bottom of Exmouth Gulf to Port Hedland.[1]

Exmouth (at the top of Northwest Cape) is not a mining centre. It has a relatively clement climate and is a holiday resort town at the northern most point of the Ningaloo reef. Its primary industry is tourism, and thousands of Pilbara miners holiday there on a regular basis to seek respite from the torrid Pilbara climate. Exmouth is therefore not considered a part of the Pilbara region and consequently has not been examined in this study.

The local government names and boundaries of the Pilbara are based on the towns existing at the time of Federation in 1901. They bear little reference to the present localities and townships. For example the Shire of Roebourne, on the coast, encompasses Dampier, Karratha, Wickham, Port Samson, Cossack, and Roebourne, as well as the hinterland to Tom Price and Paraburdoo (which are both in the Shire of Ashburton). The administration centre for the Shire of Roebourne is now Karratha, and the town of Roebourne is shown as a small village east of Karratha, while Cossack, the original port, is long abandoned and does not appear.

Initially districts were referred to by the river systems that flowed through them—Murchison, Gascoyne, Ashburton, Fortescue and De Gray (from south to north). In modern times most of those appellations are meaningless and have fallen into disuse. The southern Shires of Murchison and Upper Gascoyne are vestiges of the post-colonial era and consist of hamlets of less than 50 people, though they continue to service the pastoral industry.

The first observation to be made by a visitor to the Pilbara is the distance between communities. The Great Northern Highway from Newman to Port Hedland is 450 kilometres, or about five hours' drive. From Onslow to Port Hedland it is 540 kilometres or about six and a half hours; it is over 650 kilometres from Onslow to Newman, over eight hours by road. There are few communities between the towns. There are none between Newman and Port Hedland, only

1 Refer to the map of Western Australia.

Karratha and Roebourne between Onslow and Port Hedland, and Tom Price or Paraburdoo (depending on the route taken) between Onslow and Newman.

Early European settlers, who arrived in the 1880s, discovered what they thought to be endless grassy plains ideal for the burgeoning pastoral industry. What they had in fact found was open Spinifex plains of coarse and almost unpalatable grasses. Their livestock were forced to graze around the few natural perennial waterholes along seasonal watercourses.

Vegetation that had taken hundreds, perhaps thousands, of years to establish was virtually wiped out in little over sixty years, from settlement in the 1880s to the outbreak of World War II. A handful of small settlements were established as ports to service the pastoral industry at Carnarvon, Onslow, Point Samson (Cossack), Port Hedland, and Broome. Apart from a few small mining 'shows' at Marble Bar, Whim Creek and the now infamous Wittenoom Gorge asbestos mine, the region was generally considered 'Blackfella country'—a reference to the indigenous Australians who inhabited the region around the few permanent water holes and mission settlements and who were 'employed' on the scattered pastoral stations. Broome and Carnarvon, respectively north and south of the Pilbara, relied on their pearling and fishing fleets with intensive, irrigated agriculture at Carnarvon.

The following temperature map shows that the average annual maximum temperature is between 30 °C in the south and 33 °C in the north. The lower temperatures of 24 °C north-west of Newman are misleading as this is due to a mountain range that is too rugged for any human occupation. It is these Hamersley ranges that provide the main source of iron ore that attracts the large mining companies and produces employment for the Pilbara blue-collar workers.

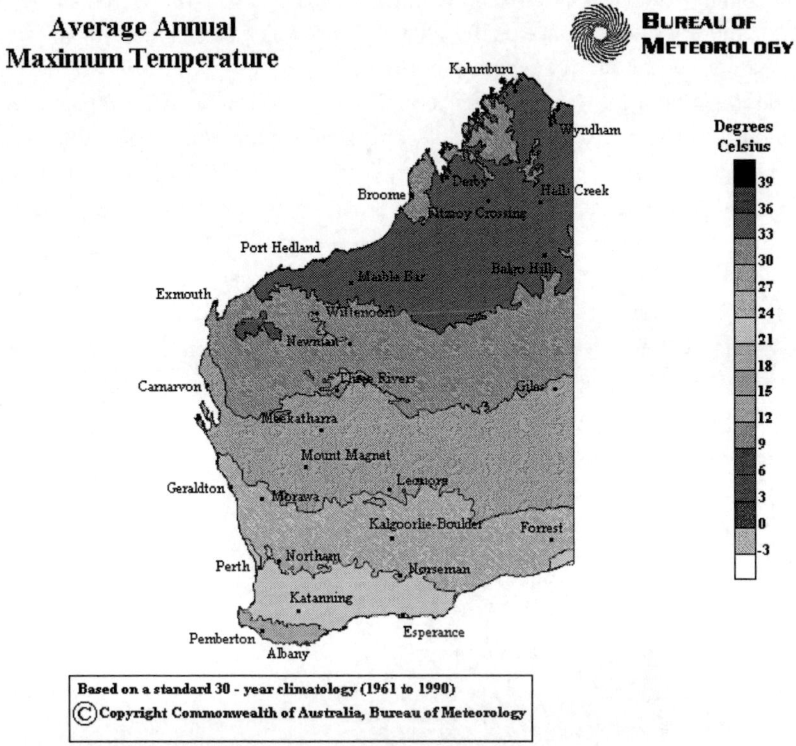

Figure 2 Western Australia's average annual maximum temperatures
Note: the original map is in colour. Isotherms are all above 15 °C and not under 12 °C (which are similar shades of grey in this reproduction)

The mining communities of Paraburdoo, Pannawonica, and Tom Price are to the west of Newman. The ports of Dampier (and its service town of Karratha), Wickham and Port Hedland—despite being on the coast, which should result in cooler climates—are all within the 33 °C zone. There are a few roadhouses for fuel and water, but generally it is no place for the inexperienced traveller. With summer daytime temperatures in excess of 50 °C, humans can perish very quickly. Traffic is generally limited to the major highways, and straying away from them can be fatal.

The community of Pannawonica, arguably the most isolated community in the Pilbara, is of particular interest in this study. Pannawonica is some 46 kilometres off the North West Coastal Highway and is a final destination as there is no other land access other than the railway that serves the iron ore trains to Cape Lambert

(Wickham). The nearest town to Pannawonica is Karratha, which is a comparatively short distance of 200 kilometres or two and a half hours drive.

Despite being mid-way between Newman and Exmouth, Pannawonica is situated within a 33 °C zone, even though surrounded by a cooler temperature zone. This is also due to the topography of the land in that it is situated on a plain at the end of a re-entrant or gully that prevents surface airflow from the sea. The Cape and Rough Ranges to the west also provide a localised barrier to prevailing south-westerly winds.

As shown in the following temperature map, the average annual daily temperature does not appear excessive, with an average maximum temperature of around 33 °C for the most part. However, daily maxima in the summer months reach over 40 °C and climatic conditions are most unpleasant.

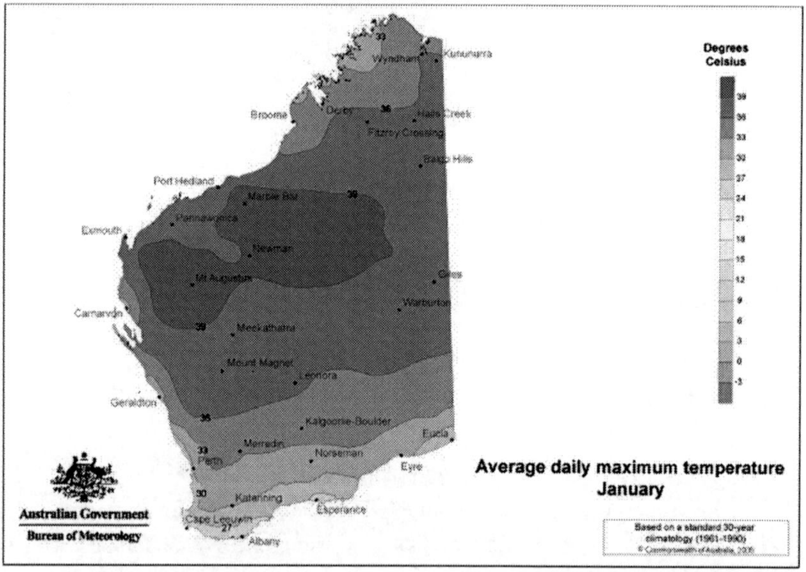

Figure 3 Western Australia's average daily maximum temperature for January
Note: the original map is in colour. Isotherms are all above 15 °C and not under 12 °C (which are similar shades of grey in this reproduction)

The north west of Western Australia is largely a barren, stony desert landscape with sparse vegetation. It has long periods of drought coupled with flooding rains when rotating tropical storms cross the northern coastline. At times, the desert is flooded, vegetation blooms and then the land returns to its parched state for months and sometimes years.

The rotating tropical storms (known as cyclones) bring rain to the region, but they also bring devastating tempests and flash flooding. The damage can be considerable: lives are lost, stock destroyed, and communities isolated for days, sometimes weeks, due to damage to transport infrastructure.[2]

As indicated in the map of cyclone tracks below, tropical cyclones can cross the coast anywhere between Carnarvon and Broome, but the Pilbara region is under the greatest threat. As many as six cyclones a year can occur in the Pilbara. In contrast, Carnarvon may not be subject to cyclone threats in many years.

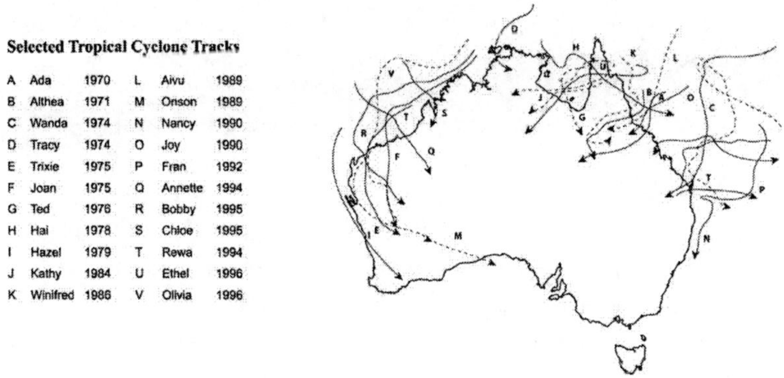

Figure 4 The pattern of tropical cyclone paths in Australia

The seasonal cyclones bring with them another discomfort. Generally the heat of the Pilbara is a 'dry heat'. While it is uncomfortable, humans can survive in temperatures of up to 50 °C. However, the sudden influx of moist tropical air brought with the cyclones raises the humidity to extremely uncomfortable levels. Periods of high humidity can last for days, weeks or even months if successive cyclones pass through the region.

The inhospitable region of the Pilbara was largely ignored by European Australians until the 1960s. Two significant events occurred then, which directly affected the Pilbara region. Firstly, the embargo by the Australian government on

2 Some cases are: tropical cyclone 'Tracy', Darwin, December 1974, 65 killed, 650 injured, 35 000 evacuated, $837 million insured damage total estimate over $4.1 billion; tropical cyclone 'Bobby', Onslow, February 1995, seven killed; tropical cyclone 'Olivia', Pannawonica, April 1996, ten injured, power installation and 55 houses destroyed; tropical cyclone 'George', Fortescue Metals campsite south east of Port Hedland, March 2007 two killed, 28 injured and $8 billion insured damage (Charles Sturt University Australian Emergency Management Forum Hazards Disasters and Survival <http://www.csu.edu.au/faculty/arts/sslib/aemf/HDS/chapter_7.htm> at 13 March 2008).

the sale of iron ore to Japan was lifted. Secondly, discoveries of large iron ore deposits were made in the Pilbara. A report by the National Conference of Public Works and Environment Committees in 2003 noted that:

> The Pilbara had long been known to contain immense deposits, and a boom began which was to see the establishment of nine new towns in the region by 1970 (Dampier, Tom Price, Paraburdoo, South Hedland, Newman, Wickham, Pannawonica, Goldsworthy (now closed) and Shay Gap (now closed)). Almost over-night the Pilbara's population increased tenfold.[3]

In addition to that, in the late 1970s discoveries of oil and natural gas off the north-west shelf were also made and '[i]n the '70s and '80s the development of these resources expanded the region's economy and population enormously'.

1.2. The Pilbara's socio-economic and working environments

This book covers the 30-year period from 1977 to 2007 with a particular focus on the 1990s. It is not intended to reflect subsequent changes to work practices by industry and / or public services and infrastructure by governments that may have influenced social and economic conditions after that time.

Since the 1960s, the effect of mineral and later gas / oil exploitation has been enormous and spectacular. In 1961, the population of the Pilbara was estimated at 3,240; in 1997 it was 41,225.[4]

The native inhabitants of the region, both European and indigenous Australians, were largely ignored by the newcomers. It is noted that few 'locals' are employed by the mining companies, and locals generally continue in the employment they engaged in prior to the 'new arrivals'. Pastoral properties continue to exist with minor changes to livestock management, and the locals enjoy the amenities that the larger population has attracted, but social intercourse between the two groups is limited.

---

3 Legislative Assembly of the Australian Capital Territory, Report on 2003 National Conference of Public Works and Environment Committees The Sustainability of Regional Development Addressing The Triple Bottom Line Vicki Dunne MLA Chair 8 August 2003 <http://www.legassembly.act.gov.au/committees/reports/pe22conference.pdf> at 3 September 2005.

4 Australia State of the Environment Report 2001 (Theme Report) Prepared by: Ann Hamblin, Bureau of Rural Sciences CSIRO Publishing on behalf of the Department of the Environment and Heritage <http://www.deh.gov.au/soe/2001/land/land01-10.html> at 3 September 2005.

It was not only the enormous increase in the number of people that has affected the social structure of the Pilbara, but also the focus of age and sex. The stabilising influence of a broad spectrum of individuals, normally found within a community able to provide social and educational guidance to younger individuals, did not exist:

> The aged population for the Pilbara has typically been low, and this trend is expected to continue. In 2001, 3.1 per cent of the population were over 70 years of age. The median age for Pilbara in 2001 was 31 years.[5] The Pilbara has the second youngest population of the state after the Kimberley- it has a strong bias towards young families.[6]

The following quote from Scadding,[7] who focussed on the development of the US Navy communications base in Exmouth in the 1960s, gives an indication of what happened in the 1970s in the Pilbara:

> From the 1960s onwards, the Pilbara was to undergo rapid development, and this had considerable impact on social developments of living in the Pilbara. There were two primary social change drivers occurring: firstly, the US Navy Communication Station was established in 1963 at Exmouth and '...a thriving community of over 3,000 mostly single personnel with a lot of money and little else to do'[8] integrated with the local population and enabled such industries as tourism to rapidly develop; secondly, the iron ore mining boom with so many single men seriously changed the social scene in the Pilbara.

The economic background of the Pilbara blue-collar worker is quite different from that of similar classes of workers engaged in other regions of Australia. As shown in the following table, they receive remuneration up to nearly 70 per cent higher than the national average in compensation for the dangerous working conditions that they have to endure, as well as the isolation and the harsh natural environment that confronts them.

The explosion of mining activities in the 1970s and onwards not only led to higher incomes but was accompanied by income tax rates significantly higher than previously experienced by Pilbara blue-collar workers or their peers. The phenomenon of high remuneration for such work and conditions is not

---

5 Australian Bureau of Statistics, 2001.0, 2001a, Basic Community Profile for Pilbara—Community Profile Series (2002).

6 Australian Bureau of Statistics, 2001g, A Profile of the Region, Development Commission Region of Pilbara, Western Australia, <http://wwwistp.murdoch.edu.au/Susty_case_studies/Pilbara/socio-cultural/Demographics.htm> at 3 September 2005.

7 Garry Scadding Non-Indigenous History of the Pilbara (undated) http://www.istp.murdoch.edu.au/Susty_case_studies/Pilbara/socio-cultural/Non-Indigenous_History.htm#mining at 3 September 2005.

8 Anna Vitenbergs, and Loreen Brehaut, Pilbara Journey through the Twentieth Century (2000) 226-7.

uncommon and is often experienced in similar types of activities (such as oil production and exploration) in other regions of Australia and the world.

Comparisons of income in the following table reveal that Pilbara blue-collar workers are paid significantly more than their occupational peers in the Goldfields, Western Australia and the nation generally. For example, in 1999 the average annual taxable income in Paraburdoo in the Pilbara was $52,191, compared with averages of $41,191 in Kalgoorlie-Boulder in the Goldfields, $34,360 in Western Australia and $34,798 in Australia generally.

Town	Post code	Mean Average Annual Taxable Income in $A							
		1995	**1996**	**1997**	**1998**	**1999**	**2000**	**2001**	**2002**
Goldfields									
Coolgardie	6429	32 414	36 357	35 443	37 101	37 968	38 961*	38 699	42 092
Kalgoorlie-Boulder	6430	35 410	36 788	38 382	39 867	41 191	41 338	43 168	44 429
Pilbara									
Dampier	6713	44 702	44 612	45 647	47 495	50 434	50 957	54 286	55 153
Karratha	6714	38 261	38 294	39 751	41 912	43 578	44 231	47 186	49 836
Newman	6753	47 191	47 473	48 653	49 203	50 540	50 650	51 282	53 896
Paraburdoo	6754	42 716	42 752	46 176	46 918	52 191	55 092	59 187	56 290
Pannawonica	6716	43 688	41 875	43 328	45 599	45 631	50 162	58 121	67 412
Port Hedland	6721	38 764	41 396	42 387	45 541	46 917	47 772	49 310	53 641
Tom Price	6751	43 777	44 855	45 492	46 889	50 769	52 379	55 262	53 957
Wickham	6720	38 305	37 562	40 448	42 142	43 939	45 160	48 086	52 169
Gascoyne									
Carnarvon	6701	26 378	27 193	27 746	28 832	31 098	32 295	34 203	34 828
Kimberley									
Broome	6725	27 970	29 104	29 658	31 216	34 888	35 069	35 748	36 484
Metropolitan									
Perth	6000-6175	29 146	30 129	31 133	32 825	34 622	35 750	37 779	38 681
WA		29 204	30 268	31 120	32 735	34 360	35 379	37 318	38 330
Australia		29 339	30 344	31 345	32 902	34 798	36 161	38 539	39 254

Table 1 Goldfields and Pilbara taxable income comparisons 1995–2002[9]

* Figures not available for Coolgardie, this is for the surrounding Yellowdine- Marvel Loch region.

9 Years from 1994 to 1999 available on compact disc: ATO, Taxation Statistics 1994-95 (1997); ATO, Taxation Statistics 1995-96 (1998); ATO, Taxation Statistics 1996-97 (1999); ATO, Taxation Statistics 1997-98 (2000); ATO, Taxation Statistics 1998-99 (2001). Years 1999-2000 to 2005-06 available from, ATO, Home > Corporate> General Accountability Information> Taxation statistics>Personal Tax (2008) Australian Taxation Office <http://www.ato.gov.au/corporate/content.asp?doc=/content/00117625.htm&page=33> at 23 June 2008.

The Australian Bureau of Statistics (ABS) referred to this in its feature article 'Regional Wage and Salary Earners in Western Australia':

> In 2000-01, four of the ten SLAs [Statistical Local Area] with the highest average annual wage and salary income in Western Australia were located in regions with significant mining activity, including Ashburton, East Pilbara, Coolgardie, and Port Hedland. Average annual incomes in these regions ranged from $44,770 in Port Hedland to $51,781 in Ashburton—the highest of any region in the state—reflecting the comparatively high earnings of those working in the state's mining industry. The proportion of wage and salary earners in these SLAs earning in excess of $52,000 per year ranged from 37.0 per cent in Port Hedland to 47.6 per cent in Ashburton—compared to 16.6 per cent across Western Australia.
>
> In comparison to the metropolitan SLAs in the top 10, these mining regions had relatively few Professionals and Managers and administrators and relatively more 'blue-collar' workers. More than half of the wage and salary earners in these regions were employed as either Tradespersons, Plant and machinery operators and drivers, or Labourers and related workers in 2000-01. These workers earned higher incomes than those working in the same occupations elsewhere in the state. Between 52.4 per cent (Port Hedland) and 67.8 per cent (Ashburton) of Tradespersons in these regions earned more than $52,000 in 2000-01, compared to 18.7 per cent of all Tradespersons in the state. Over half of the Labourers and related workers in Coolgardie and East Pilbara earned over $52,000 in 2000-01, compared to the state average of 12.0 per cent.
>
> Among the ten SLAs with the highest average wage and salary incomes in Western Australia, Ashburton recorded the highest proportion of Plant and machinery operators and drivers (82.0 per cent), Professionals (53.0 per cent) and Managers and administrators (51.9 per cent) earning in excess of $52,000 a year.[10]

From Australian Taxation Office (ATO) statistics, comparisons can be made with other occupational groups such as agricultural labourers, who are among the lowest paid workers in the nation. Workers engaged in primary production have an average income of $29,966 compared with fellow workers in the mining industry whose average wage was $45,008 in 1997-98.

Numerically, the trade qualified and unskilled, blue-collar workers are a vastly larger social group than the, tertiary qualified, professionals of the Pilbara. An example of that proportion is demonstrated by statistics extracted from a report of the Burrup Skills Taskforce.[11] They reveal the population of engineers engaged on the Burrup project,[12] in 2006, to be approximately 40 of a total operational workforce in excess of 1,000.

---

10 Australian Bureau of Statistics, 1367.5 Western Australian Statistical Indicators Labour Feature Article—Regional wage and salary earners in Western Australia (2004).

11 Emerging Industries on the Burrup: Skill Needs and Strategies <http://www.training.wa.gov.au/resources/docs/Burruppercent20Taskforcepercent20Report.pdf> at 11 June 2006.

12 A Pilbara industrial project serviced by the town of Karratha and the port of Dampier.

Information from a regional real estate agent[13] indicates a stratification of Pilbara society on an occupational basis. There exists a stable, long-term blue-collar resident population and a transient, short-term professional resident population. In general, professionals and supervisors such as engineers, surveyors, and senior administrative staff are engaged on a 'fly-in-fly-out' basis and have little personal contact with the resident blue-collar workers.

In addition, those professionals, and others, such as medical practitioners, accountants, and teachers are generally paid the same rates as their city dwelling peers, though they do receive small compensatory benefits such as subsidised housing, remote area allowances and the like. In most cases, however, they attend the Pilbara on a very short-term basis and are generally domiciled in Perth.

Professional residents do not generally interact with the long-term blue-collar residents and have other social and sporting interests. Some temporarily move their families to the Pilbara, but the terms are generally limited to 12 months to two years. In contrast the blue-collar workers view themselves as long term residents with some of them having been there since the early days of mining construction in the 1970s. Sales and rental data kept by real estate agents in the Pilbara also confirm the transient nature of the professional population and the comparative permanence of the blue-collar workers.

Blue-collar workers interact amongst themselves and have a general distrust of the professional classes. In the words of one professional '[t]hey [the blue-collar workers] don't have much to do with us. They are either on shift, asleep or out fishing. At work, we are in the office and they are outside.'[14]

According to the manager of college information systems of Karratha College of Technical and Further Education (TAFE), a third-year trades apprentice employed by a mining company receives an income approximately equal to that of his teachers. The social outcome is that, at least as to income, the Pilbara blue-collar worker perceives himself to be the social equal, if not superior, to the equally or lower paid professional. Consequently retention rates of students are very low with most students preferring to discontinue studies to work as blue-collar workers with the mining companies.

A consequence of this disruption from general Australian social structure is indicated in the table below. According to the census of 1996, the general population of the Pilbara is not as well-educated as the general population of the

---

13 Interview with Lindsay Gibson, Principal Ray White Karratha (Karratha, 7 June 2006).

14 Interview with Glen Jennings, Manager, College Information Systems, Pilbara TAFE Karratha Campus (Karratha, 8 June 2006).

state of Western Australia and is well below that of the nation. More particularly, on average only 9.36 per cent of Pilbara residents have received a tertiary education compared with Western Australian and Australian averages closer to 13 per cent.

Town	Postcode	Founded	Population 1996	Tertiary qualified (%)[a]
Goldfields				
Coolgardie	6429	1893	5 652	8.12
Kalgoorlie-Boulder	6430	1894	29 685	9.24
Total			35 337	9.06
Pilbara				
Dampier	6713	1972	1 424	9.68
Karratha	6714	1969	10 057	9.68
Newman	6753	1972	4 790	9.68
Paraburdoo	6754	1972	1 980	9.68
Pannawonica	6716	1972	779	9.23
Port Hedland	6721	1896[b]	12 846	8.92
Tom Price	6751	1965[c]	3 872	9.23
Wickham	6720	1971	1 649	9.68
Total			37 397	9.36
Gascoyne				
Carnarvon	6701	1883	8 620	7.70
Kimberley				
Broome	6725	1883	13 714	10.89
Metropolitan				
Perth	6000-6175	1829	1 244 320	13.87
WA		1829	1 726 095	12.38
Australia		1788	17 892 423	12.84

Table 2 Goldfields and Pilbara educational comparisons 1996
(a) Associate Diploma and above; (b) Developed existing town and port facilities 1972; (c) Private town established 1965 not gazetted until 1985[15] [16]

15 Department of Land Administration, History of Country Town Names (2006) <http://www.dli.wa.gov.au/corporate.nsf/web/History+of+country+town+names> at 19 February 2006.

16 Australian Bureau of Statistics, 1996 Census of Population and Housing—Basic Community Profile (2000).

Despite earning higher than average incomes, in the 1990s the Pilbara blue-collar workers tended to increase their spending on consumer products and recreational activities rather than investing the extra income or purchasing assets to improve their living standards after leaving the Pilbara. Some purchased rental properties in cities, chiefly Perth as it was the nearest, with a view to some 'negative gearing' and investment advantages,[17] but in the main the higher than average costs of living,[18] the purchase of consumer products such as four-wheeled drive vehicles, recreational boats,[19] electronic entertainment systems, and frequent holidays to nearby Asia, consumed most of their disposable income.

As noted above, one indicator of this economic activity is demonstrated by the propensity for recreational boat ownership. The Pilbara has a considerably higher recreational boat ownership density than any other region in Western Australia. The table of recreational boat registration in Western Australia 2001, prepared from information provided by the Western Australian Department for Planning and Infrastructure, shows that in that year the highest density of boat ownership in Western Australia was in the Pilbara region (identified as the North West in this table). A map showing the density of recreational boat ownership in Western Australia is provided in Appendix A.

---

17 Negative gearing is the financial practice of deliberately operating an investment property at a revenue loss in order to offset that loss against other taxable income. It is anticipated that the net loss after tax will be compensated by a capital gain which is taxed at more favourable rates than income according to ordinary concepts in Australia.

18 Gareth Parker, 'It's $1000 a week or rent a tent in Karratha', The West Australian (Perth, Western Australia) 17 June 2006, News 7.

19 Refer to boat ownership in Table 3 and to Appendix 'A'. In 2006 the population of the Shire of Roebourne (Dampier, Karratha and Wickham) was 15 273 (Australian Bureau of Statistics, Census Data <http://www.abs.gov.au/AUSSTATS/abs@.nsf//web+pages/Census +Data> at 1 April 2008.) yet in 2004 between 1 500 and 2 000 recreational boats were registered in that shire (more than one boat for every 10 persons). This compares with 68 495 registered recreational boats for the entire population of Western Australia of 1.9 million (less than one boat for every 30 persons).

Region and postcode	Boat registrations	Population	Ownership density (%)
Metropolitan (6000–6199)	45 581	1 397 000	3.26
South West (6200–6299)	8 672	191 100	4.54
Great Southern (6300–6399)	4 208	80 500	5.23
Eastern (6400–6499)	1 575	85 600	1.84
Central West (6500–6599)	3 449	77 200	4.47
Central North (6600–6699)	254	12 200	2.08
North West (6700–6799)	4 756	82 700	5.75

Table 3 Recreational boat registration in Western Australia 2001

It is also noted that a sharp growth of real estate investment by the mining communities of the Goldfields and Pilbara occurred in the early 2000s. There are likely to be many other social and economic factors which influenced Western Australia's growth in the real estate market in the early 2000s, but the sharp growth of real estate investment by the mining communities of the Goldfields and Pilbara may not be regarded as merely being coincidental.

That investment may reflect a switch from mass-marketed tax avoidance schemes (which were under intense ATO scrutiny at the time) to other tax-effective investment strategies. However, the further analysis of 'negative gearing' activities of the blue-collar workers is outside the scope of this book.

1.3. The Pilbara: political environment

Taylor has argued that '[p]erceptions of the ATO are affected by perceptions of the government. Illegitimacy of one implies some illegitimacy of the other.'[20] Therefore the political attitudes and voting patterns of residents of the Pilbara may also be an important factor in determining their attitudes to tax avoidance and aggressive tax planning.

In Australia the Liberal Party (LP) tends to represent conservatism or the 'right' and the Australian Labor Party (ALP) social democracy or the 'left'. Heywood[21]

---

20 Natalie Taylor, 'Understanding Taxpayer Attitudes Through Understanding Taxpayer Identities' in Valerie Braithwaite (ed), Taxing Democracy: Understanding Tax Avoidance and Evasion (2003) 71.

21 Andrew Heywood, Political Ideologies—An Introduction (2nd ed, 1998).

defines the 'right' as being 'a broad ideological disposition that is characterised by sympathy for principles such as authority, order, hierarchy, and duty.' The 'left' is 'a broad ideological disposition that is characterised by sympathy for principles such as liberty, equality, fraternity and progress.'

In general terms, the Liberal Party tends to represent industry and the industrialists, while the ALP tends to represent the populace and the workers. However in modern times those lines are beginning to blur, as both parties seek to represent the majority of electors and have both become more moderate in their views.

The pre-1960 population of the Pilbara was predominantly British colonial. These descendants of the early settlers of the 1880s have more in common with the indigenous Australians through their connections to the land than they do with the Labor voting, trade unionists of the mining industry. The pastoralists tended to be fervent Liberal / National Party supporters and view membership of the party as a social necessity.

However the indigenous Australians tended to support the ALP, often simply out of spite to the 'White Bosses', or they did not vote at all. With the influx of blue-collar workers into the Pilbara in the 1970s support for the Liberal Party became almost non-existent north of Exmouth, save for the vestige of pre-1960 inhabitants. Until the recent rise of the National Party, all Western Australian state parliamentary seats north of the Gascoyne have been held by the ALP since that time, often with large majorities.

The state electoral results for the district of Pilbara are illustrated in the table below. It indicates the level of political support of Pilbara blue-collar workers for the ALP. The percentage of blue-collar workers is based on census information provided by the ABS. Voter turnout is based on the number of electors enrolled in the Pilbara electoral district. All voters may not be workers, but all workers are entitled to be voters.

A further disparity is that the electoral boundaries have not been consistent. In 2001, the major mining towns of Dampier and Karratha were not in the seat of Central Kimberley-Pilbara. This table is indicative of the general trend of voting patterns only.

Election	14 December 1996 (%)	10 February 2001 (%)	26 February 2005 (%)
Labourers, production, tradespersons, transport and related workers (as a percentage of voters)	48.31	53.22	40.90
Turn out	68.08	68.41	68.57
ALP	63.82	26.82	50.12
Liberal	29.26	12.36	27.39
National	6.93		
Ind (ex-ALP)		54.57	
One Nation		6.26	1.55
CDP			1.41
Ind			10.51
Green			9.02

Table 4 Election results Western Australian district of Pilbara[22]

Voters generally do not discern between State and Federal issues and simply view 'the party' as being responsible for government decisions. In 1996 the Howard Liberal government was elected to Federal Parliament, and ATO action to combat the mass-marketed tax avoidance schemes began in 1997. To the Labor voting Pilbara electors it appeared that the Liberal Party had stopped the mass-marketed tax avoidance schemes and that the ALP had done little to oppose it.

In summary, the above analysis suggests that Pilbara miners are not only geographically but also socially isolated. They live and work in one of the harshest climates in Australia and are subject to the highest marginal rates of personal income tax in the Australian taxation system. They also demonstrated the highest propensity of all Australian taxpayers to participate in the mass-marketed tax avoidance schemes of the 1990s.

It is also noted that the Pannawonica taxpayers demonstrated the highest propensity to engage in the mass-marketed tax avoidance schemes of all the Pilbara communities. Arguably, not only is Pannawonica the most isolated community in the Pilbara, but it also has the harshest physical environment of the region. What is more, Pannawonica taxpayers enjoy some of the highest annual

22 Western Australian Electoral Commission, State Elections, <http://www.waec.wa.gov.au/elections/> at 3 February 2013.

incomes in Western Australia and consequently most of them are on the highest rate of personal income tax.

This background information about the extreme climate as well as the living and working conditions in the Pilbara and its political environment provides a necessary context for the central arguments of this book: that the propensity to engage in tax avoidance activity may be significantly influenced by the level of the tax rates and the nature of the working environment in which income is derived.

This section has given an overall view of the physical and social environments of the living and working conditions endured by the blue-collar workers of the Pilbara in the 1990s. Generally, most of those working conditions in the Pilbara remain unaltered from those in the 1990s.

Against this background, this book focuses on taxpayers who were engaged in mining and related activities in the Pilbara region of Western Australia in the 1990s. In particular it focuses on blue-collar workers who engaged in the mass-marketed tax avoidance schemes identified as such by the ATO. It examines the operation of a range of schemes identified by the ATO as being 'tax-effective'[23] mass-marketed tax avoidance schemes and attempts to identify the key factors that attracted the blue-collar workers of Western Australia's mining communities in such large numbers.

In the past, certain high wealth individuals have taken advantage of boutique or specifically tailored tax avoidance schemes, but the mass-marketed tax avoidance schemes of the 1990s in Australia were mass-produced. Economies of scale, resulting from the implementation of the mass-production process, reduced costs. This made such schemes available to a very broad range of taxpayers. Through these schemes the blue-collar workers of the mining industry were able to enter tax avoidance arrangements which were previously only the domain of high wealth individuals (HWIs).

Tax avoidance schemes are generally an artificially created commercial entity, and / or a series of financial transactions, which serve no purpose other than to reduce an individual's taxation burden. They may be legal structures, such as incorporated companies, that are formed to take advantage of deliberately legislated tax concessions to particular economic activities, or mere contrivances structured to appear as though they are legitimate operations. Some of the mass-marketed tax avoidance schemes of the 1990s took the form of afforestation operations or other agricultural enterprises granted favourable taxation

23 The ATOs term for financial structures established primarily to reduce tax.

concessions, but in fact they were not. Tax avoidance schemes which function for no other purpose than to artificially avoid tax are illegal.

Earlier tax avoidance schemes were not usually marketed commercially but were generally available to all high income individuals. In contrast, the mass-marketed tax avoidance schemes of the 1990s appear to have been specifically targeted at salary and wage earners. The 1990s schemes developed from more or less genuine investments into little more than shams that converted taxpayers' refunds into income for the promoters. Employees with tax credits, and therefore eligible for refunds, as well as sub-contractors, usually tradespeople operating as small business entities and subject to tax withholding or provisional tax credits,[24] were the primary targets of the promoters. For these reasons the scope of this book is primarily concerned with that class of taxpayer, the blue-collar workers of Western Australia.

Once the ATO had become aware of the magnitude of the mass-marketed tax avoidance schemes in the late 1990s, it began to take steps to counter them. The ATO response included disallowing scheme related tax deductions previously granted under Australia's 'self-assessment' tax return filing system. The ATO re-assessments met with great resistance, particularly in the Goldfields region of Western Australia. However, it is interesting to note that the Pilbara miners—though faced with exactly the same ramifications of the ATO re-assessments as was the case in the Goldfields—generally accepted the decision and appeared comparatively compliant with the recovery action taken by the ATO.

The general attitude in Western Australia's Goldfields region to the ATO's subsequent rejection of mass-marketed tax avoidance scheme deductions was 'you gave me the money, why should I give it back?' A campaign of resistance was established in the Goldfields—with slogans like 'Say No to the ATO'. The protests

24 'Provisional tax' was levied pursuant to Division 3 of the Income Tax Assessment Act 1936. It was not a tax, according to ordinary concepts, but rather was the collection of tax in advance based on the subject year's investment or business income imposed on certain individuals. It was an estimation of what the tax liability would be in the succeeding year. Once the assessment of the succeeding year was made the 'provisional tax' was adjusted by way of a further payment to meet the actual tax liability or by a refund in the case where actual assessable income was less than the estimate. It was intended to operate in a similar way to 'pay-as-you-earn' instalments for salary and wage earners. The advance payment was held as a credit by the ATO. Both were replaced by the 'pay-as-you-go' system under the A New Tax System legislation in 2001.

became the subject of an Australian Broadcasting Commission (ABC) Four Corners program in 2001[25]

The Prime Minister addressed public meetings, and ATO officers visited Kalgoorlie, the centre of the Goldfields region. Many of the submissions to a subsequent Senate inquiry[26] were from affected Kalgoorlie taxpayers.

In response to that resistance a survey was commissioned in 2002 by the ATO to investigate taxpayer attitudes to its handling of taxpayers engaged in the schemes.[27] Murphy, who conducted the survey, stated that 'to date, there has been little empirical research conducted on the attitudes and beliefs of taxpayers actually known to be engaged in aggressive tax planning'.[28] Aggressive tax planning is essentially a euphemism for tax avoidance activity.

A further survey was therefore conducted in the Goldfields, particularly in Kalgoorlie, enquiring to why taxpayers resisted ATO efforts to recover the lost revenue. That survey briefly addressed the circumstances of how investors became involved in the mass-marketed tax avoidance schemes. Hobson conducted the second survey and put forward the view that the population of Kalgoorlie had a unique culture which caused its population to rebel against the payment of taxation. However, the survey was inconclusive. Hobson states in her report 'research can never truly uncover individuals' motivations for investing in schemes, [e]ven though many interviewees admitted wondering if they had been foolish and inept in their [tax avoidance] actions, they were reluctant to take the blame for events.'

Apart from a few exceptions, such as Hobson's survey, little research has been carried out as to why so many blue-collar workers engaged in mass-marketed tax avoidance schemes.

The Senate inquiry touched on how the mass-marketed tax avoidance schemes were marketed but did not examine taxpayers' motivation to participate in the schemes. This book seeks to contribute to the body of knowledge in this area by

---

25 ABC Television, 'The Crackdown', Four Corners, 18 June 2001 <http://www.abc.net.au/4corners/stories/s312807.htm> at 17 August 2013,

26 The Senate Economics References Committee, Parliament of the Commonwealth of Australia, Inquiry into Mass Marketed Tax Effective Schemes and Investor Protection Interim Report (2001) 21, (Senate Inquiry).

27 Kristina Murphy and Karen Byng, 'A User's Guide to "The Australian Tax System Survey of Tax Scheme Investors"' (Working Paper No 39, Centre for Tax System Integrity, 2002).

28 Kristina Murphy, 'An Examination of Taxpayers' Attitudes towards the Australian Tax System: Findings from a Survey of Tax Scheme Investors' (2003) 18 Australian Tax Forum 209.

undertaking an examination of taxpayer participation in the mass-marketed tax avoidance schemes of the 1990s. It focuses in particular on the participation in those schemes by blue-collar workers of the mining industry in the Pilbara region of Western Australia.

The author suggests that the Pilbara taxpayers were highly motivated towards participating in the mass-marketed tax avoidance schemes by the combination of two key factors. Those two factors were high personal income tax rates and the physically harsh living environment and heavy working conditions endured by the blue-collar workers engaged in the mining and associated industries of the Pilbara region in the 1990s.

The extent of taxpayer participation in mass-marketed tax avoidance schemes was revealed in 1997, when the Australian Taxation Office detected a 'surge'[29] in the number of taxpayers participating in such activities throughout Australia. The surge was highlighted by the increase in the volume of tax deductions claimed by wage and salary earning taxpayers as indicated in the following graph.

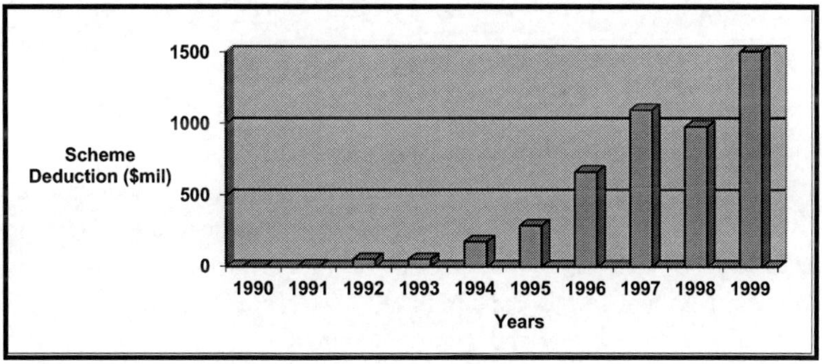

Figure 5 The growth of mass-marketed tax avoidance scheme deductions in the 1990s

It was estimated by the ATO that in the 1997-98 financial year there was over $1.0 billion of assessable income on which income tax should have been paid but was avoided. That figure increased further to over $1.5 billion in the 1998-99 financial year. The significant growth in tax deductions claimed through the use of the mass-marketed tax avoidance schemes ultimately represented nearly 2 per cent of Australia's annual tax revenue.

ATO statistics, tabled below, reveal that while the schemes were available to all Australian taxpayers it was the taxpayers of Western Australia who accounted

29 The term 'surge' was used as a description of the volume of refunds generated by the use of such schemes in the Senate Inquiry.

for over 40 per cent of all Australian participants in mass-marketed tax avoidance schemes in the period 1996-99. It is of significance here, that Western Australians made up only roughly 10 per cent of the Australian population.

State	Population of scheme participants	Scheme participants (%)
Australian Capital Territory	559	1.72
New South Wales	7 423	22.84
Northern Territory	364	1.12
Queensland	4 365	13.43
South Australia	1 817	5.59
Tasmania	192	0.59
Victoria	4 032	12.41
Western Australia	13 741	42.29
TOTAL	**32 493**	**100.00**

Table 5 State by State distribution of tax scheme investors 1996–99

The ATO later identified the largest population of scheme participants to be the highly paid tradespeople and labourers (blue-collar workers) of the mining industry in remote and rural Australia. In 2000 the ATO issued a media statement which said '[the promoters] have recruited the largest number of investors in WA followed by NSW, Victoria, Queensland, and South Australia with smaller numbers in Tasmania, Northern Territory and [the] ACT'.[30]

In 2002, the ATO collaborated with the Centre for Tax System Integrity (CTSI) to investigate taxpayer attitudes to its recovery processes. As a result, further information, provided by the ATO, identified that it was not only Western Australia that was the focus of the tax avoidance, but that it initially appeared to be especially focussed on the mining centre of Kalgoorlie, the principal town of the Goldfields region of Western Australia.

However, as shown in the next table, further analysis of ATO statistics revealed that the propensity to engage in the schemes was considerably higher in the Pilbara than it was in the Goldfields. Therefore, while the Goldfields region, which is spread around its central town of Kalgoorlie and geographically well-removed

30 Australian Taxation Office, 'New Warning for Tax Scheme Investors' (media release 2000/101, 30 October 2000).

from the Pilbara, shares a very similar harsh physical environment with the Pilbara region, as well as having a heavily mining-based economy, the focus of this study is centred on the Pilbara region. It is also noted that the living environment and working conditions experienced in the Pilbara are harsher, and the population more isolated, than those of the Goldfields region.

Town	Postcode	Population 1998	Taxpayers	Scheme participants	Density of scheme participants (%)	
					Taxpayer population	Total scheme participants
Goldfields						
Coolgardie	6429	1 258	467	38	8.14	0.12
Kalgoorlie-Boulder	6430	28 087	11 162	363	3.25	1.12
Total		29 335	11 629	401	3.45	1.23
Pilbara						
Dampier	6713	1 424	734	49	6.68	0.15
Karratha	6714	10 057	5 330	244	4.58	0.75
Newman	6753	4 790	2 507	135	5.38	0.42
Paraburdoo	6754	1 980	712	70	9.83	0.22
Pannawonica	6716	779	332	60	18.07	0.18
Port Hedland	6721	12 846	2 350	124	5.28	0.38
Tom Price	6751	3 872	1 428	97	6.79	0.30
Wickham	6720	1 649	887	76	8.57	0.23
Total		37 397	14 280	855	5.99	2.63
Gascoyne						
Carnarvon	6701	8 616	2 636	0	0.00	0.00
Kimberley						
Broome	6725	11 368	4 324	49	1.13	0.15

Town	Postcode	Population 1998	Taxpayers	Scheme participants	Density of scheme participants (%)	
					Taxpayer population	Total scheme participants
Metropolitan						
Perth	6000 / 6175	1 334 992	619 920	9 600	1.55	29.54
WA		1 726 095	838 114	13 741	1.64	42.29
Australia		17 892 423	8 251 120	32 493	0.39	100.00

Table 6 Detailed regional distribution of Western Australian tax scheme investors 1998

As illustrated in the table, nearly 6 per cent of taxpayers in the Pilbara region participated in mass-marketed tax avoidance schemes in 1998. That is a remarkably high proportion when compared with the national average of less than 0.4 per cent. In particular, over 18 per cent of taxpayers resident in the Pilbara mining community of Pannawonica engaged in the mass-marketed tax avoidance schemes, a rate nearly 46 times higher than that of the average Australian taxpayer.

This book seeks to fill gaps in the broader knowledge of taxpayer compliance behaviour and to further develop an understanding as to why taxpayers engage in tax avoidance activity. The principal aim of this book is to investigate the motivational factors which may have influenced individual taxpayers to engage in tax avoidance activity in the context of the participation of the blue-collar workers of the Pilbara region of Western Australia in the mass-marketed tax avoidance schemes of the 1990s.

To conduct the investigation, this book specifically explores and analyses the influencing factors grouped into four major categories; *demographic, socio-psychological, economic, and legal and administrative factors*. This is to establish those factors most dominant in influencing so many blue-collar workers—located in such a small, yet harsh, region and from a particular, and also harsh, industry—to be attracted to the schemes.

The key influencing factors remain significant on taxpayer motivation towards tax avoidance activity. The findings of this book therefore, may assist in earlier detection of such schemes and the process of countering such widespread avoidance activity from being repeated in the future.

1.4. The research

An overview of the research design is provided here to place the following chapters in context.

Generally, *what* happened can be quantified and analysed empirically using a 'positivist' or 'scientific' research approach. However, this book seeks to investigate *why* the particular behaviour was focussed in a particular region. Therefore a 'non-positivist' research approach is also used to interpret *socio-psychological influences* that contributed to the particular tax compliance behavioural posture under investigation.

This research philosophy viewpoint has influenced the decision to adopt a mixed-method research design, which combines both quantitative and qualitative research approaches. A combination of aspects of both positivist and non-positivist, or a 'middle ground' research approach, is required.

A pragmatic research approach considers elements of both 'positivist' and 'non-positivist' research approaches. Therefore, a pragmatic research approach has been adopted in order to investigate the phenomenon under scrutiny and to understand its causes and antecedent conditions.

A *quantitative* approach is used to analyse statistical data gathered by the ABS and the ATO. In addition, data collected from previous research conducted by CTSI is used for corroborative analysis. A survey is also conducted using the ABC's internet 'On-line opinion' polling resource facility.[31] The ABC 'On-line' internet survey is examined to provide evidence to support or refute the findings of the previous research and statistical data of the ABS and the ATO.

The main aim of the quantitative research is to provide support and a basis for the qualitative research approach to be conducted. The quantitative examination establishes participation rates and reveals the disproportionate involvement of the Pilbara 'blue-collar' workers in the mass-marketed tax avoidance schemes.

A *qualitative* approach is used to investigate the phenomenon of the 'surge' in mass-marketed tax avoidance schemes in the 1990s and in particular the disproportionately high rate of involvement by taxpayers in the Pilbara region of Western Australia. Specifically, the discovery of theory through methods of data analysis, known as grounded theory, is used to provide a basis or grounding for the theory that taxpayer motivation towards tax avoidance activities is

31 Details of internet polling resources are available at <http://www.onlineopinion.com.au> or by contacting the Chief Editor On-Line Opinion, Mr Graham Young at <graham.young@onlineopinion.com.au>.

exacerbated by high personal income tax rates—particularly when coupled with a physically harsh living environment and heavy work.

The qualitative survey includes taxpayers' attitudes to the ATO's response and manner of dealing with the matter to explore the likelihood of those taxpayers re-engaging in such activities. To do this, in-depth interviews with taxpayers who participated in the schemes have been undertaken. Those responses were compared and contrasted with taxpayers of similar occupations and taxpayers of similar income streams who did not participate in mass-marketed tax avoidance schemes.

Investigations, carried out by way of 37 semi-structured, in-depth interviews with four base cohorts of taxpayers, are analysed in the book as follows:

- Cohort 1 – A group of 11 taxpayers, blue-collar workers engaged in the Pilbara mining industry who participated in the mass-marketed tax avoidance schemes. The responses of this group are examined to provide an indication of motivations for participating in the schemes.
- Cohort 2 – A group of 10 taxpayers, blue-collar workers engaged in similar occupations to those in Cohort 1 from outside the mining regions and who did not participate in the mass-marketed tax avoidance schemes. Taxpayers in this group are engaged in similar occupations as those in Cohort 1. However, they do not experience the same harsh physically harsh living environment and heavy working conditions, nor experience the same high rates of personal income tax. Primarily, this group serves as a benchmark group to indicate the influence of harsh living and heavy working conditions on taxpayer attitudes to aggressive tax planning. Secondly, this group also serves as a control group to indicate the influence of taxation rates on taxpayer attitudes to tax compliance.
- Cohort 3 – A group of 10 taxpayers from urban professional backgrounds, such as university professors, stockbrokers, and engineers, with similar annual income and taxation rates to the blue-collar workers in the Pilbara are examined primarily to indicate the influence of personal income tax rates on their attitudes to aggressive tax planning. This group also serves as a benchmark to help identify the impact that physically harsh living environment and heavy working conditions may have had on taxpayer attitudes to tax compliance in the Pilbara.

- Cohort 4 – A group of 6 taxpayers who do not fit into the parameters of the three cohorts above. These are Pilbara professionals, such as mining engineers and chemists, who participated in the mass-marketed tax avoidance schemes, and blue-collar workers from within the region, who did not participate. Despite not fitting the selection criteria these taxpayers came forward to participate in the study and to safeguard the integrity of this research they are included as a separate category.

The findings allow a comparison of the attitudes of similar samples of taxpayers involved in similar occupations and other taxpayers on similar income levels to the taxpayers engaged in the Pilbara's mining industry. The findings are then compared with ATO responses to mass-marketed tax avoidance schemes by way of analysing published ABS data, the report of the Auditor-General[32] that investigated the ATO's recovery procedures, and other relevant literature.

In addition, and in order to provide appropriate context, the operation of two of the mass-marketed tax avoidance schemes is closely examined. The two schemes serve to illustrate the range of mass-marketed tax avoidance schemes from arguably genuine investments to almost fictitious schemes with no substance.

The first is Main Camp Tea-Tree Project No. 4. Tax deductions claimed for investments in that scheme were disallowed under the general deductions provision, Section 51 of the *Income Tax Assessment Act 1936* (ITAA 1936). However, this scheme also used non-recourse loans to inflate the deductions claimed and was also disallowed under the general anti-avoidance provisions of the ITAA 1936. The second is Satcom Electronic Commerce Services Pty Ltd, which had little or no purpose other than to avoid tax.

The book also involves an examination of court transcripts and decisions of litigation relating to the ATO's denial of tax deductions claimed through the use of the mass-marketed tax avoidance schemes of the 1990s. Evidence given by parties and witnesses under oath is examined to reveal motivational factors for engaging in the schemes.

The rationale for the chosen research design is that a theory to establish the relationships between taxpayer attitudes to compliance with the law cannot be solely supported through the examination of statistical data in isolation. The

32 The Auditor-General, Audit Report No.23 2003-04 Performance Audit, The Australian Taxation Office's Management of Aggressive Tax Planning <http://www.anao.gov.au/Web Site.nfs/Publications> at 31 March 2005.

quantitative analysis identifying the phenomenon requires qualitative research support to produce robust findings.

The following chapter provides further context relating to the development of mass-marketed tax avoidance schemes and their use by Australian taxpayers in the 1990s. It examines the concepts of tax evasion, tax avoidance and tax planning. It then examines the recent history of tax avoidance schemes in Australia from the 1970s, when they were tailored for HWIs, to the mass-marketed tax avoidance schemes of the 1990s. It examines the cyclical pattern of design and promotion of schemes, the administrative, judicial and legislative anti-avoidance responses and the reaction of taxpayers to those responses.

Chapter Three reviews published literature relating to tax compliance behaviour. It considers the literature on the subject of taxpayer motivation to comply with taxing authorities and to pay tax. In particular it focuses on key motivational influences that are relevant to the cohort groups examined in this research.

Chapter Four examines data collated from this research. In particular it examines documents gathered from participants in mass-marketed tax avoidance schemes, the findings of cases relating to the ATO's litigation to close the mass-marketed tax avoidance schemes of the 1990s, and interviews with participants conducted in this research.

The outcomes of the research methods are examined and compared and contrasted to highlight influencing factors that were present in the population of taxpayers in the Pilbara in the 1990s. The findings are further examined to highlight influencing factors which were significant in motivating the blue-collar workers in the Pilbara to engage in the mass-marketed tax avoidance schemes of the 1990s.

Chapter Five reviews and concludes the book. It places this research within the context of previously published literature and states its contribution to the literature. It recognises limitations to the research and suggests areas for further research into issues that were encountered during the research but were beyond the scope and focus of this study.

In conclusion, it suggests that increased physical isolation and heavy working conditions exacerbated a feeling of social distance by the taxpayers of the Pilbara region from the broader Australian population, government, and taxing authorities. Further, it also suggests that the very high levels of remuneration paid to the blue-collar workers in the mining industry were accompanied with correspondingly high personal income tax rates. It may have been the combination of those influences which led to the phenomenon of increased avoidance activity investigated in this book.

2. CHAPTER TWO: TAX EVASION, TAX AVOIDANCE AND TAX PLANNING IN AUSTRALIA

'The difference between tax avoidance and tax evasion is the thickness of a prison wall.'
Denis Healey, British politician, (1917–)

The previous chapter included an outline of the physical, social and political environment of the mining communities of the Pilbara in the 1990s. It provided the necessary background to some key social and economic factors that affected the residents of the Pilbara as taxpayers relative to 'mainstream' Australian society.

The overall aim of this chapter is to provide necessary background and context relating to the development of tax avoidance activity in Australia which led to the mass-marketed tax avoidance schemes of the 1990s. Within this overall aim, the chapter has three specific objectives.

Firstly, it provides working definitions of the concepts of tax evasion, tax avoidance and tax planning. Given that the focus of this book is on *why* taxpayers engage in tax-reducing activity and not *how* they reduce their tax, the distinction between the concepts is not critical to this book. However the definitions are examined to place them within the broader framework of tax-reducing activities.

Secondly, it examines the history of tax avoidance schemes in Australia from the early 1970s to the late 1990s to illustrate how mass-marketed tax avoidance schemes developed.

Thirdly, and as part of the examination of tax-reducing activities in the last decades of the twentieth century, this chapter will examine taxpayers' responses to the ATO's subsequent review of deductions claimed through the use of tax avoidance schemes and recovery action of refunds issued by way of the ATO's self-assessment programme. This examination is undertaken to establish the impact of the responses of the taxation administration to the tax-reducing activities of participants in tax avoidance schemes on the attitudes of taxpayer to tax compliance.

2.1. Tax evasion, tax avoidance and tax planning

Taxpayers often demonstrate a willingness to engage in tax-reducing activities of one form or another. The methods used by taxpayers to reduce their tax liability may involve tax evasion, tax avoidance or tax planning. The choice of method used is determined by the morality, economic viability and / or legality of the various methods available in a particular society or jurisdiction combined with the views, economic circumstances and risk profiles of the individual taxpayer.

Compliance with taxation law is a subset of compliance with the law generally. Tyler found that people obey the law primarily because they believe in respecting legitimate authority.[33] He suggests that people obey the law if they believe it is legitimate, not because they fear punishment.

The focus of this research concerns the motivational factors that influence taxpayers' behaviour to engage in tax-reducing activities. It is contended that the common factor for all taxpayers in engaging in tax evasion, tax avoidance and / or tax planning is the desire to pay less tax than they are otherwise burdened with. Therefore the distinction between tax evasion, tax avoidance and tax planning is instructive though not critical to this book.

Tax-reducing activities do not have clear or distinct boundaries and generally shade from one to the other. Commentators such as Seldon,[34] for example, see no economic distinction between tax avoidance and tax evasion. Seldon referred to the practice of reducing tax burdens by any means as 'avoision' being an amalgam of the two terms. However the three concepts of tax evasion, tax avoidance and tax planning do require a working definition to place them within the broader context of the development of mass-marketed tax avoidance schemes.

Another view is that of commentators such as Prebble and Prebble who argue that tax evasion and tax avoidance activities are morally wrong and see no moral distinction between the two concepts.[35]

Against this background, **Tax evasion** may be defined as the practice of reducing taxation liabilities by concealing income or declaring expenses or

33 Tom R Tyler, Why People Obey the Law (2006).

34 Arthur Seldon, 'Avoision: The Moral Blurring of a Legal Distinction without an Economic Difference' in Arthur Seldon (ed), Tax Avoision (1979) 1.

35 Zöe Prebble and John Prebble, 'The Morality of Tax Avoidance: Why the Legal Difference between Evasion and Avoidance is Insufficient to Ground a Moral Distinction' (Paper presented at the Australasian Tax Teachers Association Annual Conference, University of Tasmania, 24 January 2008).

claiming tax offsets that do not exist.[36] Individuals and organisations that engage in activities outside of the law, in pursuits such as drug trafficking, are also unlikely to comply with the taxation laws of a particular jurisdiction. Despite the unlikelihood of tax compliance '[assessable] income has been accepted as including the proceeds of criminal activities'.[37] Therefore those individuals and organisations are not only in breach of the law generally, but are also tax evaders.

Tax evasion may arise from an inadvertent error, omission or unintentional mistake, however if it is fraudulent it is regarded as a crime.

Tax avoidance differs from tax evasion in that a person engaged in tax avoidance may comply with the letter of the law while at the same time be trying to gain a taxation benefit not intended by the legislature. Tax avoidance can also be unlawful. Freedman examines the situation where tax avoidance shades into fraud.[38] She cites 'high profile cases in [the United Kingdom] where individuals, including tax professionals, have been successfully prosecuted for what they claimed were unsuccessful avoidance rather than evasion schemes'.[39] Freedman observes that '[t]he test for dishonesty depends on a combination of findings of fact about what the defendant knew and believed and an application of the current standards of ordinary decent people'. She also points out that 'engagement in an avoidance scheme can encourage taxpayers to be economical with the truth'.

Complex or otherwise non-commercial and artificial business structures, such as interposed entities that are used to disguise transactions to obtain an unintended benefit from tax relieving provisions, are sometimes referred to as 'unacceptable' avoidance. A concise definition of unacceptable tax avoidance was provided by Lord Goff in *Ensign Tankers (Leasing) Ltd v Stokes*:

> Unacceptable tax avoidance typically involves the creation of complex artificial structures by which, as though by the wave of a magic wand, the taxpayer conjures out of the air a loss, or a gain, or expenditure, or whatever it may be, which otherwise would never have existed.[40]

36 Valerie Braithwaite, 'Dancing with Tax Authorities: Motivational Postures and Non-compliant Actions' in Valerie Braithwaite (ed), Taxing Democracy: Understanding Tax Avoidance and Evasion (2003) 17.

37 Commissioner of Taxation v La Rosa [2003] FCAFC 125, para 5.

38 Judith Freedman, 'Defining Taxpayer Responsibility: In Support of a General Anti-Avoidance Principle' (2004) 4 British Tax Review 332.

39 See for example R v Charlton [1996] STC 1418, as cited in Freedman.

40 [1992] 1 AC 655.

Taxation systems often contain provisions deliberately targeted at stimulating certain commercial activities within the economy. Legitimate business structures may receive favourable taxation treatment and are referred to as 'acceptable' avoidance, generally termed tax planning.

Tax planning is the practice of arranging 'the affairs of a taxpayer so that, within the bounds of the law, the incidence of income tax may be minimised'.[41] The basic premise of tax planning is best described by Lord Upjohn when he stated '[n]o commercial man in his senses is going to carry out transactions except on the footing of paying the smallest amount of tax [possible]'.[42]

The research underpinning this book focuses on mass-marketed tax avoidance schemes in Australia during the 1990s. Therefore a closer examination of the concept of complex artificial structures is required to place them into the broader context of this study.

The techniques of tax minimisation using such artificial transactions are termed 'schemes'. They vary from transactions that 'are inherently worthless and which need no [legislative] provision to strike them down'[43] to deliberate commercial contrivances that exist for no reason other than to avoid tax, or for which the 'dominant purpose'[44] is to avoid tax.[45]

Tax avoidance schemes take many forms, however often they involve the promotion of non-existent or valueless projects, legally structured to provide income tax deductions, or similar tax benefits, to their subscribers. The deductions allowed for tax purposes are often greatly in excess of the sums outlaid by the taxpayers, hence the attraction to the tax avoider.

Tax avoidance schemes typically include monetary transactions, or the appearance of monetary transactions, which make little or no common or commercial sense. Examples of detected tax avoidance schemes are found in the cases of *Spotless*[46] and *Meredith*.[47] In the former case a deposit of funds was purportedly made to a bank in the Cook Islands. The reasonable person would find

---

41 Robin Woellner et al, 1997 Australian Taxation Law (7th ed. 1997) 1416. The 1997 reference has been used as it was the handbook available to tax avoidance scheme designers and tax professionals at the time of the mass-marketed tax avoidance schemes of the 1990s. The use of later references for this purpose may distort contemporary thought.

42 IR Commissioners v Brebner (1967) 43 TC 718.

43 See eg Jacques v Federal Commissioner of Taxation (1924) 34 CLR 328, 358.

44 Income Tax Assessment Act 1936 (Cth) sub-s 177A (5).

45 Income Tax Assessment Act 1936 (Cth) Pt IVA.

46 Federal Commissioner of Taxation v Spotless Services Ltd (1996) 34 ATR 183.

47 Meredith v Federal Commissioner of Taxation [2002] FCAFC 271.

it odd that an Australian company might deposit funds in an Australian bank with a branch in some remote South Pacific country, unless the person was aware that the Cook Islands held itself out as a 'tax haven' at the time. As to the facts in the case of *Meredith*, taxpayers paid $3,000 in return for an invoice made out for $64,000. Again, a reasonable person would find such a transaction odd.

The relevance of the distinctions between unacceptable tax avoidance and tax planning to this research is that mass-marketed tax avoidance scheme designers, promoters and taxpayers rely on 'blurring' the distinctions to enable their unacceptable tax avoidance scheme to appear to be legitimate tax planning.

2.2. The recent history of tax avoidance schemes in Australia

A brief background to the development of the mass-marketed tax avoidance scheme reveals that it is a relatively modern economic concept. Tutt[48] attributes the first design of an 'off-the-peg' mass-marketed tax avoidance scheme to Bernard Kimble, an English accountant. According to Tutt, such schemes began in 1965 with a 'boutique'[49] scheme designed to turn taxable income into non-taxable capital gains. These involved a complex dividend-stripping[50] array of trusts and companies that were set up for the English actress Julie Christie, wealthy from her success in Hollywood films.[51] Such structures had been used by his firm for high income taxpayers such as film stars, composers and actors in England during the 1950s. However until 1965 each case had been individually crafted rather than set up from a standard template.

In Australia 'off-the peg' tax avoidance schemes also began in the 1960s. Australian scheme designer and promoter Peter Clyne referred to 'off-the-peg' tax avoidance schemes[52] in 1969, when he warned that they should not be used. He said '[the tax avoidance scheme] must be tailored to measure, individualised,

48 Nigel Tutt, The Tax Raiders: The Rossminister Affair (1985).

49 Designed for or directed to a small, specialised, fashionable market (Macquarie Concise Dictionary).

50 The practice of purchasing shares in a private company with the intention of declaring dividends from the company's accumulated profits to the new shareholder, and then selling the shares in the company once the dividend has been paid (Macquarie Concise Dictionary).

51 Tutt states, 'The scheme was consummated at a meeting at the Grosvenor House Hotel in Park Lane, London on December 22 1965'.

52 Peter Clyne, The New Techniques of Tax Avoidance (1979).

applicable to only one client ... thus it will not present a broad front for the "fiscal fiend"[53] to attack and cannot be shot down as easily as the *Curran* scheme.'[54]

Evidence of taxpayer attitudes of the era to tax avoidance is indicated in Clyne's 1969 comments that:

> Paying taxes is rather like alcohol, tobacco, heroin or wild women. It is simply a habit . . . costly, addictive, soul-destroying and unnecessary. But in one way it does differ from alcohol, tobacco, heroin and wild women—It offers no compensating element of pleasure, satisfaction or tranquility. So one ought to kick the habit of paying taxes and develop the anti-habit of tax avoidance.

Despite these personal attitudes of taxpayers, when Australia joined the Organisation for Economic Co-operation and Development (OECD)[55] in 1971, the federal government adopted the recommendation of the OECD on tax evasion and avoidance wherein the Council required the governments of member countries:

- To strengthen, where necessary, their legal, regulatory or administrative provisions and their powers of investigation for the detection and prevention of tax avoidance and evasion, with regard to both their domestic and international aspects, and to exchange experiences with respect to such action;
- To facilitate, improve and extend exchanges of information between their national tax administrations, with a view to combating tax avoidance and evasion, notably by making more intensive use of international conventions or instruments in force and by seeking new arrangements of a bilateral or multilateral character, with due regard to the provision of adequate safeguards for taxpayers;
- To exchange experiences on a continuing basis on tax avoidance and evasion practices, on techniques for detecting and preventing them and on ways and means of improving tax compliance in general.

---

53 Clyne's term for the Commissioner of Taxation.

54 Clyne's book was published in 1979 but the warning referred back to an earlier book by him, published in 1969. The Curran scheme concerned a taxpayer who acquired shares in a company with substantial capital profits. The profits were then credited in payment of bonus shares. The effect of the issue of bonus shares was to devalue the original shares acquired by the taxpayer. He sold them at a loss, which was held to be deductible, while on the sale of the bonus shares it was held proper to treat the amount of the dividend applied to them as the amount paid by the taxpayer for them. This was widely regarded as an artificial scheme. Curran v Federal Commissioner of Taxation (1974) 131 CLR 409.

55 Organisation for Economic Co-operation and Development, 'International Tax Avoidance and Evasion' Issues in International Taxation (1987,1).

The book now examines tax avoidance activity in Australia from 1971 onwards. It is suggested that the development of tax avoidance schemes is a cyclical sequence of actions and reactions between taxpayers, scheme designers and promoters and tax administrators, the judiciary and legislators, depicted in the figure showing the cyclical pattern of tax avoidance scheme development in Australia illustrated below.

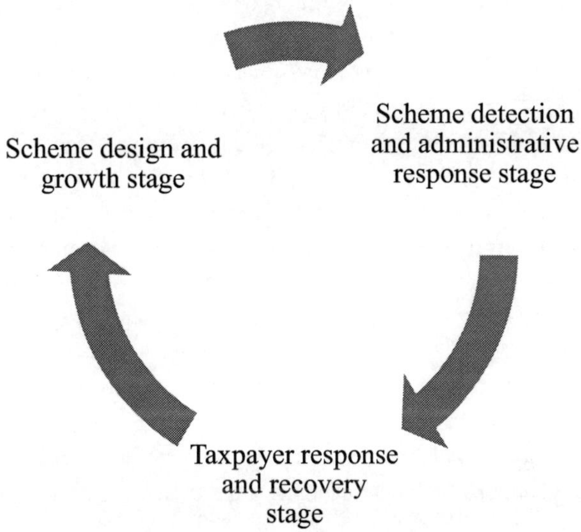

Figure 6 The cyclical pattern of tax avoidance scheme development in Australia

This examination is undertaken to illustrate how tax avoidance schemes evolved from individually-tailored schemes—used by HWIs in the 1970s—to broaden in scope, both in terms of their complexity and application and to extend to the mass-marketed tax avoidance schemes used by high income earning blue-collar workers in the 1990s. The schemes did not supersede each other but rather developed from previous schemes that often remained in use by tax planners and taxpayers.

The scheme design and growth stage is the period of scheme development during which accountants and other tax and financial professionals react to taxpayer demands to find structures and methods of reducing their taxation burden. It often involves investigation of legislation and anti-avoidance rules developed during the previous cycle as tax administrators, the judiciary and legislators respond to such schemes. An important characteristic of the transition from the taxpayer response and recovery stage to the scheme design and growth stage is an apparent lack of tax avoidance activity.

Successful tax avoidance schemes are developed and are taken up by taxpayers until they reach a volume, either by way of value or participants, which draws the attention of tax administrators. It is noted that each cycle tends to result in increased complexity of the tax system. As stated by Browne, tax professionals do not exclusively act on the demands of taxpayers. He suggests 'during the 1970s the avoidance industry mushroomed. "Taxation planning" was actively promoted by professional lawyers and accountants.'[56]

The scheme detection and administrative response stage begins when tax revenue losses and / or taxpayer involvement reach a detectable point and become significant. Tax administrators often note a fall in revenue that cannot be explained by other economic factors such as high unemployment. In Australia in the 1990s, for example, it was the significant volume and value of taxpayer refunds that triggered the detection and response stage.

Tax administrators take action to prevent further losses and / or recover the losses—which escalates to litigation. The impact of judicial decisions is included in this stage as the outcome of litigation is critical to the administrators' ability to prevent further losses and / or recover tax revenue. Weaknesses in legislation and action to prevent further similar schemes may then be enacted by law-makers who change or make further laws to support the tax administrator's position. This stage may not necessarily consist of stricter enforcement measures but could result in other actions such as amnesties[57] or lowering of tax rates[58] to improve compliance.

---

56 Peter Browne, 'Fair Shares' (1985) 52 Legal Services Bulletin as quoted in Ivan Potas, 'Thinking about Tax Avoidance' (1993) 43 Australian Institute of Criminology: Trends & Issues in Crime and Criminal Justice.

57 Amnesties can have a negative as well as positive impact on tax compliance; Benno Torgler and Christopher A Schaltegger, 'Tax amnesties and political participation' in Benno Torgler (ed), Tax Compliance and Tax Morale: A Theoretical and Empirical Analysis (2007).

58 There are considerably more factors affecting tax compliance. However a relationship between compliance and tax rates has been identified by a number of researchers: John Braithwaite, 'Through the Eyes of the Advisers: A Fresh Look at High Wealth Individuals' in Valerie Braithwaite (ed), Taxing Democracy: Understanding Tax Avoidance and Evasion (2003) 245; Joel Slemrod and Shlomo Yitzhaki, 'Tax Avoidance, Evasion, and Administration' in Alan J Auerbach and Martin Feldstein (eds), Handbook of Public Economics (2002) 3, 1423; Benno Torgler, Tax Compliance and Tax Morale: A Theoretical and Empirical Analysis (2007).

The taxpayer response and recovery stage occurs as taxpayers are prevented from using the hitherto established schemes and reconsider their attitudes to the payment of taxes. It may also involve fiscal reconstruction to cope with tax compliance resulting from debts caused from the previous stage or future restriction of after-tax income. A pause in overt tax avoidance activity marks this stage as compliance is, or appears to be, raised.

In the Australian experience it appears that the cycles take around 10 years to go through the three stages. Each cycle produces a new set of schemes that are a little more complex than the previous ones. The cycles should be viewed not as a flat plane of repetitiveness but rather as three dimensional, as the cycle gains momentum and moves through time. It should also be noted that the boundaries of the cycle are not clear and distinct points in time but rather move through a gradual metamorphosis from one stage to another.

It is convenient, however, for illustrative purposes, to treat the examination in decades. This examination will therefore look at the tax avoidance schemes of each of three decades (from 1970 to 2000) sequentially.

2.3. The 'bottom of the harbour' schemes of the 1970s

(i) The scheme design and growth stage

The schemes of the 1970s chiefly consisted of the asset stripping of profitable trading companies incorporated specifically for the purpose of trading for one accounting period only. The assets were stripped out of the company by way of dividends and the corporate shell wound up.

The schemes were not sophisticated in an accounting or legal sense. They simply consisted of incorporating a 'trojan' company through which the profits of successful trading enterprises were directed. The 'trojan' companies were then stripped of their profits by way of declaring dividends to shareholders. The businesses' trading names were transferred from one company to another each year, to give the public appearance of continuity of the particular enterprise.

The then worthless companies were wound up. The directors of the 'trojan' companies were ordinary people with little or no knowledge of corporations law or the implications of what they were doing. Often they were housewives or labourers 'lending' their names and addresses for a small fee.

The schemes were targeted at HWIs with corporate trading structures with well-known trading companies. The schemes originated in Victoria and ultimately spread to all Australian States. According to Grabosky, the 'bottom of the harbour' schemes particularly flourished in Western Australia and were 'employed by hundreds of the more affluent members of the community to avoid paying taxes'.[59]

By the 1980s the overall lost tax revenue from the 'bottom of the harbour' schemes was estimated to be as much as $10 billion, or equivalent to 25.94 per cent of Australia's Gross Domestic Product in 1970.[60]

Grabosky stated:

> When the 'bottom of the harbour' schemes were in full flower, the sums involved were millions of dollars, not hundreds of thousands. Indeed, the full cost of this chapter of Australian criminal history ran to thousands of millions of dollars. Some 7,000 companies were involved.

'The 1986-87 *Annual Report* of the ATO stated that these [1970s] schemes involved some 6,688 companies and resulted in tax evasion of between $500m and $1 [billion].'[61] 'The numbers are significant but a casual glance at the range of financial estimates implies that the true loss is incalculable. ATO statistics are merely those detected; many schemes would have been undetected.'[62]

A number of reasons have been advanced for the growth of these schemes in the 1960s and 1970s. Myers pointed specifically to the sympathetic view shown towards the taxpayer by the Barwick High Court[63] for the growth of Australian tax avoidance activity in the 1960s and 1970s. He uses an excerpt from Sir Garfield's memoirs as evidence of judicial attitudes of the 1960s and 1970s, in which Sir Garfield stated:

> The liability to pay income tax is wholly derived from the law imposing and providing for the assessment of that tax. The obligation to pay it is a legal one. Some politicians try to treat it as a moral obligation. But it is not. The citizen is bound to pay no more tax than the statute requires him to pay according to the relevant state of his affairs.

---

59 Peter N Grabosky, 'The Deputy Crown Solicitor and the Bottom of the Harbour Scheme' in Peter N Grabosky (ed), Wayward governance: illegality and its control in the public sector (1989).

60 Australia's GDP for 1970 was $38.546 billion. Australian Bureau of Statistics, Australian National Accounts: National Income, Expenditure and Product, (Catalogue 5206.0, Table 7, 2012).

61 Ivan Potas, 'Thinking about Tax Avoidance' (1993) 43 Australian Institute of Criminology: Trends & Issues in Crime and Criminal Justice, 2.

62 Michael D'Ascenzo, 'In Defence of the Rule of Law' (Speech delivered at the Taxation Law Workshop, Aitken Hill, Victoria, 26–28 October 2001).

63 Allan J Myers, 'Tax Avoidance and the High Court since Sir Garfield Barwick' (Lecture delivered at the Melbourne Law School, University of Melbourne, 12 April 2005).

He cited Sir Garfield Barwick's statement as evidence of the reason for the 'boom' in the tax avoidance industry in Australia in the 1970s. Indeed Sir Garfield's findings in *Curran*[64] tend to support the view that he focussed on the form of the transactions rather than the substance or intent behind them, applying a literal rather than purposive statutory interpretation.

Potas also considered that, after 1970, tax avoidance activity was fuelled by a very restrictive interpretation of tax legislation adopted by the Australian courts. Judicial attitudes were such that virtually any tax avoidance scheme 'appears to have been outside the reach of the Commissioner of Taxation'.

However Grabosky stated '[t]he proliferation of extremely artificial tax avoidance schemes in the 1970s was to a large extent encouraged by members of the legal and accounting professions,' and that '[t]he medium in which these massive frauds on revenue flourished was "bureaucratic inertia"'.

(ii) The scheme detection and administrative response stage

'Phantom' or 'dummy' directors were an integral part of the incorporation of 'trojan' companies. The provision of 'dummy' directors became a very lucrative business and attracted some very large organisations. In Victoria, the Federated Ship Painters and Dockers Union (FSDU) was more than capable of providing 'dummy directors in the companies involved in those schemes'. What was more than likely a mere 'sideline' for the FSDU became the thread by which the 'bottom of the harbour' schemes were discovered.

Detection of the schemes, and administrative response, was very slow. It appears that the schemes had existed for more than 10 years before they were detected. Further the schemes were detected almost by accident, when the Royal Commission established in 1980[65] as an investigation into the criminal activities of the FSDU in Victoria exposed the existence of 'a massive tax avoidance industry'.

Grabosky's chapter on the involvement of the Deputy Crown Solicitor's (DCS) office in the 'bottom of the harbour' schemes lays much of the 'bureaucratic inertia' at the hands of the DCS office in Perth, Western Australia, and specifically one Abe Gleebman. In his defence, Gleebman asserted that despite being advised of the frauds by the ATO in 1973, it was not 'until [that advice] was discovered in

---

64 Curran v Federal Commissioner of Taxation (1974) 131 CLR 409.

65 Commonwealth of Australia and Victoria, Royal Commission on the Activities of the Federated Ship Painters and Dockers Union, Final Report (1984) vol 1, 91. This report became known as the 'Costigan Report'.

the course of inquiries by the Costigan Royal Commission in 1982' that action took place.

It is suggested that while some of the blame for the 'bureaucratic inertia' that lead to the time delay may rest on the DCS, the ATO must also accept some of that burden. Support for the ATO's part in the 'bureaucratic inertia' factor may be found in evidence given later to the 2001 Senate inquiry, when Michael D'Ascenzo, the then Second Commissioner said:

> There is a reality about pursuing prosecution. I remember being involved in some of the bottom-of-the-harbour situations, where we had a Commonwealth task force involving a whole range of agencies. We did end up putting into jail a handful of promoters, but there were many that—[escaped] ... it just got too late in the piece.[66]

Braithwaite[67] identifies three other factors[68] in addition to bureaucratic inertia as being responsible for the tax avoidance boom typified by the bottom of the harbour schemes, some of which have already been alluded to above. They were:

- Federal and High Court decisions unsympathetic to ATO enforcement that emboldened the promoters;
- Payment of commissions to accountants and solicitors who referred vendors; and
- Increased willingness of the community to participate in tax avoidance.

A factor that may have caused excessive delays in pursuing prosecution was a largely held belief that the general anti-avoidance provisions of s 260 of the ITAA 1936 were ineffective.[69] This view of s 260 is reasonable given the sympathetic view towards the taxpayer of the Barwick High Court. Braithwaite suggested that

---

66 Senate Inquiry, second report 11. 'Bureaucratic inertia' remains a problem for legal administrators and is not confined to tax administration. In a public statement in November 2008 WA Director of Public Prosecutions Robert Cock referred to a 10-year delay in prosecuting perpetrators of WA's 'finance brokers' scandal: 'The criminal justice system just didn't deliver. We got a few convictions; a few people spent a couple of years in jail. But really, we didn't achieve what the system is supposed to achieve.' (Paul Lampathakis, 'Justice Scandal: Brokers let off', The Sunday Times (Perth WA) 30 November 2008).

67 John Braithwaite, Markets in Vice; Markets in Virtue (2005).

68 The fourth reason is that of Arie Freiberg, 'Ripples from the Bottom of the Harbour: Some Social Ramifications of Taxation Fraud' (1998) 12 Criminal Law Journal 136, 137, as quoted in Braithwaite above.

69 Jeffrey Waincymer, 'The Australian Tax Avoidance Experience and Responses: A Critical Review' in Graeme S Cooper (ed), Tax Avoidance and the Rule of Law (1997) 247.

the attitude of the courts in the 1970s had reduced the ATO to no more than a 'token enforcer'.

The 'bottom of the harbour' schemes were closed by legislation and the strengthening of Australia's General Anti-avoidance Rules (GAARs) with the replacement of s 260 by the introduction of Pt IVA of the ITAA 1936 in 1981. Section 15AA of the *Acts Interpretation Act 1901* (Cth) was also enacted in 1981 to require the courts to prefer a *purposive* approach to statutory interpretation rather than the *literal* approach that had frustrated many ATO prosecution cases.[70]

(iii) The taxpayer response and recovery stage

The introduction of Pt IVA of the ITAA 1936 and s 15AA of the *Acts Interpretation Act 1901* (Cth) addressed one of Braithwaite's reasons for the growth of tax avoidance schemes (the problem of unsympathetic courts) but the other three factors were not addressed by those amendments to legislation. The 'bottom of the harbour' schemes of the 1970s reflected community attitudes and perceptions towards the use of tax avoidance techniques, at least in terms of public visibility. The delay in detecting and responding to the 'bottom of the harbour' schemes resulted in negligible direct impact on taxpayers. According to Grabosky there were only two prosecutions, and one of those convictions was later set aside.

The combination of rising tax rates, judicial permissiveness and apparent lack of action by the ATO had led to a surge in tax avoidance schemes—so much so that it was suggested in 1978 in the Commonwealth House of Representatives that:

70 In the interpretation of a provision of an Act, a construction that would promote the purpose or object underlying the Act (whether that purpose or object is expressly stated in the Act or not) shall be preferred to a construction that would not promote that purpose or object. (Emphasis added) s 15AA(1) Acts Interpretation Act (1901) (Cth).

> Tax dodging is taking a great deal of the talent of sections of the accountancy profession and is involving a large number of bureaucrats within the Government service in a continual game ... There is no doubt that never before in the history of Australia have we seen such concerted attacks on the revenue as have taken place in recent times. Never before have we seen such enormous volumes of revenue at risk as have been at risk in recent times. Those volumes are reaching ... extraordinary heights...[71]

Waincymer noted that 'the "Bottom of the Harbour" scandal of the 1970's [sic] was unique in its degree and impact and led a significant group in society to believe that paying tax was only for the foolish'.

However the element of criminality in the 'bottom of the harbour' schemes, highlighted by the Costigan inquiry, led many HWIs to distance themselves from involvement in schemes that were now more likely to be viewed as tax evasion or 'unacceptable' tax avoidance rather than tax planning. Taxpayers may have remained willing to reduce their tax burdens but were not so willing as to wish to go to jail over it. The taxpayer response appears therefore to be an acceptance of the 'new rules'.

However the continuation of tax-reducing activities into the 1980s indicates that the 'bottom of the harbour' schemes were not the end of tax avoidance scheme activity in Australia, but rather the beginning of the next cycle. The motivation to reduce tax remained, and the designers and promoters of tax avoidance schemes were to continue to develop and market tax-reducing structures in the 1980s. Taxpayers sought other methods of reducing their taxation burden and scheme designers were more than happy to oblige. Lawyers and accountants continued to refer clients to scheme designers. Taxation administrators remained outwardly tardy to react to tax avoidance activity and taxpayer demand to reduce taxation burdens had correspondingly increased.

2.4. Tax reducing activities of the 1980s

Two particular tax-reducing methods were employed by scheme designers in the 1980s and were the more significant tax-reducing activities used by employees. The first method consisted of the payment of private and domestic expenses by employers for and on behalf of, rather than to, employees thus reducing employees' assessable income. This method became known as 'salary sacrifice' and came to be used extensively by blue-collar workers.

71 Michael Baume, Member for Macarthur, 5 May 1978, as quoted in Woellner et al.

Subsequent tax administration action to restrict salary sacrifice arrangements encouraged the development of the second method by way of the use of 'interposed entities'. This section looks at those activities and the respective administrative responses in turn.

(a) Salary sacrifice

(i) The scheme design and growth stage

A characteristic of the transition from the taxpayer response and recovery stage to the scheme design and growth stage is an apparent lack of tax avoidance activity. Tax avoidance activity in the early 1980s was not readily apparent. Braithwaite stated '[w]hat is clear is that aggressive tax planning became much less aggressive during the 1980s and into the 1990s'. He endorsed Levi's[72] belief that voluntary compliance with Australian tax law improved during the 1980s as a result of the Hawke government's rebuilding of public confidence in the tax system as well as unprecedented public consultation and high profile prosecutions of the designers and participants of the 'bottom of the harbour' schemes. He considered these as plausible but unverifiable reasons for the apparent decline in tax avoidance activity.

However, schemes did continue to develop in the 1980s. The schemes of the 1980s involved various forms of reducing direct payments to individual taxpayers. They often involved making payments on behalf of employees rather than directly to the employees as salaries or wages. For their part employees accepted reduced salaries and wages in return (salary sacrifice). Many private and domestic expenses such as travel to and from work, entertainment and other domestic household expenses were paid for and on behalf of employees.

The activity later became known as 'salary sacrifice' arrangements. The employer was able to deduct the payments made on behalf of employees from its assessable income as labour expenses. The employee received an undisclosed or 'fringe benefit' in lieu of a direct assessable income payment. The employee thus avoided declaring the income and did not have to pay any tax on the benefit. These arrangements were contained in very simple 'employment agreements' that set out the terms and conditions of payments to be made on behalf of the employee.

---

72 Margaret Levi, Of Rule and Revenue (1988), as quoted in Braithwaite.

Use of the schemes tended to focus on high income earning professionals in private practice but also extended to taxpayers engaged in other trading entities. The development of the North West oil and gas fields off the Pilbara coast in the mid 1980s[73] provided a previously un-encountered kind of tax avoider—the high income earning blue-collar worker.[74]

The 'blue-collar' sectors included heavy industry, manufacturing, transport, fishing, agricultural and service industries. With the assistance of co-operative employers who permitted the use of 'employment arrangements', blue-collar workers were able to defray some of their taxed income with non-taxed 'employee benefits'.

Tax avoidance activity in the 1980s therefore extended its taxpayer base beyond the HWIs and the primarily professional classes. These classes of taxpayers had previously been the major participants in avoidance activity. The numbers of taxpayers involved, and the extent of losses to taxation revenue, were significant. According to ABS labour statistics for 1985 around 50 per cent of male employees and 25 per cent of female employees received a non-wage benefit.[75]

(ii) The scheme detection and administrative response stage

Braithwaite proposed the view 'that aggressive tax planning became much less aggressive during the 1980s and into the 1990s' may have overlooked the practice of salary sacrifice as it was considered 'acceptable tax avoidance' until 1986. The volume of tax avoided in this manner of tax planning was not accounted for and

---

73 North West Shelf LNG Pty Ltd, 'A Brief History of the North West Shelf' (Press Release, June 2003) <http://www.australialng.com.au/downloads/NWSALNG_brochure.pdf> at 15 February 2006.

74 Wage conditions calculated from the Mechanical and Electrical Contractors (North West Shelf Project Platform) Award 1984, No. A 10 of 1984 and compared with employment advertisements placed in The West Australian in March and April 1983, show that trades people in the Pilbara oil industry were paid around $50 000 per annum (pa) plus the provision of free accommodation, clothing, tools and travel to and from work. At the same time the vacancy for the Deputy Crown Solicitor in Perth was advertised with a remuneration of $45 200 pa. A senior computer systems officer with the State Health Computing Services was offered a mere $29 067 pa. The State Energy Commission advertised for an engine driver in Derby WA for $250.70 per week or $13 036 pa on 30 March 1983.

75 Australian Bureau of Statistics, 6101.0 Labour Statistics Australia (1985).

thus may have given rise to his belief, which is also expressed by Levi, and Devos,[76] that voluntary compliance with Australian tax law improved. It may have been that compliance did not improve, but rather 'unacceptable tax avoidance' activity had crossed the boundary to be reconfigured as 'acceptable tax planning'.

'Salary sacrifice' did reach a detectable level, however, and taxation administrators reacted to end the practice. As a measure to combat loss of taxation revenue through the use of 'salary sacrifice' employment agreements, the *Fringe Benefits Tax Assessment Act* was introduced to tax 'fringe benefits' (FBT) in 1986. This made the employer liable for the avoided tax that would have been paid by the employee had the income been paid directly to the employee.

FBT further penalises employers in that it not only imposes the tax avoided by the employee through direct expense payments, but also recovers the tax deductibility of the expense that would otherwise have been of a private and domestic nature. The payment is 'grossed-up'[77] to increase the approximate value of the payment that the employee would have had to receive before tax to acquire the goods or services purchased on the employee's behalf.

A rate of 48.5 cents in the dollar was then applied to the 'grossed-up' payment.[78] Hence a payment of $100 was 'grossed-up' to the value of $194.17. A tax rate of 48.5% was applied to the $194.17. In this way the payment of $100 on behalf of an employee attracted a tax liability of $94.17 upon the employer.

The result was that employers remained free to make payments on the employee's behalf, but became liable for almost the same amount in tax. Also limits were placed on the sums permitted to be defrayed through 'salary sacrifice' and the values of fringe benefits received were required to be disclosed on employees' income tax returns.

(iii) The taxpayer response and recovery stage

FBT affected the blue-collar workers directly in that employers were limited in the ways they could pay tax exempt salaries. FBT resulted in employers becoming less

---

76 Ken Devos, 'Penalties and Sanctions for Australian Taxation Crimes and Their Effect on Taxpayer Compliance' (paper presented at the 5th International Conference on Tax Administration, Atax UNSW, Sydney, 4 April 2002) as quoted in Braithwaite.

77 Prior to 2006-07 year the FBT rate was 48.5% and the grossed-up rate was $\frac{1}{1 - 48.5\%} = 1.9417$

78 This was reduced to 46.5% as of 1 April 2006.

enthusiastic to participate in the agreements and generally encouraged them to resort to paying salaries or wages direct to employees as before.

A number of exemptions to FBT are included in the legislation, such as payments to employees' superannuation to a limited extent.[79] The exemptions have resulted in salary sacrifice continuing, albeit in a less attractive and limited manner. However, in general the introduction of FBT caused taxpayers to seek other ways of reducing their taxation burden and the concept of interposed entities was introduced to taxpayers by the tax professionals. That concept is examined in the following section.

(b) Interposed entities

(i) The scheme design and growth stage

The introduction of FBT curtailed the use of 'salary sacrifice' arrangements but it stimulated the use of 'interposed entities' and 'income splitting'. This involved interposing a legal entity between the employer and the employee. Initially employees argued that they were contractors being paid for the provision of services rather than employees being paid under contracts of service.

There were other taxation benefits to the interposition of a separate legal entity between the employer and employee for both parties. As a contractor the employee was able to claim certain expenses as 'business expenses' that were deductible against assessable income. An example of this is travel to and from work—which for an employee is of a private and domestic nature. However a tradesman working as a contractor from home is able to deduct the expense of travel to the job as a business expense. Another example is the responsibility and cost of workers' compensation insurance which could be passed to the employee in his role as a contractor.

After 1992, the superannuation guarantee charge could be avoided through the use of an interposed entity in some circumstances. A good example of the

79 The case of Ryan v Federal Commissioner of Taxation [2004] ATC 2181 dealt with superannuation payments made by an employer husband to an employee wife. The case also considered interposed family entities and income splitting arrangements. The Commissioner of Taxation sought to set aside the 'arrangement' under Pt IVA however the court found in favour of the taxpayers. Detailed examination of the case is outside the scope of this thesis but the exception is noted.

practice of attempts made to circumvent the FBT is illustrated in the facts surrounding the case of *Vabu Pty Ltd v Federal Commissioner of Taxation*.[80]

It did not take scheme designers and taxpayers long to realise that if they could interpose an entity to avoid FBT by changing an employee into a contractor, then perhaps the entity could be made up of, at least nominally, a number of individual taxpayers and thereby take advantage of lower tax rates provided for under Australia's progressive tax rate system. Other income-splitting techniques, designed to take advantage of the structure of 'progressive' tax rates using family trusts, partnerships and other interposed entities, were employed by taxpayers and their employers.

The advantage of 'income-splitting' in the 1984 taxation year is demonstrated by the following example. An individual solicitor earns $40,000[81] and the taxation assessed, ignoring rebates and other levies, is $14,491. By simply splitting that income with his wife—who has no other income—by way of a trust, the net tax on the same income can be reduced to $9,403, representing 12.5 per cent of gross income and a tax saving of over 35 per cent.

Examples of income derived by personal exertion being substituted as business income, illustrated in the cases of the activities of welders, plumbers, electricians, architects, accountants, and the like, where no other family members take an active part in the enterprise, reveal the interposed entity to be no more than a taxation minimisation scheme.

(ii) The scheme detection and administrative response stage

Again detection of the schemes by the taxation authorities was comparatively slow. Indeed the detection processes upon which administrators relied showed a decline in tax avoidance activity. Braithwaite quotes Devos, who notes a report that 'non-compliance detected in audits fell from a high of 87 per cent in 1984-85 to a low 59 per cent in 1990-91 after which it gradually began to increase again'.

A possible explanation for the reduction in the detection of interposed entity schemes prior to 1984 is that until the decision was made in *Tupicoff v*

---

80 [1996] ATC 4898.

81 ATO statistics for 1984 are unavailable at this time however in Tupicoff v Commissioner of Taxation, where the taxpayer was an insurance salesman, the sums involved were gross income of $35 000 and $10 492. The sums relate to activities in the 1978 year, therefore the example of a solicitor earning $40 000 in 1984 is considered reasonable for the purposes of this example.

Commissioner of Taxation,[82] the ATO was not targeting income-splitting arrangements. The ATO had stepped back from strict application of Pt IVA to what are considered 'family' partnerships.[83] However Evans warns '[a] cynic might suggest that this decision owes more to a pragmatic acceptance that there are simply too many such partnerships to challenge rather than the application of a principled approach to the issue'.[84] Ultimately the numbers of individuals involved and amounts of tax avoided reached detectable levels and drew the attention of tax administrators and legislators.[85]

These early attempts at tax minimisation through income-splitting using trusts or other 'interposed entities' were addressed by the ATO in 1984. Taxation Ruling IT 2121 set out official views in the light of a decision of the Federal Court of Australia handed down on 21 November 1984 in the case of *Tupicoff v Commissioner of Taxation*.

Limitations were placed on infant beneficiaries under div 6AA of the ITAA 1936 as to the tax impositions on income over $416 per annum. This effectively prevented advantage from income distribution to minor family members for the purpose of tax minimisation.

These limitations were in response to a financial practice of changing the form or structure of an enterprise that enabled the proprietor(s) to distribute income to family members who were not otherwise involved in the business. The structures often had no other function than to reduce the incidence of tax. Often, funds distributed to non-working family members were never placed in the control of the family member concerned. The funds remained in the control of the 'owners' and were 'paper' transfers only.

(iii) The taxpayer response and recovery stage

'Bureaucratic inertia' delayed the final clarification of interposed entity arrangements until the late 1990s. However early in the 1980s the ATO's opinion was that the wages of employed blue-collar workers were from personal exertion

82 [1984] ATC 4851 and (1984) 15 ATR 1262.

83 Australian Taxation Office, Taxation Ruling TR 94/8; Australian Taxation Office, 'Practical Guide to Part IVA' (Media Release 2005/70, 13 December 2005).

84 Chris Evans, 'The Battle Continues: Recent Australian Experience with Statutory Avoidance and Disclosure Rules' in Judith Freedman (ed), Beyond Boundaries: Developing Approaches to Tax Avoidance and Tax Risk Management (2008) 37.

85 ATO Taxation Ruling TR 2006/2, <http://law.ato.gov.au/atolaw/view.htm?docid=TXR/TR20062/NAT/ATO/00001> at 15 June 2008.

and not 'business' income. This effectively stopped those schemes from proliferating. Generally tax professionals were aware that they could not arguably support the income-splitting structures and the schemes lost favour in the late 1980s.

However many professionals and tradespeople established trusts to enable income-splitting with family members to reduce taxation burdens. Examples of interposing trusts to split assessable income remain despite the ATO crackdown on 'personal services income' and the introduction of the *New Business Tax System (Alienation of Personal Services Income) Act 2000* (Cth).

The introduction of the alienation of personal services income provisions did restrict the use of interposed entities. However the rules can be circumvented through the use of 'service trusts'. Such tax avoidance structures may have been limited but they continue to be used. Numerous professionals such as medical practitioners, dentists, lawyers, accountants and the like continue to circumvent such controls that forbid splitting income with their spouses by way of partnership, by establishing 'service' trusts.[86]

It should also be noted that non-taxation legislative factors apply to such enterprises and business structures. There are licensing, regulatory and other legal or ethical requirements placed on some trades and professions. Rules of regulatory bodies such as the Legal Practitioners Board, the Medical Practitioners Board and professional organisations such as the Australian Medical Association require partners to be qualified in the profession in order for the partnership to be valid. However the 'service trust' can also circumvent some of those rules.

As with the end of the 'bottom of the harbour' schemes and the tax avoidance activity of the 1970s, the cycle of tax avoidance scheme development was to move to another level. A significant outcome of the development of the tax avoidance structures of the 1980s was that the concept of tax minimisation structures had been introduced to the blue-collar workers of Australia.

Braithwaite's fourth factor[87] had increased in its scope to encompass another class of taxpayer, and the focus of this research—the blue-collar worker in addition to the previously targeted HWIs. Therefore as well as continuing to

---

86 The legal validity of 'service trusts' was the principal issue in Phillips v Federal Commissioner of Taxation [1978] ATR 783. See also Federal Commissioner of Taxation v Everett (1980) 10 ATR 608 as to splitting income by way of partnership structures. The introduction of Capital Gains Tax rendered partnership structures less effective as tax reducing methods.

87 'Increased willingness of the community to participate in tax avoidance.'

'service' HWIs, scheme designers and promoters began to 'service' a previously untargeted taxpayer, the high income-earning blue-collar worker. Market forces continued to stimulate demand for tax-reducing schemes.

However the broadening of the tax base in the 1980s, and the removal of many of the concessions and preferences that had previously permitted effective tax reducing structures, removed some of the avenues of legitimate tax-reducing schemes. Legislative and administrative restrictions on the use of salary sacrifice arrangements and interposed entities as vehicles for tax minimisation meant that the tax professionals—integral to the supply of tax-reducing opportunities—had to look for alternative possibilities.

This examination now moves on to the development of tax avoidance schemes in the 1990s.

2.5. Mass-marketed tax avoidance schemes of the 1990s

(i) The scheme design and growth stage

The mass-marketed tax avoidance schemes of the 1990s used a mixture of existing corporate structures, taxation law and ATO procedures to contrive complex and effective taxation avoidance schemes. The introduction of 'self-assessment' introduced a further factor to the development of mass-marketed tax avoidance schemes which appeared to give the appearance of legitimacy. The schemes evolved into many 'business structures' and ultimately over 196 were reviewed by the ATO in 2001.

The ATO published a list of schemes deemed to be 'eligible schemes' on its website and used the list as part of the Commissioner's response to the Senate Committee inquiry into mass-marketed schemes and investor protection. However the ATO removed the list of eligible schemes when the Commissioner's offer to settle was finalised.[88]

The mass-marketed tax avoidance schemes of the 1990s were broadly categorised by the ATO into three groups:

88 The list of schemes is appended to the author's thesis published by the University of New South Wales at <http://www.unsworks.unsw.edu.au/primo_library/libweb/action/dlDisplay.do?docId=unsworks_11537&vid=UNSWORKS> at 23 June 2014.

- The creation of artificial deductions through a system of exchange of loan contracts (round-robin financing and non-recourse loans) whereby the funds for 'deductible' business expenses were 'loaned' to taxpayers to be repaid out of future profits from the respective 'business' venture;
- Certain film and other investments granted favourable taxation treatment by Australian tax legislation; and
- Employee-benefit arrangements.[89]

Examples of business structures used in tax avoidance schemes ranged from those in the first category that were outright contrivances with little or no regard for substance whatsoever, to those in the second category which were arguably not tax avoidance schemes and had some basis of substance, such as the tea tree plantations operated by Main Camp Tea Tree Project No. 4.

A common thread of many of the schemes, in particular those in the first category, was that 'investors' were claiming tax deductions for monies they had not paid. The 'business debts' were financed by way of 'loans' from the promoters and were never legally valid.

Through the system of self-assessment participants deducted the invalid business expenses from their taxable income. Many taxpayers, who participated in the schemes, applied for a variation of their tax withholding amount under s 221D of the ITAA 1936. This gave the participating taxpayers immediate cash flow benefits. Where taxpayers did not reduce their tax withholding amounts, the ATO consequently over-refunded the participating taxpayers with pay-as-you-earn (PAYE), and other tax credits, withheld from their income. This additional factor was not only exploited by the taxpayers, who were ultimately liable to repay the refunds, but also by the promoters who, in at least one case, expropriated the tax refund from the taxpayer to themselves.

The third category, which involved employee benefit arrangements, was significantly different from the mass-marketed tax avoidance schemes that are the focus of this book. Participants needed to be employers, rather than employees, to set up the appropriate financial structures. In addition their average tax liability was significantly higher than that of the average participants in mass-marketed tax avoidance schemes. Given those differences, examination of this category is outside the scope of this book.

---

89 ATO Submission No 845, 1 to the Senate Inquiry.

The mass-marketed tax avoidance schemes were marketed extensively throughout Australia. However they received considerable acceptance in Western Australia and particularly in the mining regions of the Pilbara and the Kalgoorlie goldfields. The high income earning, highly taxed and hard-working blue-collar worker appeared to be particularly attracted to the schemes.

Promoters were quick to note the market demand in the Pilbara and Kalgoorlie goldfields. They used extensive marketing campaigns to promote their 'products'. These included seminars for groups of investors as well as door-to-door sales and telephone canvassing of entire towns to sell the schemes. The schemes were, in the truest sense, 'mass-marketed'.

The introduction of self-assessment permitted the deductions related to mass-marketed tax avoidance schemes submitted in individual taxation returns to be processed by the ATO without query. This created a belief by scheme participants that the schemes were genuine. Further, tardiness by the ATO in reacting to the schemes, or 'bureaucratic inertia', consolidated the perception that the schemes were genuine tax planning financial arrangements.

According to the ATO, over $4 billion in taxable income representing nearly $2.5 billion in lost taxation revenue was identified to have been avoided.

The following details of two of the schemes are provided to give further background and context to the design, operation and promotion of the mass-marketed tax avoidance schemes of the 1990s. The two examples provide an indication that there was a continuum in the range of schemes, from the earliest, and almost legitimate, 'investments' producing tangible products to the later, intangible schemes, which were little more than corporate contrivances. The two examples represent the ends of that continuum.

They are examples of mass-marketed tax avoidance schemes offered to the Pilbara blue-collar workers in the 1990s. They are examined to indicate how the schemes functioned.

Much of the supporting evidence was provided by interviewees to this research and participants in the schemes. This also includes references to related litigation and evidence given to the Senate Inquiry.

Main Camp Tea Tree Project No. 4, mentioned above, was a genuine agricultural project for the production and export of tea tree oil in the 1990s and 2000s. It was registered in Sydney, New South Wales, on 28 February 1992[90] and

90 Extracted from Australian Securities and Investments Commission's database <http://www.search .asic.gov.au/cgi-bin/gns030c> at 8 July 2008.

its primary business was the establishment and operation of large-scale tea tree plantations.

The tea tree plantations were established by:

> Glendon Michael Stotter, the Chairman of Directors of B[usiness] a[nd] R[esearch] M[anagement Limited]. From March 1992 to October 1995, Mr Stotter was involved in the establishment of the Main Camp Tea Tree Oil Projects Nos 1–4, which had raised funds from the public pursuant to registered prospectuses, for the purpose of establishing tea tree plantations on property at Main Camp near Casino in northern New South Wales. The development of that property was described by Mr Stotter as successful.[91]

Despite being considered an 'eligible scheme' and the 'investment' disallowed by the Commissioner of Taxation in 2002,[92] Main Camp Tea Tree Limited continued to be a genuine, thriving business. In 2004 it featured on the ABC's *Landline* television programme.

> The world's largest tea tree plantation, Main Camp, is also trialing alternative production methods. Founded in 1992, the main camp project accelerated the growth of what had been a cottage industry. It is a massive 4,440 hectares and 22 kilometres in length with 147 kilometres of internal roads. About half the industry's entire production comes from Main Camp, about 400 tonnes of oil a year.[93]

Despite being considered an 'eligible scheme', and losing the bulk of its investors, the Main Camp tea tree oil projects continued to trade until 2008 when they became insolvent. Main Camp Corporation Pty Ltd applied for voluntary deregistration on 27 February 2008.

It is possible that a lack of financial support brought about by the loss of the tax incentive to agricultural investments, which was exploited by the promoters and later withdrawn by the decision of the Commissioner of Taxation to consider the projects 'eligible schemes', contributed to the ultimate failure of the plantations.

In his examination of the mass-marketed tax avoidance schemes the Commissioner of Taxation found that many of the schemes, though apparently genuine in the production of the end product, involved a series of non-recourse

---

91 Howland-Rose and Ors v Federal Commissioner of Taxation [2002] FCA 246 [5].

92 Letter from Michael Carmody, Australian Commissioner of Taxation, to Thomas Anderson, 28 March 2002 (held by the author). In the context of the ATO treatment of mass-marketed tax avoidance schemes 'eligible' meant eligible to be considered as a tax avoidance scheme not eligible in a positive sense as a deduction.

93 Shoebridge, Joanne, 'Tea tree growers confident better times are just around the corner', Landline, 11 April 2004 <http://www.abc.net.au/landline/content/2004/s1081381.htm> at 4 May 2010.

loans to shareholders. The non-recourse loans had the effect of artificially inflating otherwise genuine, and legitimately deductible, expenses.

As well as being funded by way of cash from public subscriptions, Main Camp Tea Tree Project No. 4 also engaged in a system of non-recourse loans which created investment packages to the value of $23,500. An investor's contribution was paid by way of $3,525 in 'prepaid' interest and a 'seed fee' of $200.[94] The balance of the $23,500 was made up by way of a 'non-recourse' loan. Therefore the investor made a cash contribution of $3,725 but appeared to contribute $23,500 into a 'genuine' agricultural project.

Though it was an agricultural product which received favourable taxation treatment, the use of the non-recourse loans therefore placed the operation of Main Camp Tea Tree Project No.4 in the first group of mass-marketed tax avoidance schemes categorised above. Main Camp Tea Tree Project No. 4 was considered to be a mass-marketed tax avoidance scheme. It became a forerunner of the plantation industry-based mass-marketed tax avoidance schemes.

The value of the loans was disallowed as a tax deduction by the ATO. However it is noted that not all investors contributed to the project entirely by way of non-recourse loans, some contributed much more than $3,725 in cash. Despite this all Main Camp Tea Tree Project No 4 investors had the sum of $19,775 disallowed.

Later, investors who had contributed more than the required minimum of $3,725 were granted deduction for all monies they had actually paid. In one case as much as $14,200 was paid by 10 April 2002 of the original non-recourse debt of $23,500 taken out on 30 June 1995. However the balance of the loan, being $9,300, was never recovered by the company. It is noted that no loan statements were issued to the investor after 10 April 2002 nor did the administrator make any claim on the investor on winding up the project.

It is also noted that in statements given in evidence *Howland-Rose and Ors v Federal Commissioner of Taxation* it was evident that the financiers, who were engaged by the project managers to raise funds for the project, had raised considerably more funds than were passed on to the project managers.

At the other end of the continuum, **Satcom Electronic Commerce Services Pty Ltd** operated as a franchise business structure which sold licences to access a search engine on the Internet. This scheme was a mixture of a genuine attempt to

94 Facsimile from Peter Marshall, General Manager, Main Camp Tea Tree Oil Ltd, to Alexander R Fullarton, 10 April 2002.

produce and market a computer-based information technology system and a blatant fraud.

It was registered in Perth, Western Australia, on 28 February 1997. [95] With its registered office in Osborne Park, Western Australia, it operated chiefly in that State. Satcom was heavily promoted in the Pilbara region and most of its investors were Pilbara blue-collar workers.

The designers and promoters of the scheme consisted chiefly of four people, though a substantial office complex was established in Perth. The designers of the search engine were information technologists who developed a search engine program for use on the Internet. However the designers and promoters of the corporate structure (scheme) were tax professionals and salesmen who engaged in the marketing of the scheme to taxpayer / investors.

In order to avoid the requirements of the Australian Securities and Investments Commission (ASIC) relating to incorporated companies, promoters turned to yet another corporate entity—the franchise. A proprietary limited company was established and a series of franchise agreements marketed. The overt purpose of the franchise businesses was to distribute registrations to access the search engine on the Internet.

In order to market the registrations the investor became a distribution franchisee and executed legal documents evidencing the transaction. The franchisee committed to sell the access to the Internet search engine by way of marketing access rights to the general public. The access was registered with Satcom by way of an annual subscription.

Funding for the scheme was raised by soliciting investors to purchase franchises. The investor was charged administration and legal costs, as well as stamp duty and franchise business name registration fees of $4,000. In addition a franchise fee of $60,000 was also charged. The $4,000 was to be paid in cash and the remaining $60,000 was financed by a related party as a non-recourse loan. The franchisee received written evidence of the transaction and was instructed to claim the total fee of $64,000 in the following year's income tax return.

Investors claimed the $64,000 as business expenses and, subject to their marginal income tax rate, received a refund of up to nearly $32,000. The first refund was transferred to the promoters as a repayment of a 'loan'. The refund

---

95 Company registration details: Satcom Electronic Commerce Services Pty Ltd. ACN 077 650 269. Extracted from Australian Securities and Investments Commission database <http://www.search.asic.gov.au/cgi-bin/gns030c> at 22 December 2005.

was transferred to the promoter on the grounds that the tax saving would be indefinite.

In almost all cases the franchisees never attempted any business transactions to support their argument of conducting genuine businesses. It is likely that the participating investors were not entirely aware of the existence of the franchise business and that they were expected to market the product, being the Internet search engine.

The successful marketing of this scheme may also have been influenced by the actual existence of the program, which could be readily demonstrated to prospective clients by way of accessing the Internet. This scheme not only relied on the attraction of tax avoidance, with the usual promotion of non-recourse loans and self-assessment to produce inflated tax deductions, but also the timing of the fervour for information technology in the late 1990s stock market boom.

In any event, in the north-west mining town of Paraburdoo it would have been almost impossible to carry on a viable business due to the number of the franchises that were sold into a very small community. It is also doubtful that a blue-collar worker in the Pilbara, working 12-hour shifts on a mine site in over 50 °C conditions, would have the desire or the resources to 'actively engage in business pursuits'.

It is interesting to note that the Satcom scheme was actively promoted in 1998 and after the ASIC had issued warnings as to 'shonky' tax scheme promoters in April 1997. The ATO also established its 'schemes task force' in July 1997 and issued its warning on 'tax effective' schemes in October of that year.[96]

Shortly after 1999 the promoter disappeared from Western Australia. The company applied for voluntary deregistration on 30 January 2001 and the company was wound up on 5 September 2002. Its only asset, an internet search engine, was sold to the Commonwealth Bank by the liquidator. Subsequently, the operations of Satcom were central to the test case of *Meredith v Federal*

---

96 Australian Taxation Office, 'Tax Office on target' (media release 97/50, 30 October 1997). The media release makes reference to 'aggressive tax planning' but it is, at best, a veiled threat rather than notice that the ATO intends to address the matter. Merely making a statement that 'We are experiencing the increasing globalisation of business and a great deal of legislative activity to counter aggressive tax planning' does not imply action will be taken, particularly when it wasn't. Only an astute observer would have perceived the threat. The more emboldened promoter may even have viewed it as tacit approval of the mass-marketed tax avoidance schemes.

Commissioner of Taxation and Ors[97] and the subsequent appeal case of *Meredith v Commissioner of Taxation*.[98]

The book now turns to the ATO's action to recover the 'over refunds' that emanated from the schemes and the taxpayer responses to that recovery action.

(ii) The scheme detection and administration response stage

As with the transition from the 'bottom of the harbour' schemes of the 1970s to the interposed entities of the 1980s, tax avoidance activity appeared much less aggressive in the early 1990s. It was not until 1996 that authorities began to notice 'termites' in the fiscal structure.[99] It is difficult to determine accurately when the mass-marketed tax avoidance schemes of the 1990s commenced but it is likely to have been in the late 1980s to early 1990s.

Detection of the schemes was quicker than those of earlier decades, perhaps less than 10 years. This earlier detection could have been due to enhanced organisational capacity and action to reduce 'bureaucratic inertia' by the ATO or the design of the mass-marketed tax avoidance schemes themselves.

Unlike previous schemes that solely sought to reduce tax liability and therefore tax payable, these mass-marketed tax avoidance schemes—some identified as 'eligible schemes'– targeted a different class of taxpayer and operated in a different fashion. The focus of the mass-marketed tax avoidance schemes of the 1990s was to recover tax credits paid by employers and contractors to the ATO through the PAYE system.

The mass-marketed tax avoidance schemes of the 1990s created 'business' losses which were deducted from other wage or salary income. The high income earning blue-collar worker typically has tax payments deducted and remitted to the ATO prior to his / her annual assessment. The deductions claimed by way of the schemes resulted in those tax credits being refunded to the taxpayer. The ATO was alerted to the presence of the schemes by the 'surge' in tax refunds.

In 1996 tax deductions related to mass-marketed tax avoidance schemes exceeded $666 million. That was a significant increase from $288 million in 1995 and $176 million in 1994, and a phenomenal increase when compared with just $2 million in 1990.

---

97 [2001] FCA 1135.

98 [2002] FCAFC 271.

99 A term coined by Vito L Tanzi, 'Globalization, Technological Developments, and the Work of Fiscal Termites' (Working Paper No. 00/181International Monetary Fund, November 2000); and used by Braithwaite.

The ASIC issued warnings as to 'shonky' tax scheme promoters in April 1997. The ATO established its 'Schemes Task Force' in July 1997 and issued its warning on 'tax effective' schemes in October of that year.

In 1998 the ATO issued some 57,000 amended assessments under Pt IVA of the ITAA 1936 to recover taxes which had been avoided, in the Commissioner's opinion, through the use of contrived schemes. One hundred and sixty-five schemes were deemed 'eligible schemes' and taxpayers had many millions of dollars of income tax deductions retrospectively disallowed.

(iii) The taxpayer response and recovery stage

There was considerable taxpayer angst and a great deal of political, professional and taxpayer resources were directed at resisting the Commissioner's action. Generally taxpayers involved in the mass-marketed tax avoidance schemes protested openly and strongly against the amended assessments. However, as noted in Chapter One, the Pilbara blue-collar workers tended not to join the public protests.

The protests ultimately resulted in a Senate Inquiry into the mass-marketed tax avoidance schemes and the resultant ATO recovery action. A Senate Economics References Committee was established on 29 June 2000 with terms of reference to consider:

- The adequacy of measures to promote investor understanding of the financial and taxation implications of tax effective schemes;
- The conduct of, and the adequacy of measures for controlling, tax effective scheme designers, promoters and financial advisers; and
- The ATO's approach towards, and role in relation to, mass marketed tax effective schemes.

The committee reported that '[o]ne of the critical factors in the debate over MMS [mass-marketed tax avoidance schemes] is the apparent time delay between growth of the MMS market and the ATO decision to crackdown on the schemes'. The Senate inquiry also noted that one of the key issues taken into account was '[t]he time delay between the growth of the [mass-marketed tax avoidance schemes] market and the ATO's decision to disallow deductions associated with mass marketed arrangements'.

Legal action was taken to challenge the Commissioner's decision to disallow deductions related to mass-marketed tax avoidance schemes, of which six 'test cases' are examined below to illustrate the type of scheme and the number of taxpayers affected by each case.

Howland-Rose v Federal Commissioner of Taxation[100] dealt with expenditure on research and development of the Main Camp tea tree plantation mentioned above. Given that the income relating to the expenditure was to be received more than 13 months after the date of the expenditure, it was held that the expense was not relevant or incidental to the production of assessable income and so the deductions were disallowed. The general anti-avoidance provisions of the ITAA 1936, Pt IVA were not applied in this case.

Vincent v Federal Commissioner of Taxation[101] dealt with the validity of business expenses incurred by way of debts to financiers through the use of non-recourse loans. It was held that the dominant purpose of the transactions was to enable the taxpayer to obtain a tax benefit in connection with the scheme. It was therefore held that Pt IVA of the ITAA 1936 applied to the scheme and that deductions previously allowed (under the self-assessment program) were correctly disallowed.

Meredith v Federal Commissioner of Taxation[102] dealt with the Commissioner of Taxation's powers to issue amended assessments. The plaintiff asserted that the amended assessments issued to the participants of the Satcom 'investment' mentioned above were invalid. It was held that the Commissioner was authorised to issue amended assessments.

Krampel Newman Partners Pty Ltd v Federal Commissioner of Taxation[103] dealt with investment in a 'film investment' pursuant to div 10BA. The film never completed final production. It was held that the investors had not acquired the copyright in the relevant film in the year of expenditure and therefore they were not entitled to any income tax deduction.

Puzey v Federal Commissioner of Taxation[104] dealt with an investment in a sandalwood plantation. Unlike the findings in *Vincent v Federal Commissioner of Taxation* [2002], it was held that the taxpayer was carrying on business and that, but for Pt IVA, the expenses would have been deductible. Although management fees of $800 were allowed as a revenue expense, all other expenses were disallowed, utilising the provisions of Pt IVA.

---

100 [2002] FCA 246.
101 [2002] FCAFC 291.
102 [2002] FCAFC 271.
103 [2003] FCA 123.
104 [2003] FCAFC 197.

Federal Commissioner of Taxation v Sleight[105] dealt with the concept of carrying on business as a primary producer as a partner in a 'managed farm investment' and business expenses paid by way of a non-recourse loan disallowed. It was held that actual cash expended was deductible but only against capital gains and not deductible against ordinary income. The deduction against ordinary income was therefore disallowed. As with Howland-Rose v Federal Commissioner of Taxation the provisions of Pt IVA were not utilised in disallowing the deductions.

The table showing the impact of the ATO's 'test cases' on participants in mass-marketed tax avoidance schemes indicates how widespread the marketing of the schemes was and the number of taxpayers involved in the particular schemes covered by the above 'test cases'.

Scheme	**Case**	**Year decided**	**Number of taxpayer's re-assessed**[106]	**Total participants (%)**[107]
Main Camp Tea Tree Project	Howland-Rose	2002	9 710	29.88
Active Cattle Management	Vincent	2002	642	1.98
Satcom	Meredith	2002	1 017	3.13
Film Investment Mephisto's Web[108]	Krampel Newman	2003	34	0.10
Kununurra Sandalwood	Puzey	2004	287	0.88
Northern Rivers Tea Tree	Sleight	2004	20 454*	62.95

Table 7 The impact of the ATO's 'test cases' on participants in mass-marketed tax avoidance schemes (* Includes those taxpayers affected by the Puzey decision) [109]

105 [2004] FCAFC 94.

106 Letter from the Director, Aggressive Tax Planning, Australian Taxation Office to Alexander R Fullarton, 16 December 2008.

107 Based on the total number of scheme participants of 32 493 as identified by Murphy.

108 Not on list of schemes.

109 Aggressive Tax Planning section, Australian Taxation Office, Moonee Ponds, Victoria.

The Kununurra Sandalwood, Main Camp and Northern Rivers Tea Tree Projects involved by far the majority of scheme participants. Arguably the tangible evidence of the existence of the projects by way of many hectares of plantation trees was a strong influence in substantiating the 'genuineness' of the 'investments'.

There also appears to have been some promoter involvement in the litigation. Documents obtained from scheme participants confirm that legal practitioners and accountants who were involved in the design, promotion and implementation of at least two schemes—the Satcom and the Kununurra Sandalwood projects—established 'fighting funds'. The fighting funds were conducted by companies incorporated for the purpose of financing the legal actions of David Meredith (a participant in Satcom)[110] and Noel Puzey (a participant in Kununurra Sandalwood).[111]

Scheme participants were solicited to contribute to the fighting funds and in one case, that of Resolution Holdings Pty Ltd, participants continued to be asked to contribute to the fund for some time after the company had been wound up in December 1999.

After much political pressure and public protests, agreement was reached with the tax administrators. Penalties and interest were remitted and taxpayers given time to repay the 'over-refunded' sums.[112] Legislation was introduced to provide for prosecution of the promoters of mass-marketed tax avoidance schemes[113] and tax avoidance activity subsequently lapsed.

It is noted that, as of 2008, tax avoidance activity by way of mass-marketed tax avoidance schemes appears to have declined. It is suggested that it may not be a period of inactivity but rather a point in the cycle wherein such avoidance is undetected by taxation administrators.

---

110 Resolution Holdings Pty Ltd; Meredith v Federal Commissioner of Taxation [2002].

111 Australians for Tax Justice Incorporated; Puzey v Federal Commissioner of Taxation [2004].

112 ATO, 'Most mass marketed scheme investors set to benefit from interest reduction' (media release 2001/58 23 July 2001); ATO, 'Tax Office announces settlement offer for mass marketed scheme investors' (media release 2002/07, 14 February 2002).

113 Division 290 of Schedule 1 to the Taxation Administration Act 1953 introduced in 2006.

2.6. Summary

The history of tax avoidance schemes of the 1970s, 1980s and 1990s in Australia provides evidence of a cycle of actions and reactions by taxpayers, tax planners and tax administrators. Tax avoidance schemes developed and broadened in scope from 'boutique' schemes, individually-crafted to suit HWIs in the 1970s, to the mass-marketed tax avoidance schemes of the 1990s which were mass produced to suit any taxpayer wishing to participate in tax avoidance, and which were particularly successfully targeted to blue-collar workers in the mining regions of Western Australia.

Each cycle has not only led to the development of the subsequent schemes but, as well as retaining most of the participants of previous schemes, new classes of taxpayers were attracted as the 'avoidance market' broadened. Increases in the rates of income tax payable by some taxpayers, brought about by rising incomes of unskilled, semi-skilled and tradespeople, particularly in the mining industry of Western Australia, motivated those new classes of taxpayers to engage in tax avoidance. The schemes of the 1990s, though available to all Australian taxpayers, proved particularly attractive to taxpayers employed in the harsh and inhospitable Pilbara region of Western Australia.

An examination of the literature relating to taxpayer compliance will be undertaken in the next chapter, with a particular focus on key socio-psychological behavioural factors of relevance to the cohort groups under analysis in this book.

3. CHAPTER THREE: INFLUENCES ON TAXPAYER COMPLIANCE

'"The horror of that moment" the King went on, "I shall never, never forget!" "You will, though." the Queen said, "If you don't make a memorandum of it."'
Lewis Carroll, Through the Looking-Glass, and What Alice Found There (1871), British author, Anglican clergyman and photographer (1832–1898)

3.1. Overview

This chapter reviews the literature on the factors influencing taxpayer compliance behaviour.

Researchers including Tyler have considered acceptance of, and compliance with, decisions made by authorities and the obedience to laws and legitimacy of authorities generally. Tyler explored 'the everyday behaviour of citizens toward the law and examine[d] why people obey or disobey it'. He considered refusing to pay tax as part of a raft of behavioural practices such as using illicit drugs, engaging in illegal sexual practices and driving when drunk. Tyler's investigations were therefore far broader than public compliance with taxation law.

However the imposition of tax, or compulsory extraction of payments from one's income or wealth, creates an aversion, or resistance, to those payments particularly where there is no overt return. Therefore the critical issue for this part of the book is to understand why taxpayers comply (or do not comply) with prevailing taxation law.

This book focuses specifically on individual taxpayer attitudes to the impost of taxation in their lives. The particular focus is on key motivational factors of relevance to individual taxpayers. Past research has identified a range of factors influencing individual taxpayer compliance and they are specifically reviewed in this chapter.

Before commencing a review of the literature it is instructive to consider what we mean by tax compliance. The *Macquarie Dictionary* defines *tax* as:

1 A compulsory monetary contribution demanded by a government for its support and levied on incomes, property, goods purchased, etc.
2 A burdensome charge, obligation, duty, or demand.

It also defines *compliance* as:

> The act of complying; an acquiescing or yielding.

It defines *acquiescence* as:

> To assent tacitly; comply quietly; agree; or consent.

Considered in those terms *tax compliance* is the action of taxpayers agreeing with, and consenting to behave in accordance with, the taxation legislation and supportive administrative rules of a particular taxing jurisdiction. *Formal compliance* is identified by taxpayer registration with taxation administrators, lodgement of complete and accurate forms and documents, payment of taxes in a timely fashion and maintaining all records as required.[114]

For the purposes of clarity and the structure of this book, the factors have been grouped into the same four basic categories outlined in Chapter One—*demographic*, *socio-psychological*, *economic* and *legal and administrative*.

The following figure depicts the factors considered in this research and the categories in which they are dealt with. This is similar to, but not quite the same as, the ATO's Business Industry Sociology Economy Psychology Systems of compliance (BISEPS) model.[115] The BISEPS model considers all taxpayers, including complex business structures; the type of business structure, industry engaged in and economic factors such as interest and inflation rates are considered. As this book focuses on individual taxpayer behaviour, the factors that relate to business, trade and other commercial entities are not considered.

---

114 Margaret McKerchar and Chris Evans, 'Sustaining Growth in Developing Economies through Improved Taxpayer Compliance: Challenges for Policy Makers and Revenue Authorities' (2009) 7 eJournal of Tax Research 171.

115 ATO, 'Cooperative Compliance Model' <http://www.ato.gov.au/Businesses/content.aspx?menuid=0&doc=/content/22630.htm&page=13&H13> at 9 September 2011; Kristina Murphy, 'Moving Forward Towards a More Effective Model of Regulatory Enforcement in the Australian Tax Office' (2004) 6 British Tax Review 603.

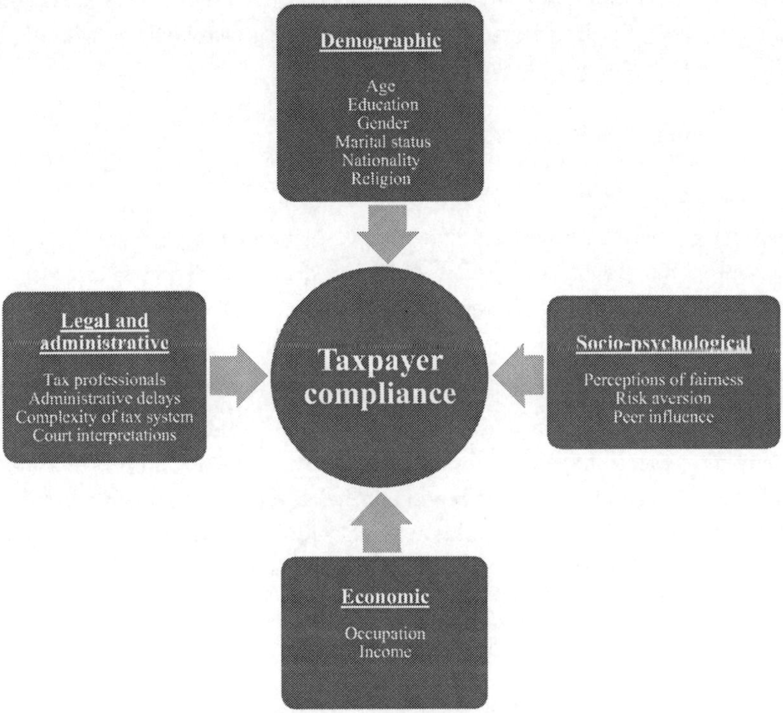

Figure 7 Factors affecting tax compliance behaviour by individuals

For convenience of analysis the categorisation of factors in the groups shown in the illustration has been adopted in this book, though it is acknowledged that it is not without difficulties. It is recognised that there is a degree of overlap between categories and some factors could be considered to belong in other categories. For example, occupation is often considered as a demographic factor. In this model it is viewed as an economic factor as it often relates directly to levels of income which in turn affect personal income tax rates.

Similarly, the influence of tax professionals could be viewed as a socio-psychological rather than as a legal factor. However as tax professionals tend to focus on the application of tax law rather than the intention of the legislature it has been placed in the group of legal factors in this book.

Each of the factors may also consist of related factors and they are considered under the one heading. For example 'risk aversion'—an individual's intrinsic acceptance of a level of risk—is influenced by the chances of being detected (audit rates), the implications of being detected (penalties) and the anticipation of those penalties being forgiven (amnesties). The influencing factors are now examined within the four categories of factors described.

3.2. Demographic factors

This section examines the literature on the influences of demographic factors on taxpayer compliance behaviour. It is used to highlight the demographic factors relevant to the groups of taxpayers studied in this research and to establish the degree of significance of those influencing factors.

Age

Research suggests that age can be a key factor in determining attitudes to compliance. More particularly it is suggested that compliance is likely to increase with age, as illustrated in the indication of the relationship between age and tax compliance in the figure below, although other research casts some doubt on the strength of the age factor as a key determinant of compliance behaviour.

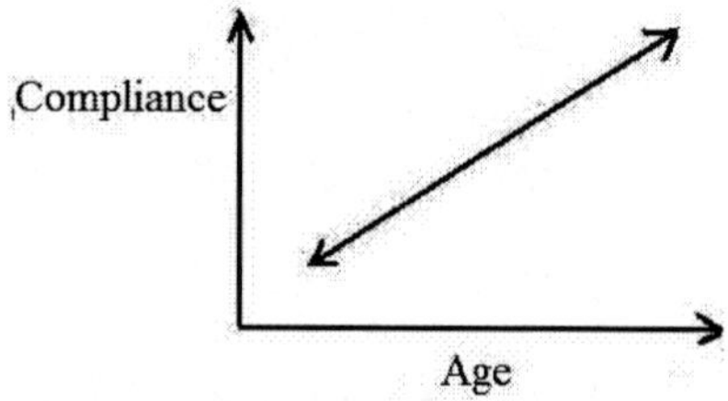

Figure 8 Effect of age on tax compliance

Earlier research, such as Becker's study,[116] acknowledged that penalties and the risk of detection have less of a deterrent effect on the young. A decade and a half later, Wallschutzky referred back to a study in the United States (conducted in 1974) which found '[t]he most important background variable was age, with increasing age being positively related to lower [tax] resistance'.[117] He followed this up a year later, writing '[i]n fact age was the third most "influential" factor'.[118]

---

116 Gary S Becker, 'Crime and Punishment: An Economic Approach' (1968) 76 Journal of Political Economy .

117 Ian G Wallschutzky, 'Possible Causes of Tax Evasion' (1984) 5 Journal of Economic Psychology 371.

118 Ian G Wallschutzky, Taxpayer Attitudes to Avoidance and Evasion (1985).

Erard,[119] Smith and Kinsey,[120] Wadhawan and Gray,[121] and Witte[122] also point to age as having a consistent correlation with non-compliance—the younger the person, the less compliant they were found to be.

Research published in 1998 by Fjeldstad and Sembojas supported the view that compliance was lowest for their youngest age group, but they suggested that generalisations based on age are questionable due to the small number of respondents in the younger and older age groups of their study.[123] Also in 1998, Andreoni, Erard and Feinstein pointed to previous 'experimental studies generally [which] find that age is positively associated with compliance'.[124] Willott and Griffin's publication in 1999 on their research on criminality noted that over 86 per cent of their research population of male offenders was less than 30 years of age.[125]

However, Webley, Adams and Elffers state '[y]ounger respondents were more likely to be non-compliant and, as Adams and Webley (1996) have argued in other contexts, this is more likely to be a cohort effect, whereby people are generally becoming less respectful of the law and official bodies, than an age effect'.[126] Webley later suggests that there may be alternative influences, other than a cohort effect, that change people's compliance behaviour as they age.[127]

Murphy's research also suggests that compliance improves with age. However, the findings from her research survey of participants in mass-marketed tax

---

119 Brian Erard, 'Taxation with Representation: An Analysis of the Role of Tax Practitioners in Tax Compliance' (1993) 52 Journal of Public Economics .

120 Kent W Smith and Karyl A Kinsey, 'Understanding Taxpaying Behaviour: A Conceptual Framework with Implications for Research' (1987) 21 Law and Society Review 639.

121 Satish C Wadhawan and Clive Gray, 'Enhancing Transparency in Tax Administration: A Survey' (Discussion Paper No 3, United States Agency for International Development, Bureau for Africa, Office of Sustainable Development, 1998).

122 Ann Dryden Witte, 'What Factors Affect Voluntary Compliance? The Impact of Tax Laws, Tax Administration and Taxpayer Attitudes on Taxpayer Behaviour' (Paper presented at the Tax Compliance Intensive Weekend Workshop, Bowral NSW Australia, 25-27 August 1989).

123 Odd-Heige Fjeldstad and Joseph Semboja, 'Why People Pay Taxes: The Case of the Development Levy in Tanzania' (Working Paper No 1998:5, Chr. Michelsen Institute, 1998).

124 James Andreoni, Brian Erard and Jonathan Feinstein, 'Tax Compliance' (1998) 36 Journal of Economic Literature 818.

125 Sara Willott and Chris Griffin, 'Building Your Own Lifeboat: Working-class Male Offenders Talk about Economic Crime' (1999) 38 British Journal of Social Psychology 445.

126 Paul Webley, Caroline Adams and Henk Elffers, 'VAT Compliance in the United Kingdom'(Working Paper No 41, Centre for Tax System Integrity, 2002).

127 Paul Webley, 'Tax Compliance by Business' in Hans Sjögren and Göran Skogh (eds), New Perspectives on Economic Crime (2004) 95.

avoidance schemes of the 1990s did suggest that the participants were in fact nearer to middle age (at an average age of 46 years). A partial explanation for this apparent anomaly is that the survey was conducted in 2002. Her questionnaire asked the current age of the participants and not their age at the time of engaging in the mass-marketed tax avoidance schemes some four to six years earlier. It is also noted that only 3.6 per cent of respondents in Murphy's quantitative approach were less than 30 years of age at the time of the survey.

More recently, in 2005, Devos found that age had important implications for tax evasion generally.[128] However, he adds the cautionary rider that his study was limited and that age groups of 40 and over were not represented. He also refers to previous research where he reports 'the age variable found that older taxpayers tended to be more compliant than younger taxpayers'. He then describes other research which found no relationship between age and compliance. He concludes that 'the interaction of age with other compliance variables could be problematic'. However he notes that his research sample was restricted to university students and 'was not representative of the whole taxpayer population [and that] the findings need to be appropriately qualified'.

In 2007 Torgler stated '[t]he findings of the tax compliance studies show that the impact of age on compliance is still uncertain'. He cites nine studies ranging from 1974 to 1991 which found that age increases the level of compliance, with eight further surveys implying that there is no influence of age on tax compliance, with only one showing a significant curvilinear relationship between age and tax compliance. He concludes '[t]o clarify the importance of the age variable, more empirical evidence is needed'.

Houston and Tran's survey of Australian taxpayers who lodged tax returns in the 1997-98 year rejects age as a significant influencing factor.[129] Meriküll and Staehr also find 'age does not appear to influence the probability of tax evasion'.[130]

According to Ashby, Webley and Haslam, age is one of the six significant predictors of tax compliance. However, contrary to the above research, in 2009

---

128 Ken Devos, 'The Attitudes of Tertiary Students on Tax Evasion and the Penalties for Tax Evasion—A Pilot Study and Demographic Analysis' (2005) 3(2) eJournal of Tax Research 222.

129 Jodie Houston and Alfred Tran, 'A Survey of Tax Evasion Using the Randomized Response Technique' (2001) 13 Advances in Taxation 69.

130 Jaanika Meriküll and Karsten Staehr, 'Unreported Employment and Tax Evasion in Mid-transition: Comparing Developments and Causes in the Baltic States' (Working paper No 6/2008, Bank of Estonia, 2008).

they found that those who 'minimized their tax bills' were in the older group of taxpayers.[131]

There are likely to be a number of social, psychological and economic reasons which contribute to the effect of age on compliance. Kornhauser[132] suggests it may be that as a person ages he or she becomes more risk averse, social influences become stronger and older people may simply have more to lose by way of assets accumulated through life.

As the median age of the population of the Pilbara was the second youngest in Western Australia, at 31 years in 2001, the impact of the influence of age may be an important determinant of taxpayer involvement in the mass-marketed tax avoidance schemes. This factor is therefore further explored in the research analysis which is undertaken in Chapter Four.

Education

In 1987, Smith and Kinsey hypothesised that the demographic variable of education was consistently related to 'admitted' non-compliance. Later researchers, including Devos; Gupta;[133] and Kasipillai, Aripin and Amran,[134] have found the relationship to be a positive connection between increased education and increased tax compliance. However Meriküll and Staehr's Estonian research revealed two different conclusions: 'For 1998, a higher education level increases the probability of evasion, but this effect is not present in 2002'.

Some researchers, such as Becker; Witte; and Agell and Persson,[135] suggest the impact of education tends initially to increase compliance behaviour then, as education advances, taxpayers become less compliant, as illustrated in the figure below.

---

131 Julie S Ashby, Paul Webley, and Alexander S Haslam, 'The Role of Occupational Taxpaying Cultures in Taxpaying Behaviour and Attitudes' (2009) 30 Journal of Economic Psychology 216.

132 Marjorie E. Kornhauser, 'Normative and Cognitive Aspects of Tax Compliance: Literature Review and Recommendations for the IRS Regarding Individual Taxpayers' (2007) 2 National Taxpayer Advocate Annual Report to Congress 138.

133 Ranjana Gupta, 'How the Perceptions of Tax Evasion as a Crime Mirror the Penalties' (Paper presented at the Australasian Tax Teachers' Association Conference, Brisbane Qld, 23 January 2007).

134 Jeyapalan Kasipillai, Norhani Aripin and Noor Afza Amran, 'The Influence of Education on Tax Avoidance and Tax Evasion' (2003) 1 eJournal of Tax Research 134.

135 Jonas Agell and Mats Persson, 'Tax Arbitrage and Labour Supply' (Working Paper No 6708, National Bureau of Economic Research, 1998).

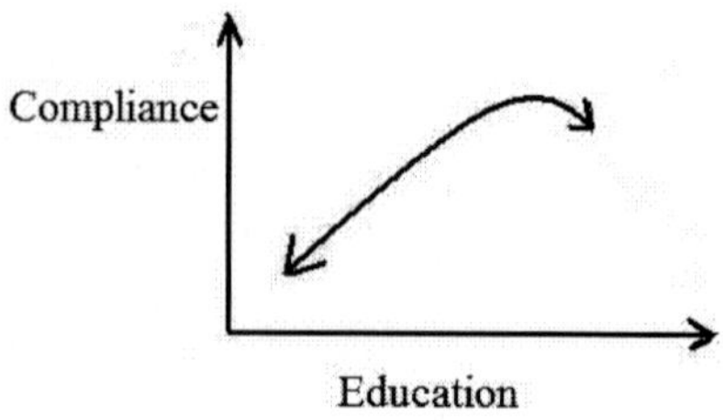

Figure 9 Effect of education on tax compliance

They suggest that education leads to a better understanding of taxation law and the role of taxes in society, particularly in social democracies. However, as level of education advances, taxpayers become more familiar with the intricacies of taxation law and are able to employ resources which enable them to reduce their taxation burden. This may be due to taxpayers learning how to become successful at avoidance techniques.

Torgler supports the concept that increased education levels lead to increased tax awareness or 'tax knowledge'. He suggests taxpayers 'may be less compliant because they better understand the opportunities for evasion and avoidance, and they might be more critical about and more aware of how the state uses tax revenues'.

Loo, McKerchar and Hansford also found that 'tax knowledge had the most effect in determining individual taxpayers' compliance behaviour'.[136] Education was not only significant in contributing to taxpayers' knowledge of taxation law, but it also influenced other factors, 'particularly in the case of salary and wage earners, [it] was affecting their choices of occupation and as a consequence, affecting their level of income, and eventually affecting their financial positions'. It is noted that in Murphy's research, over 57 per cent of participants in the mass-marketed tax avoidance schemes of the 1990s had tertiary qualifications.

The above research suggests that education, by leading to increased knowledge about taxation, is a significant factor in determining a taxpayer's propensity to comply with tax obligations. On the other hand, Houston and Tran indicate that while there is some negative relationship between education and tax evasion, they reject education as a significant influence.

136 Ern Chen Loo, Margaret McKerchar and Ann Hansford, 'Tax Compliance Behaviour: Findings Derived from a Mixed Method Design' (Paper presented at the 8th International Tax Administration Conference, Sydney, 28 March 2008).

As noted in Chapter One, the permanent population of the Pilbara was only slightly better educated than the population of the Goldfields, and was less educated than three-quarters of the metropolitan population of Perth. Therefore research on the influence of education indicates that the blue-collar workers of the Pilbara should have demonstrated a propensity toward non-compliance.

The influence of education is further examined in Chapter Four as the literature indicates levels of education may provide a partial explanation for the participation in the mass-marketed tax avoidance schemes but not at such high propensity as demonstrated by Pilbara taxpayers in the 1990s.

Gender

Previous researchers such as Smith and Kinsey, Hasseldine,[137] Barnett and Grown,[138] Gupta, and Torgler have consistently indicated that males, and Witte found, in particular, younger males, were generally less compliant than females, as illustrated in the figure showing the effect of gender on tax compliance. Willott and Griffin and Webley found this applied not only to compliance with tax law but the law generally.

Figure 10 Effect of gender on tax compliance

Becker also noted that gender varies the propensity to engage in illegal activity. However Devos found that gender was a weaker influence when associated with other variables such as education. Meriküll and Staehr found 'gender does not appear to influence the probability of tax evasion.' However their Latvian studies revealed that, in Latvia, males are more prone to evade tax than women.

Houston and Tran found that women displayed a higher propensity toward tax evasion than men but noted that 'the differences are not statistically significant'.

The findings of research undertaken by Wadhawan and Gray which showed 'participation rates in the underground labor market are greater among males,

137 John Hasseldine, 'Gender Differences in Tax Compliance' (1999) 3(2) Asian-Pacific Tax Journal 73.

138 Kathleen Barnett and Caren Grown, Gender Impacts of Government Revenue Collection: The Case of Taxation (2004).

craftsmen, middle-aged cohorts, and persons with nonworking spouses' may be significant to this book. Interestingly, they considered the combined influence of gender and occupation—and this coupling effect of influences will be explored further and in greater detail in Chapter Four of this book.

It is also noted that Murphy's survey of participants in mass-marketed tax avoidance schemes shows that males made up 82 per cent of the total number of respondents.

However it may be that the apparent influence of gender is co-incidental. There are other examples where females demonstrate a lower propensity for tax compliance than males. For example, in the timeliness of the lodgement of income tax returns, ATO statistics reveal a differing indication of male tax compliance behaviour. In 1997, ATO statistics for 1994[139] showed that the percentage of late lodgers was 15 per cent for males compared with 25 per cent for females. This trend is confirmed in other years.

However it is noted that a primary function of the mass-marketed tax avoidance schemes was to obtain a refund of tax credits. Timely lodgement of income tax returns was an essential element of the process. Therefore the population of females who do not lodge timely returns, as indicated above, were not included in the population of mass-marketed tax avoidance schemes participants. There may also be many other reasons why females showed a consistently higher propensity to lodge tax returns later than males.[140]

Marital status

Wadhawan and Gray and Torgler have specifically investigated the influence of marital status on compliance behaviour. Their research indicates married persons are more likely to comply than single persons, as indicated in the following illustration.

139 ATO, Taxation Statistics 1994-95 (1997).

140 Females are often the main family carer and have child care and household concerns which far outweigh tax compliance. This may particularly be the case if they are also engaged in casual or part-time paid employment. It may also be that they have taken an extended period away from paid employment, for family reasons, and are prompted to lodge belated income tax returns only after returning to paid employment.

Figure 11 Effect of marital status on tax compliance

However that influence appears to be quite weak. Murphy's research indicates that 94 per cent of participants in the mass-marketed tax avoidance schemes of the 1990s were, or had been, married. Erard points to research by Clotfelter and Alexander and Feinstein[141] which revealed mixed results and found that married taxpayers demonstrated a relatively high level of non-compliance. However Erard finds that married taxpayers tend towards non-compliance only in certain circumstances.

The above research indicates other demographic factors such as age, education and gender could have a greater influence than the marital status of taxpayers. Chapter Four will consider whether marital status had an impact on the compliance behaviour of the blue-collar workers of the Pilbara region in the 1990s.

Nationality

The terms race, nationality and ethnic origin have been used interchangeably by researchers. 'Race' has fallen into disuse in modern times but it was used by earlier researchers. Likewise in the context of this research 'nationality', or belonging to a particular society at large, should be distinguished from 'ethnic minority' as in belonging to a particular ethnic group within a larger society.

Becker notes that race has an effect on the elasticity to engage in illegal activity from person to person. His research indicates that nationality has little influence on tax compliance, however.

Willott and Griffin are dismissive of ethnic origin as an influence on compliance with the law and point to gender as a far more significant factor affecting compliance. In a study of tax evasion in Lithuania, Latvia and Estonia, Meriküll and Staehr found ethnicity did not appear to be of importance as a determinant factor

141 Charles T Clotfelter 'Tax Evasion and Tax Rates: An Analysis of Individual Returns' (1983) 65 Review of Economics and Statistics ; Craig Alexander and Jonathon S Feinstein, A Microeconomic Analysis of Income Tax Evasion (1987) cited in Erard 190.

affecting tax evasion. In 2002, however they found that Estonians had a 'lower probability of evasion than other ethnic groups'.

Devos suggests nationality has a significant influence but found it only to be as to attitudes of power of administrators and feelings of sorrow and remorse. Torgler also refers to research which found 'evidence that individuals in the United States have a statistically significant higher tax morale than those in Spain'.

However, belonging to an ethnic minority may have some influence. This is likely to affect a feeling of social distance from the general community and the government. Witte did not consider nationality as such but noted that members of minority groups tend to be less compliant.

Murphy's survey of participants in Australian mass-marketed tax avoidance schemes revealed that the race or nationality of participants generally followed the racial mix of the population of Australia. Her survey indicated that nearly three quarters of respondents were native born Australians. Therefore participation in mass-marketed tax avoidance schemes was unlikely to have been biased toward an ethnic minority. The influence of race, nationality or ethnic origin is not considered to be a critical factor in this research and accordingly will not be examined further.

Religion

A review of the compliance literature revealed insufficient evidence to form a conclusive indication of the influence of religion on compliance. However there is an inference that if people comply with religious law then they are likely to comply with the secular law.

In 1998 Fjeldstad and Semboja noted a difference between the compliance of Christians and Muslims in Tanzania. They also noted there were other variables such as ethnicity influencing the outcomes and that the differences were not significant. Torgler concludes 'strong evidence has been adduced that religiosity factors exert a systematic influence on tax morale.' Tax morale is an intermediary factor affecting tax compliance. He further states '[t]his effect tends to persist even after controlling for factors such as corruption, trustworthiness, age, economic situation, education, gender, marital status and employment status'.

ATO statistics do not include data on taxpayers' religion. Murphy's research did not include questions as to religion. However Torgler's conclusion indicates that religiosity may be a significant factor in influencing tax compliance. Therefore, ABS data will be examined to compare the percentage of those with declared religious affiliation of the population of the Pilbara to that of the Western Australian and the national population to indicate if there was a significant difference.

Summary on the influence of demographic factors

Previous research on the influence of demographic factors has been extensive and is relatively well settled. The conclusions of a behavioural simulation experiment conducted by Marriott, Randall and Holmes, presented in 2010, supported the findings of previous research in that they found: compliance increases with age; education has little strength of influence; males are less compliant than females; and differing ethnic groups demonstrate differing levels of compliance.[142]

Demographic analysis is therefore important to this research. As outlined in Chapter One, the Pilbara population of the 1990s as a sub-set of the Western Australian population tended to be younger, semi-skilled or trade qualified, less educated, male-dominated and focussed in the mining industry. Therefore focus will be on those demographic factors identified as particularly relevant to the Pilbara community in this book; age, education level, gender and religion.

This review now moves to the next category of influence factors—the socio-psychological factors.

3.3. Socio-psychological factors

This section looks at the literature on the social and psychological influences on taxpayer compliance behaviour. It is used to examine the social influences exerted on individuals within the groups of taxpayers surveyed in this research.

A large number of influencing factors have been considered by previous researchers. The present examination has been conducted under three main groupings; perceptions of fairness, risk aversion and peer influence.

As illustrated, these are incorporated within those groupings are other factors. For example, risk aversion includes sub-factors such as the chances of detection (audit rates) and the consequences of detection (penalties, amnesties). The consequences of risk taking are also likely to be affected by sub-factors such as

142 Lisa Marriott, John Randall and Kevin Holmes, 'Influences on Tax Evasion Behaviour: Insights from a Behavioural Simulation Experiment' (Paper presented at the Australasian Tax Teachers' Association Conference, Sydney NSW, 21 January 2010) 35. The experiment was conducted with 483 first-year commerce students at Victoria University of Wellington, New Zealand, and the limitations of the use of students in such experimental models are acknowledged.

social distance from government which are considered among the factors of perceptions of fairness and peer influence.

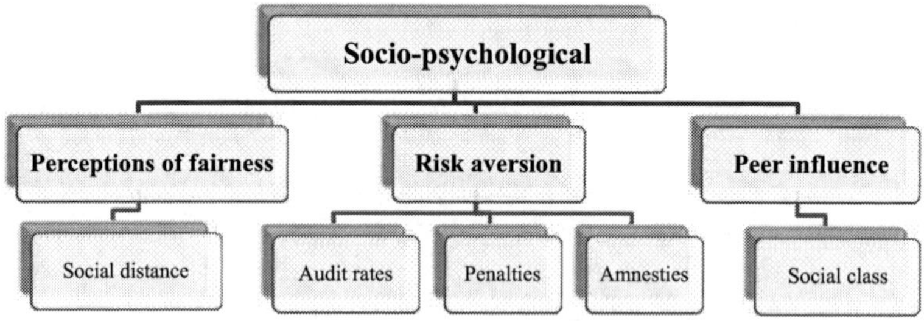

Figure 12 Groupings of socio-psychological factors

The influencing factors also interrelate with each other. Factors serve to exacerbate or negate the strength of influence of others. The influence of risk aversion may be reduced or encouraged by the influence of peers. An individual who would normally choose to refrain from doing something may be encouraged by the behaviour of others to engage in that act.

Perceptions of fairness

Previous research appears divided as to the influence of perception of fairness of the government and the taxation system. Taxpayer perceptions of unfairness may influence taxpayer behaviour either by causing non-compliance generally or by being used to rationalise tax avoidance systems or tax evasion activity.

Generally viewed by sociologists, such as Blau,[143] as an interpersonal relationship, perceptions of fairness appear to have a significant influence on compliance. However there are also some research findings that suggest perceptions of fairness have little or no effect on compliance behaviour.

The concept of taxation is not a contract or exchange, it is 'a compulsory monetary contribution demanded by a government for its support'. However despite the compulsory acquisition of funds for no return, taxpayers often feel that there is a social exchange.

Taxpayers often consider tax in the light of a perception of fairness as a 'social contract or exchange' that is—'what do I get for my money?' Therefore central to a taxpayer's perception of fairness is what the taxpayer perceives as his or her

143 Peter Michael Blau, an American sociologist and theorist 1918–2002.

part in the relationship with government. Social exchange theory, as defined by Jary and Jary,[144] suggests that individuals enter, and stay in, relationships based on perceived costs and benefits.

In 1973, Friedland, Thibaut and Walker identified the perception of fairness as a strong determinant in rule violation, especially when coupled with severity of penalty.[145] Bracewell-Milnes quotes Sandford's distinction between positive and negative evasion. He states '... taxpayers may take more pains to avoid or evade a tax they resent than one they regard as reasonable'.[146] Fjeldstad and Semboja find that '[p]eople's tax resistance is correlated to deteriorating or, in some cases, non-existent public services'.

However, Smith and Kinsey suggest that '[f]or most people, the perceived causal link between their taxpaying and the running of the government is too tenuous for opinions about the latter to have an effect on their decisions'. Their view is supported by Bosco and Mittone,[147] Witte, Wadhawan and Gray, McKerchar,[148] Webley, Adams and Elffers, John Braithwaite,[149] Valerie Braithwaite[150] and Rawlings.[151]

Karlinsky and Bankman[152] and Fjeldstad and Semboja also find that 'the perceived fairness of the terms of trade with the government is not supported'. Murphy points to '[t]he overarching aim of the [ATO's] Compliance Model to create an environment that promoted compliance' and holds that pivotal to the

---

144 David Jary and Julia Jary (eds), Collins Dictionary of Sociology (3rd ed, 2000).

145 Nehemia Friedland, John Thibaut and Laurens Walker, 'Some Determinants of the Violation of Rules' (1973) 3(2) Journal of Applied Social Psychology 103.

146 Barry Bracewell-Milnes, 'Is Tax Avoidance / Evasion a Burden on Other Taxpayers?' in Arthur Seldon (ed), Tax Avoision (1979) 105.

147 Luigi Bosco and Luigi Mittone, 'Tax Evasion and Moral Constraints: Some Experimental Evidence' (1997) 50(3) Kyklos 297.

148 Margaret Anne McKerchar, The Impact of Complexity Upon Unintentional Non-compliance for Australian Personal Income Taxpayers (PhD Thesis, University of New South Wales, 2002).

149 John Braithwaite, 'Large Business and the Compliance Model', in Valerie Braithwaite (ed), Taxing Democracy: Understanding Tax Avoidance and Evasion (2003) 177.

150 Valerie Braithwaite, 'Games of Engagement: Postures within the Regulatory Community' (1995) 17 Law and Policy 225.

151 Gregory Rawlings 'Cultural Narratives of Taxation and Citizenship: Fairness, Groups and Globalisation' (2003) 38(3) Australian Journal of Social Issues 269.

152 Stewart Karlinsky and Joseph Bankman, 'Developing a Theory of Cash Businesses Tax Evasion Behaviour and the Role of Their Tax Preparers' (Paper presented at the 5th International Conference on Tax Administration, ATAX Faculty of Law, University of New South Wales, Sydney, 4-5 April 2002), 136.

success of that strategy is the building of trust between the ATO and taxpayers through communication.

Taylor suggests that perceptions of fairness vary according to 'taxpayer social identity' and that 'an understanding of social identity processes is fundamental to understanding why particular factors might motivate behaviour in some situations and not others'. Webley cautions that '[w]hilst there is a great deal of survey evidence linking inequity with non-compliance, this may be an after-the-fact rationalisation rather than a factor which instigates evasion'.

Devos's research findings, though limited in the scope of his survey, indicate that less than one third of those surveyed felt motivated towards tax evasion by being unfairly disadvantaged by the tax system. Nearly two thirds of his respondents were ambivalent towards the 'unfairness' of the tax system. He states '[c]ertainly considerable empirical research has been conducted to examine the link of perceptions of fairness and tax evasion, but the findings of various researchers therein are inconsistent'. In 2011, 'A further empirical study by Devos[153] indicated that tax morale, tax fairness and various deterrent measures in combination had a significant impact upon tax compliance behaviour in Australia.'[154]

It is suggested that taxpayer morale exhibited through taxpayer behaviour, such as that observed in the phenomenon examined in this book, may in fact be an emotive issue influenced by feelings of isolation and social pressures rather than purely rational economic decisions.

Wenzel proposes that social norms and perceptions of fairness could be rationales for individual taxpayer behaviour rather than causal factors for non-compliance.[155] Tyler also finds that a perception of procedural fairness is a critical factor in people's acceptance of the law. This element is so strong that the outcome of dealings with authorities is irrelevant. People respect the law if they felt they have been dealt with fairly even if the ultimate outcome is not in their favour.

---

153 Ken Devos, An Investigation of the Factors which influence and Deter the Compliance Behaviour of Australian Individual Taxpayers, (Unpublished PhD thesis, Monash University, Australia, 2011).

154 Ken Devos, 'An Assessment of the Influence of Sanctions and other Factors upon International Taxpayer Compliance', (Paper presented at the Tax Governance, Vienna, 20-21 September 2012).

155 Michael Wenzel, 'Motivation or Rationalisation? Causal Relations between Ethics, Norms and Tax Compliance' (2005) 26 Journal of Economic Psychology 491.

Torgler refers to several studies which reveal evidence that '[a]n unfair tax system could enhance the incentives to rationalize cheating.' He states '[t]ax evasion may be seen as a reaction to restore equity'.

Alm, Jackson and McKee[156] consider the impact of the exchange of public goods in exchange for taxes. In their experiments on taxpayer responses as to uncertainty of tax policy and enforcement, the presence of a 'public good' becomes a major factor in determining taxpayer compliance. They find that:

> When individuals receive nothing for their tax payments, uncertainty increases compliance, a result consistent with much of the literature and the apparent views of the IRS. However, when individuals perceive that they receive a public good in exchange for their taxes, uncertainty always lowers compliance.

The conclusion to their research is that if taxpayers perceive that they receive nothing in exchange for their taxes and they are uncertain of the contributions of others, then disclosure is viewed from an individual perspective and compliance rises. However if taxpayers perceive taxes as being a contribution to a public good and they are uncertain as to the contribution of others, then disclosure is considered as being part of a larger group and compliance falls.

Their complex finding is better understood by substituting the concept of 'the provision of new public buses' for the general concept of 'a public good'. The following rationale is put. If a passenger (taxpayer) is uncertain of the compliance of other passengers (taxpayers), (are they paying their fares?) then the passenger (taxpayer) assumes they are not 'paying their fair share', and therefore he or she does not pay his or hers. It is suggested that an attitude develops of 'if they are not paying their fares, why should I?'.

On the other hand, in place of the assumption that others are not paying, it is assumed that they are—then the attitude of 'my tax is not required' develops.

In either assumption uncertainty of the compliance of others in exchange for a public good leads to lower compliance. In the event that taxes are raised for no visible benefit to the taxpayer, and he or she is unsure of the contributions being made by others, the taxpayer simply complies. The additional factor of personal benefit of a public good is removed from the taxpayer's schema.

The influence of a social exchange in relation to a perception of fairness, and its influence on compliance, is such that if an individual taxpayer views tax as an expense, for no benefit, then uncertainty of tax policy and enforcement raises

---

156 James Alm, Betty Jackson and Michael McKee, 'Institutional Uncertainty and Taxpayer Compliance' (1992) 82 American Economic Review 1018.

doubt as to detection and subsequent penalties. The risk-averse taxpayer will seek to reduce the negative effects of non-compliance by increasing compliance.

However if a taxpayer views the payment of tax as being a contribution to public good and is uncertain as to the contribution of other taxpayers then compliance falls.

Generally the perceptions of fairness of how a taxpayer views his or her position in society, and how that taxpayer is treated individually or as part of a group by his or her government, is a pivotal influence of taxpayer attitudes towards compliance behaviour. That conclusion is supported by Daude, Gutiérrez and Melguizo who, in 2012, suggested:

> In addition to better enforcement, reforms that increase transparency and the efficiency of how revenues are used (to which the quality of public services is vital) might help to increase tax morale and therefore tax compliance. [157]

This book suggests that in turn, perceptions of fairness are greatly influenced by the following socio-psychological factors.

Social distance between taxpayer and government

Previous research suggests that social distance between the taxpayer and the government is a strong influence on tax compliance. The relationship is shown below. It indicates that the greater the perceived distance, the lower the compliance. The physical distance, and social isolation, of the population of the Pilbara may have significantly influenced the participation rate in mass-marketed tax avoidance schemes.

Valerie Braithwaite refers to social distance as being '[w]hen individuals and groups decide how much they want to associate or be aligned with an authority, and how much they want to be out of reach of and out of contact with the authority'.

---

157 Christian Daude, Hamlet Gutiérrez and Ángel Melguizo, 'What Drives Tax Morale?' (Working Paper No 315, Organisation for Economic Co-operation and Development Development Centre, 2012).

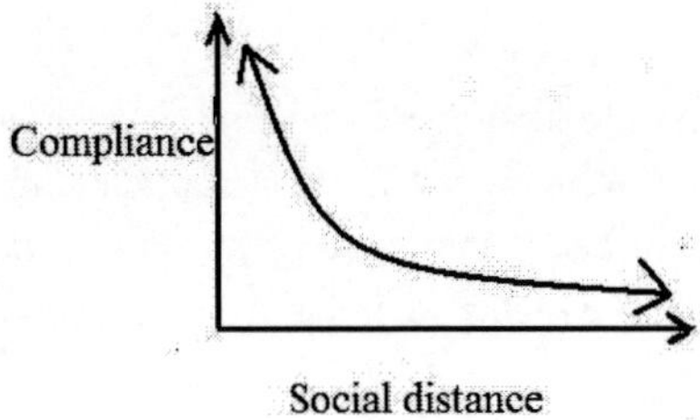

Figure 13 Effect of social distance on tax compliance

Christopher[158] and Myddelton consider the political nature of taxation. They suggest 'people avoid paying tax because they oppose it, or the reasons for it, politically'. [159] It is possible that the Howard Liberal government may have been viewed as politically distant from the ALP-supporting blue-collar workers of the Pilbara in the 1990s. That political dichotomy may have increased taxpayer resistance to compliance.

Wallschutzky and Wadhawan and Gray also find a social connection to government and its services as critical to taxpayer compliance. Webley, Adams and Elffers point to the need to 'break down some of the "them and us" barriers between the authorities and people running small businesses'. Taylor, Webley and Torgler all consider taxpayers' relationship with the government and tax morale. They find that '[p]ositive behaviour of the state towards taxpayers will increase the likelihood of compliance'.

Given the physical isolation of the main group of taxpayers under scrutiny in this book, social distance may have been a strong determinant in influencing the participation rates of blue-collar workers of the Pilbara region in the mass-marketed tax avoidance schemes.

In order to gauge their attitude to the perception of fairness, research participants in the current study were asked if they were treated fairly by the ATO. Examined in detail in Chapter Four, their responses help to establish the degree of the influence of this factor on the mass-marketed tax avoidance scheme participants compared to all respondents generally.

158 Anthony Christopher, 'The Law is the Law is the Law' in Arthur Seldon (ed), Tax Avoision (1979) 75.

159 Friedrich August Hayek, The Constitution of Liberty (1960) 438, in David R Myddelton, 'Tax Avoision—Its Costs and Benefits' in Arthur Seldon (ed), Tax Avoision (1979) 41.

Risk aversion

Risk aversion has been identified as having an impact on compliance but it has generally been found that degrees of risk acceptance vary from taxpayer to taxpayer on an individual basis. Some people are more risk averse than others. The economic factor of risk benefit also influences the degree of risk taxpayers are prepared to accept.

The findings of Becker, Stiglitz[160] and Smith and Kinsey support the view that individual differences influence those economic decisions to comply as well as looking at tax cheating as a challenge. On the other hand Hite and McGill find that taxpayers 'strongly asserted their preferences for conservative advice from their preparers'.[161]

Allingham and Sandmo take the economic view further than Becker and Stiglitz and note, '[t]here seems to be a general presumption that absolute risk aversion is decreasing with income'.[162] They consider that this is likely 'because an increase in the tax rate makes it more profitable to evade taxes on the margin'. Their conclusion implies high tax rates encourage risk taking. However they suggest that further empirical research is needed to evaluate the effectiveness of tax rates, penalty rates and expenditure on detection on the efficiency of those factors.

Slemrod and Yitzhaki point out that under the Allingham-Sandmo model, 'tax evasion occurs only if the taxpayer expects to increase his expected [after tax] income by evading taxes'. The total risk exposure includes penalties if caught. The greater the risk accepted by the taxpayer the greater the expected return. They suggest that the taxpayer and the government could be better off if an agreement could be reached whereby 'the taxpayer pays at least as much as the government currently collects, while the government ceases to audit'. The inference is that risk aversion is a factor which influences government as well as taxpayers It is noted that Singapore's GAAR provides for a 're-characterisation' of taxation reducing arrangements without penalty. It is believed the underlying policy for this is to 'keep business working'.[163]

160 Joseph E Stiglitz, 'The Effects of Income, Wealth, and Capital Gains Taxation on Risk-Taking' (1969) 83 Journal of Public Economics .

161 Peggy A Hite, and Gary A McGill, 'An Examination of Taxpayer Preference for Aggressive Tax Advice' (1992) 45 National Tax Journal 389.

162 Michael G Allingham and Agnar Sandmo, 'Income Tax Evasion: A Theoretical Analyais' (1972) 1 Journal of Public Economics .

163 Income Tax Act 1948 (Singapore) s 33.

Bosco and Mittone note, '[i]t is in fact important to underline that the variable that more strongly influences the decision to evade is the risk aversion and not the expected audit probability'. They also suggest the decision to evade will depend greatly on the taxpayer's individual attitude to risk taking.

Faure and Visser use the case of environmental crimes to illustrate the concept of risk-aversion wherein they put social reasons for polluters refraining from environmental crimes. Firms are deterred for reasons such as loss of reputation not the risk or significance of penalties.[164]

It is possible that the mostly male, socially isolated taxpayers in the Pilbara mining industry were much less risk averse than other Australian taxpayers generally. This factor was tested by asking research participants if they would consider participating in other tax minimising schemes despite the experience of participating in the mass-marketed tax avoidance schemes of the 1990s. Their responses are examined in detail in Chapter Four.

Audit rates

Researchers are divided on the significance of audit rates as a determinant on tax compliance behaviour. However taxpayers' intrinsic attitudes to risk aversion have to be coupled with the chances of detection and therefore the possibility of being audited.

Various studies have suggested a correlation between taxpayer compliance and the possibility of detection. Allingham and Sandmo suggest there is a strong correlation between penalty rates, risk aversion and the probability of detection. Witte points to previous research[165] and suggests that '[a]lmost all [theoretical] models predict that an increased probability of audit will increase compliance. The empirical literature suggests there are only small apparent specific deterrent effects of audits.'

Kirchler notes that 'the relationship between perceived audit and detection probabilities and compliance is much more complex than assumed by the neoclassical economic model'.[166] He refers to Worsham's[167] 1996 findings 'that

---

164 Micharel G Faure and Marjolein Visser, 'Law and Economics of Environmental Crime' in Hans Sjögren and Göran Skogh (eds), NewPerspectives on Economic Crime (2004) 57.

165 Jeffrey A Roth, John T Scholz and Ann Dryden Witte, 'Understanding Taxpayer Compliance: Self-Interest, Social Commitment, and Other Influences' in Jeffrey A Roth, John T Scholz and Ann Dryden Witte (eds), Taxpayer Compliance Volume 1: An Agenda for Research (1989).

166 Erich Kirchler, The Economic Psychology of Tax Behaviour (2007).

inconsistent audit rates actually increased the level of compliance'. He cites research which evidences varying degrees of the influence of perceived audit rates but notes that where no audit activity was carried out tax evasion was significantly higher. He also notes that repeated audits can increase non-compliance as taxpayers become accustomed to the experience. Not only can they learn that the audit experience is not traumatic as previously perceived but failures to detect irregularities may embolden risk-taking by what he refers to as the 'bomb crater'[168] effect. The findings of Marriott, Randall and Holmes as to the probability of audit support the previous research including that of Kirchler's 'bomb crater' effect.

In 1998 Andreoni, Erard and Feinstein cast doubt on the cost effectiveness of audits.

> Although the statutory penalties for tax evasion can in some cases be quite severe, penalties are in fact quite infrequently imposed. During the 1995 fiscal year, for example, only 4.1 per cent of all U.S. taxpayers whose federal returns were reassessed following an audit received any penalty for fraud, negligence, false withholding, failure to report tips, or other miscellaneous infractions.

In Australia, in the late 1990s, taxation administrators moved away from '[t]he traditional tax infrastructure of law, auditors, penalties, debt collectors, and court cases'[169] and saw the need to supplement that system of administration by introducing 'measures that boost taxpayers' commitment to paying tax with or without the taxing authority watching over their shoulders'.

It is noted that the mass-marketed tax avoidance schemes of the 1990s were detected by an overall loss of expected revenue by the ATO and an inordinate volume of excessive PAYE refunds. The schemes were not detected by way of audit of individual income tax returns, therefore the influence of audit rates on taxpayer compliance will not be considered further.

---

167 Ronald G Worsham, 'The Effect of Tax Authority Behaviour on Taxpayer Compliance: A Procedural Justice Approach' (1996) 18(2) Journal of American Taxation Association .

168 In war, troops under heavy enemy fire hide in the craters of recent explosions, believing it to be unlikely that the next bombs would fall in exactly the same spot in a short time span.

169 Valerie Braithwaite, 'A New Approach to Tax Compliance' in Valerie Braithwaite (ed), Taxing Democracy: Understanding Tax Avoidance and Evasion (2003).

Penalties

Previous research indicates that penalties may not be a significant factor in influencing compliance. In particular, the influence of penalties is decreased if they are not obvious to taxpayers. However after considering the chances of being caught (audit rates), the acceptance of risk may be influenced by the impact, or severity, of penalties.

Torgler, Witte and Ilersic suggest that penalties are largely ineffective in preventing tax avoidance / evasion. Ilersic takes the extreme view that 'no way, not even shooting any evaders who may be caught, will discourage such [tax evasion] practices'.[170] Davies[171] also points to a negative effect of high penalties. He states '[this] can also be extended to situations where high marginal rates of tax are imposed. People seeking to avoid paying these rates are potentially liable to end up breaking more serious legal and moral rules than those regulating taxation.'

Wenzel refers to research that suggests:

> A heavy-handed deterrence approach applied to taxpayers who would have been, or think they have been, compliant for ethical reasons could lead to reactance and undermine intrinsic ethical motivation. Conversely, strong ethical views about paying taxes honestly might make deterrence ineffective or superfluous.

Freedman also finds that penalties have little influence on taxpayer compliance and suggests:

> The only true solution to avoidance is to have a much more principle-based tax system—but this requires more than merely changes to wording. It seems that only a combination of approaches can work, but they must all have a foundation in a sensible underlying tax system to work well.[172]

However Fjeldstad and Semboja refer to research which indicates increased penalties lead to increased compliance yet their 1996 study was inconclusive, and they recommended further research to improve the robustness of the proposition. They also found that penalties had no influence in their research groups.

---

170 Alfred R Ilersic, 'The Economics of Avoidance / Evasion' in Arthur Seldon (ed), Tax Avoision (1979) 21.

171 Christie Davies, 'Can High Taxation be Enforced?' in Arthur Seldon (ed), Tax Avoision (1979) 59.

172 Judith Freedman, 'Beyond Boundaries: Developing Approaches to Tax Avoidance and Tax Risk Management' in Judith Freedman (ed), Beyond Boundaries: Developing Approaches to Tax Avoidance and Tax Risk Management (2008) 1.

Devos's 2002 research found 'that the level of taxpayer non-compliance with taxation law in Australia is not directly or solely affected by either the introduction of new tax offences or the imposition of heavier sanctions for those offences'.[173] However his later research, in 2005, found 'significant relationships with the incidence of tax evasion and the penalties for evasion'. Later still, in 2012, he found that penalties 'had limited impact upon tax compliance.'

Despite the influence of penalties being viewed as a socio-psychological influence which affects taxpayer decisions based on the fear of penalties and an aversion to risk, penalties may have the effect that they lead taxpayers into assessing risk in economic terms. Becker finds that there is an economic point where penalties influence the optimal value from a point where 'crime pays' to a point where 'crime does not pay'. Allingham and Sandmo also consider penalties as an economic factor and conclude that 'a rise in the penalty rate will lead to an increase in declared income'. However the elasticity of the influence of penalty rates is very closely affected by the probability of detection.

Kirchler notes, '[p]enalties are frequently assumed to be useful measures to prohibit undesired behaviour; consequently economic scholars have focussed on penalty schemes and their effectiveness'. He also refers to economic modelling, survey studies and laboratory experiments which indicate that 'higher punishment seems to be slightly more efficient in preventing evasion than higher audit rates'. He puts forward the findings of Fjeldstad and Semboja which cast doubt on the positive effect of fines on tax compliance. He refers to audit rates when he suggests that perceived penalties are not as significant as the perceptions of being detected in the making of tax evasion decisions.

It is interesting to note that Wadhawan and Gray's research in sub-Saharan Africa also found that '[p]rosecution and sanctions for tax fraud are few and far between'. The isolation and lack of presence of the taxing authority experienced in sub-Saharan Africa may be compared, in some respects, to the physical and social isolation of taxpayers of the remote Pilbara region in the 1990s.

Therefore the research indicates a strong relationship between penalties and audit rates in assessing acceptable levels of risk. However the impact of penalties may not have influenced the decisions of Pilbara blue-collar workers. To gauge taxpayer attitudes to the influence of penalties, participants in this research were asked if they would consider participating in other tax minimising schemes despite

---

173 Ken Devos, 'Penalties and Sanctions for Australian Taxation Crimes and the Implications for Taxpayer Compliance' (2002) 17 Australian Tax Forum 257.

their experience of having tax deductions disallowed and subsequent ATO recovery action. Their responses are considered in Chapter Four.

Amnesties

Taxpayers' assessment of the level of risk may also be influenced by the likelihood of amnesties. Once a taxpayer has made a decision as to his or her level of tax compliance and assessed the likelihood of being caught, and subsequent penalties, a following influencing factor is that of the likelihood of being forgiven—that is, an amnesty.

An amnesty was held by the ATO in 1988 for the non-lodgement of income tax returns. As the mass marketed tax avoidance schemes began to be promoted in significant volumes to the blue-collar workers of the Pilbara around the mid 1990s, the possibility of an amnesty may have been a recent memory to those taxpayers.

However the strength of influence of amnesties may be insignificant. Crane and Nourzad comment on the effectiveness of amnesties as a means of data collection but make no conclusion as to the effect of amnesties on taxpayer behaviour.[174] Wadhawan and Gray note the use of amnesties by industrial and developing countries but also draw no conclusion as to their effectiveness.

Torgler and Schaltegger conclude that 'amnesties tend to increase tax compliance'. They suggest that there is also a strong correlation with the social distance from government. They suggest that '[w]hen the government does not keep its promise [as to amnesty expectations], tax compliance decreases'. They list amnesties carried out worldwide since 1934. The list contains only 33 amnesties over a period of 70 years. The Netherlands and Portugal have had four each, and most of the other 14 countries, which have conducted amnesties, two or three. Australia's amnesties were conducted in the 1980s, one of which was targeted at participants in a specific tax avoidance scheme.

The small number of amnesties found to have been conducted is reflected in a lack of research as to the influence of amnesties. However much depends on how 'amnesty' is defined and there are many other examples of concessions being granted to taxpayers by tax administrators which were not considered by Torgler and Schaltegger as 'amnesties'.

However the small number of amnesties conducted throughout the world may be due to their long-term effectiveness. Alm, Martinez-Vazquez and Wallace

174 Stephen E Crane and Farrokh Nourzad, 'Tax Rates and Tax Evasion: Evidence from California Amnesty Data' (1990) 43(2) National Tax Journal.

question the effectiveness of amnesties. They analysed the multiple tax amnesties enacted in the Russian Federation during its main transition period of the 1990s to ascertain the impact of those amnesties on tax collections. They suggest that tax amnesties are 'fiscal gimmicks' and conclude:

> In short, an amnesty is unlikely to be any kind of fiscal panacea. It is also unlikely to be any kind of fiscal poison. On balance, it seems desirable to avoid the use of these fiscal gimmicks. The experience of the Russian Federation strengthens the overall conclusion that developing and transitional countries would be well-advised to follow a fiscal strategy that excludes tax amnesties.[175]

The concessions relieving participants in mass-marketed tax avoidance schemes in Australia in 2000 of penalties and interest might be considered an 'amnesty'. However those concessions are not on Torgler and Schaltegger's list. It is further noted that there were protest actions by taxpayers and responses of the Australian government and the ATO which tends to support the concept of a correlation between amnesties and social distance as suggested by Torgler and Schaltegger. This correlation supports the view that factors influencing compliance do not act independently.

Amnesty by way of forgiven penalties was granted by the ATO to most participants of mass-marketed tax avoidance schemes and this may have influenced compliance with the ATO's recovery action. It is possible that participants considered that if the tax avoidance schemes failed them they may have had the benefit of an amnesty. However their consideration of a forthcoming amnesty was likely to have been made after 2001 and not at the point of engaging in the schemes. Therefore the influences of amnesties are not considered further in this book.

Peer influence

Social acceptance of non-compliant behaviour may encourage tax evasion or avoidance activity. The degree of evasion or avoidance must be within the 'acceptable' standards of a community.

Christopher refers to the 'odd standards' of tax evasion. He states 'non-declaration of tips may be confided with a "nod-and-a-wink" to friends—yet few people would boast about claiming an allowance for a non-existent child'. In 1984

175 James Alm, Jorge Martinez-Vazquez and Sally Wallace, 'Do Tax Amnesties Work? The Revenue Effects of Tax Amnesties During the Transition in the Russian Federation' (2009) 39(2) Economic Analysis and Policy 235.

Wallschutzky stated, '[p]rior theory suggested that people learned how to evade from those who are successful and that peer group pressure influences behaviour. The results obtained tended to support this view and it seems that this hypothesis might explain some evasion.'

Smith and Kinsey also identify communication between taxpayers as an influence on extending the incidence of non-compliance:

> through conversations about what is and is not appropriate taxpaying behaviour. Such conversations are probably most frequent among members of occupational groups with high opportunity for non-compliance, and may serve more to reinforce norms *favouring* rather than condemning tax cheating.

Witte, Bosco and Mittone, Fjeldstad and Semboja, Karlinsky and Bankman, Wadhawan and Gray, Wenzel and Torgler all point to the influence of friends and relations on taxpayers' attitudes to compliance. In particular Ashby, Webley and Haslam point to occupational group membership and suggest that '[s]ome being occupational taxpaying norms might also be so pervasive that they are difficult to reject whatever one's level of identification'.

John Braithwaite extends the influence of peer attitudes and refers to the acceptance of sporting heroes such as Pat Rafter and Michael Jordan who 'communicate through their actions [being citizens of Bermuda] the message that avoiding tax is normal and acceptable'. He further states, '[p]eople who see themselves as poorer are less willing to pay tax voluntarily when people they perceive to be richer are believed to cheat'.

Kirchler uses the analogy of friends dining together at a restaurant and sharing the bill to illustrate the social dilemma of rational, but selfish, behaviour on the part of the person ordering an expensive meal and allowing the others to share the cost. He points out that in general society the micro approach to individualistic behaviour is far from that simple. 'A single person's contribution does not really make that much difference in the overall contribution of public goods'. He refers to research which indicates that even though an individual's rational, but selfish, behaviour harms others, the community may be considerate and sympathetic with that behaviour. If the behaviour is publicly known that sympathy actually increases.

In the isolated communities of the Pilbara the influence of peers may have had an impact on the uptake of the mass-marketed tax avoidance schemes. Marketing of the schemes could have been encouraged by 'word of mouth' advertising and social acceptance of partaking in the schemes. The research therefore explores this factor further in Chapter Four, and looks at how the taxpayers came to be aware of the schemes.

Social class

Social class presents itself in a variety of ways; education and wealth often being the most obvious. It may also be discerned by way of income and occupation. It often bears a relationship to both of those factors. The general trend appears to be the higher the social class the greater the resources that can be allocated to education. Higher education permits access to high income earning occupations which in turn leads to higher wealth and so on. In this research, education, income and occupation are considered as independent factors but it is important to note that most factors influence each other and social class is a good example of such cross influences.

Fjeldstad and Semboja note, '[a] general observation from the surveys is that the better-off respondents seem to be most compliant'. Their research revealed situations wherein the poor 'hide in the bush' to avoid tax collectors. Wadhawan and Gray have a contrary view and refer to research which indicates the influences of perceptions that rich and influential people cheat on taxes and that this 'significantly increases the likelihood that an individual will evade his or her own liabilities'. Other than the influence of publicly targeting such a class of taxpayer for evasion they have found little influence of social class on compliance. Willott and Griffin's research focuses on working-class men and their propensity to commit crime. They find that middle- and upper-class men have a similar propensity though their crimes tend to be economic. They also propose that there is no distinction of social class on the factors influencing crime.

Overall, the literature appears to be inconclusive as to the influence of social class, as an independent variable, on taxpayers' willingness to comply.

Murphy's research also examined to ascertain the social class of participants based on income and occupation. Participants' answers as to their income and occupation during the 1990s were considered as an indicator of social class on compliance, and the outcomes are discussed later in the book.

Summary

Generally researchers find that some socio-psychological factors have considerable influence on taxpayer compliance behaviour. Some researchers suggest that one of the strongest factors is the taxpayer's perception of the fairness of his or her tax burden. They also find that the perception of fairness is significantly impacted by a taxpayer's social distance from government and his or her attitudes towards risk taking. A general feeling of dissatisfaction in the social exchange between taxpayers and the government may increase the influence of the perception of fairness towards non-compliant behaviour. That dissatisfaction increases as the taxpayer feels he or she is contributing more than his or her 'fair share' towards the 'public good'.

Researchers find that other socio-psychological factors examined in this book have little effect on taxpayers' general attitude towards tax compliance, but are divided as to the impact of the influence of their peers. Some researchers find that peer influence can contribute significantly towards attitudes by a group and their relationship with authority.

Of significance to this book is the Pilbara taxpayers' perception of the fairness of their tax burden and their general feeling of social distance from the broader Australian population and government. The ethnology provided in Chapter One provides background and context to some of the socio-psychological factors which may have influenced the blue-collar workers of the Pilbara region to participate in mass-marketed tax avoidance schemes of the 1990s.

To further investigate the influence of the perceptions of fairness, and the impact of other socio-psychological factors on it, participants in this research were asked their opinion as to what they consider is a fair rate of tax and if they considered they were treated 'fairly' by the ATO. Responses to these questions are considered in Chapter Four. This review now moves to the next set of factors influencing taxpayer compliance.

3.4. Economic factors

This section looks at the published literature on the influences of economic factors on taxpayer compliance behaviour. It will be used to examine the influence that economic factors experienced by the groups of taxpayers to be surveyed in this research may have had on their decisions to engage in tax avoidance activity. In particular it looks at the factors of occupation and income.

As shown in the figure illustrating the groupings of economic factors influencing tax compliance behaviour, this book groups the economic factors of leisure and working conditions under the main grouping of occupational factors. Leisure is the converse of working hours and the type of occupation often relates to the working conditions experienced. Blue-collar workers tend to work in the field or in workshops and are exposed to climatic conditions whereas white-collar workers and professionals tend to work in environmentally controlled conditions. It also groups economic habits and income tax rates under the broader heading of income.

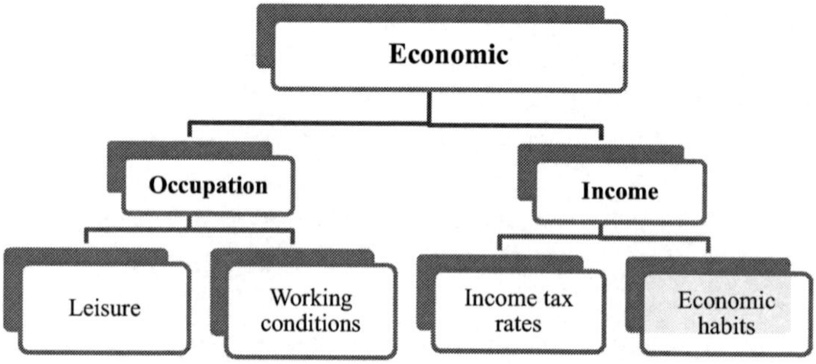

Figure 14 Groupings of economic factors

Occupation

This book focuses on the tax compliance behaviour of blue-collar workers. Therefore the influence of occupation is of particular importance. Devos notes a lack of clear research relating the variables of occupation and employment status to taxpayer compliance. He concludes 'further research needs to be done utilising occupation as an independent variable'.

Research by Ashby, Webley and Haslam found taxpayer compliance behaviour is significantly influenced 'by group memberships and the values and norms these instil'. Their quantitative survey segregated male-dominated job groups identified as financial, building, trade, farming, engineering and manufacturing sectors from other employment sectors. Their findings stressed 'the importance of occupational group membership by showing that those who belonged to a stereotypically male-dominated occupational group (irrespective of gender) were more likely to engage in tax minimization than those who did not'. They further suggested that:

> Occupational group membership is more concrete than membership with one's nation and not easy to distance oneself from. The majority of the working population spends a substantial amount of time with others in their sector. Even those who work alone cannot escape from their occupational group.

In the isolated, male-dominated, mining industry of the Pilbara region occupational group membership may have been a significant influence on taxpayer behaviour and the resultant high participation rates in the mass-marketed tax avoidance schemes.

Andreoni, Erard and Feinstein state that 'occupations may vary in the degree of evasion possible'. They found some variances in non-compliance through underreporting of income, ranging from 39 per cent in stores and restaurants to 16 per cent in real estate and insurance. However they conclude that the variations are more likely to exist as a consequence of opportunity rather than an effect of the occupation in itself, though they also note that opportunities to cheat may influence occupational choice.

Researchers such as Houston and Tran, Smith and Kinsey, Witte, Fjeldstad and Semboja, Karlinsky and Bankman, and Kirchler do not refer to specific occupations but they note 'that the self-employed and entrepreneurs are more prone to tax evasion than employed people earning a salary'. Erard also notes that taxpayers with income from 'capital gains, rents, royalties, business income or farm income [have] a significant impact on the unconditional mean level of non-compliance'.

Kirchler supports the views of the above researchers and suggests that the increased propensity towards tax avoidance by the self-employed may be due to the greater opportunity to fail to declare income or exaggerate expenses. He indicates that opportunities for evasion are more available to self-employed taxpayers than those on a salary or wages. He further suggests that exposure to greater financial risk in establishing an enterprise also influences entrepreneurs to engage in tax evasion activity. Perhaps taxpayers in similar types of occupations have similar desires to avoid tax but employed taxpayers do not have control over the finances of the enterprise to enable them to secrete income or inflate expenses. Those findings appear consistent for most researchers.

In 1997, Coleman and Freeman wrote:

> As part of its risk assessment procedures the SBI [Small Business Income Group] discovered a significant number of small trader "businesses" which also received salary and wages income in excess of $20,000. These taxpayers are found across a wide range of industries and most of them make substantial business losses. A cynic might conclude these taxpayers are determined to reduce the amount of PAYE tax they pay in a legitimate way. The SBI research has also confirmed that the small business sector is generally and substantially less compliant than salary and wage earners and larger businesses. This finding is similar to that of the United States Inland Revenue Service. It reinforces the fact that the ATO can never take away the opportunity for non-compliance in that sector, so it needs to concentrate its strategies on effecting a change in behaviour.[176]

The above researchers do not appear to have specifically considered the influence of working conditions that are associated with varying occupations or types of income. The gap in the research provides for further studies to be carried out, with particular focus on the relationship between occupation and working conditions. As this research is primarily focussed on taxpayers associated with the mining activities of the Pilbara region of Western Australia, this research will add the mining sector to the groups already surveyed by Ashby, Webley and Haslam.

Leisure

The factor of leisure is closely related to working conditions due to the substitution effect of hours engaged either at work or at leisure. However other influences, such as net income return after tax or social or family engagements, may also affect decisions to substitute work for leisure. The influence of working conditions is examined separately in the next section.

It appears that high marginal tax rates, which reduce net earnings on additional effort, significantly influence the decision to work longer. Feldstein notes that high marginal tax rates have a significant impact on taxpayers 'income-leisure' opportunity decisions.[177] Additional income, earned from additional hours devoted to employment, can be significantly eroded by higher marginal tax rates which are applied to the additional income. Taxpayers may decide that leisure and family commitments sacrificed for additional income are more important than the

---

176 Cynthia Coleman and Lynne Freeman, 'Cultural Foundations of Taxpayer Attitudes to Voluntary Compliance' in Simon R James (ed), Taxation: Critical Perspectives on the World Economy (2002) 140.

177 Martin Feldstein, 'The Effect of Marginal Tax Rates on Taxable Income: A Panel Study of the 1986 Tax Reform Act' (1995) 103(3) Journal of Political Economy 551.

earnings, particularly if the net return is regressive. Therefore taxpayers may choose to work fewer hours to avoid high marginal rates of personal tax, if possible. The blue-collar workers of the Pilbara work fixed rosters and often do not have the choice to reduce their working hours,

The influence of leisure can be viewed as a method of tax avoidance from an economic perspective. In economic terms, a point is reached where the taxpayer chooses not to earn any further income and to substitute working (taxable) hours for leisure (untaxable) hours. Brooks and Head consider a work-leisure choice analysis as a type of tax avoidance—'[b]y substituting untaxed leisure for fully taxable income ... individuals can and do avoid some tax'. [178] Their behavioural model considered the exchange of non-taxable leisure for taxable labour in economic terms. They stated that 'progressive income tax distorts the supply of labour ... [with] the greater savings enjoyed by the wealthy'. They pointed out that a 'failure to tax leisure under either income or consumption is ... [one of] the most natural and intractable constraints facing [policy makers] in the design of an equitable and efficient tax system'.

It is suggested that the impact of the loss of leisure influences tax compliance through the diminishing return of net income generated by extra work hours. The decision not to engage in extra hours of work avoids the taxation liability that would have been met on the additional income received. The blue-collar workers of the Pilbara region cannot choose to work fewer hours as they work to fixed rosters. How that influences their attitude towards tax compliance is examined in this research as part of the interviews conducted with respondents.

Further, Christopher's 1979 paper points to 'recent studies of employee job satisfaction [which] have revealed that increasing importance is attached to leisure—and at the expense, if need be, of money'. Brown extends the work-leisure substitution to include 'married women's labour supply in a household context'.[179] In this context married women may not 'work', that is earning taxable income, but non-taxable labour is being supplied to the economy. Similarly, Apps and Rees refer to the economic, but non-monetary, value of family input of 'labour supply in a household context' in their research on household production, full consumption and the costs of children.[180]

---

178 Michael Brooks and John Head, 'Tax Avoidance: in Economics, Law and Public Choice' in Graeme S Cooper (ed), Tax Avoidance and the Rule of Law (1997) 53.

179 Charles V Brown, Taxation and the Incentive to Work (2nd ed, 1983).

180 Patricia Apps and Ray Rees 'Household Production, Full Consumption and the Costs of Children' (Discussion Paper No 157, The Institute for the Study of Labor (IZA), 2000.

Brown further considers what he refers to as 'home work'. He proposes the example:

> I may paint my home—slowly and possibly badly—because if I work more to hire a painter I will have to pay him out of income on which I have already paid tax. However if I do less market [taxable] work in order to do my own painting I save this tax. The tax system thus encourages me to do work where my productivity is lower.

Working conditions

The influence of working conditions is a key factor in this book. It is noted that heavy working conditions, which can include long working hours and a resultant loss of leisure time, are closely related to occupation and this factor is therefore considered here.

A number of researchers have examined the influence of varying occupations on tax compliance and some have researched the influence of working conditions. As indicated in the figure below, the research in the area suggests that the harsher the conditions endured in earning assessable income the lower the desire to pay tax on that income.

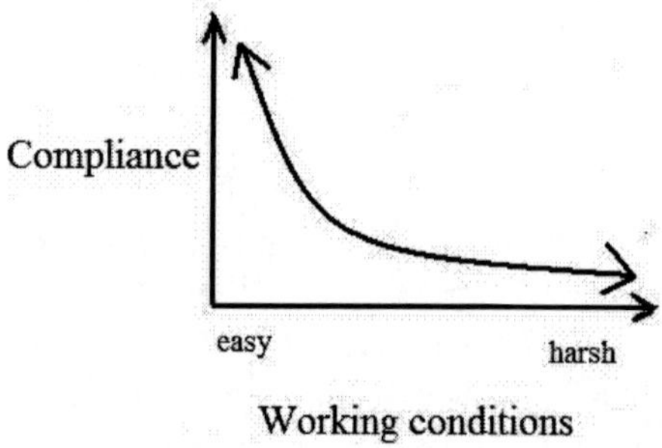

Figure 15 Effect of working conditions on tax compliance

For example, Smith and Kinsey refer to research from the early 1980s which indicated that taxpayers 'appear to be less willing to pay taxes on money resulting from entrepreneurial activity or extra effort than on income from other sources'.

In 1997 Bosco and Mittone published their conclusions of an economic experiment that they conducted on tax evasion and moral constraints. The focus of the experiment was on the influence of attitudes to risk-taking in which they considered previous research based on economic principles was unsatisfactory as it ignored the 'psychological aspects of the decision to evade tax'. Their experiment was conducted by determining the outcomes of four groups totalling 60 subjects.

However, as an adjunct to the experiment, Bosco and Mittone formed sub-groups of two categories; 'heavy workers' and 'light workers'. They worked the 'heavy workers' twice as long as the 'light workers' and paid them twice as much. Both groups were taxed at the same rate of 40 per cent. Bosco and Mittone's economic experiment found that 77 per cent of the 'heavy workers' subgroup chose tax evasion, compared with just 48 per cent of 'light workers'.

Bosco and Mittone's economic experiment conducted by way of a controlled laboratory environment was investigated further in this research. Their finding that 'hard work' increases tax evasion rates appears to strongly support the greater propensity to engage in mass-marketed tax avoidance schemes demonstrated by the taxpayers of the Pilbara region in the 1990s. The heavy working conditions experienced by the group of taxpayers under scrutiny in this book may have been a strong determinant in influencing their participation rates in the mass-marketed tax avoidance schemes. Therefore participants in the underpinning research were asked if they felt they worked hard for their income and were asked to describe why they felt their work was hard. The outcomes are explored in detail in Chapter Four.

Income

As indicated in the figure illustrating the effect of income on tax compliance, increasing income tends to have a negative influence on tax compliance. Increasing income levels are influenced by a range of other determinants such as occupation, working conditions, income tax rates, social class and opportunities to engage in tax arbitrage. As outlined in Chapter One, the blue-collar workers of the Pilbara experienced considerably higher incomes than those of their peers and also considerably higher than they had previously received before working in the mining industry.

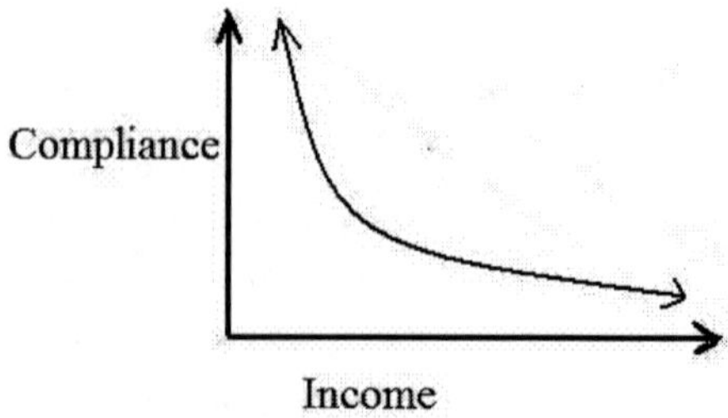

Figure 16 Effect of income on tax compliance

Previous research is limited but reveals a constant trend over a span of nearly 40 years. Becker notes that income varies the elasticity to engage in illegal activity from person to person. He states that '[o]ffenders with higher earnings have an incentive to spend more on planning their offenses, on good lawyers, on legal appeals, and even on bribery to reduce the probability of apprehension and conviction'.

Bosco and Mittone's findings reveal 'that rich subjects has [sic] always an higher evasion rate than poor ones have. Furthermore poor subjects tend to raise their evasion rate proportionally more that rich ones do when the moral constraint is removed.' Crane and Nourzad conclude that the results of their study 'also confirm the theoretical prediction that individuals with higher levels of income tend to evade more'. Kirchler points to an economic experiment which revealed that '[h]igher income level encouraged tax evasion; surprisingly, an increased tax rate did not'.

On the other hand, Houston and Tran found that respondents for their 'lower income group tended to have a higher proportion of tax evasion'. However they also state that the differences were not statistically significant.

In the current research respondents were questioned as to their income level during the period that the mass-marketed tax avoidance schemes operated. Their income position was compared in relation to the Murphy's quantitative survey data and ATO statistics. The results of this are discussed in the next chapter.

Income tax rates

As indicated in the figure below, previous research indicates that compliance has a negative relationship to increases in tax rates.

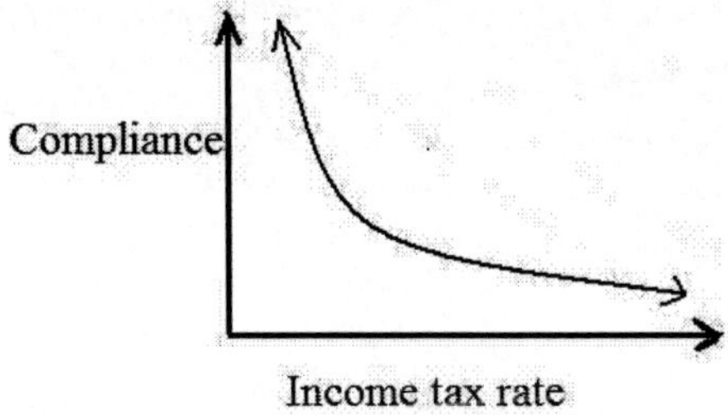

Figure 17 Effect of income tax rate on tax compliance

Wallschutzky found that the majority of evaders in his research expressed the opinion that tax rates were too high. Findings among groups of the general community were largely the same, which 'left [one] with the distinct impression that this was the major cause of most tax evasion'. Bosco and Mittone also point to research which 'shows that evasion increases with the tax rate'. John Braithwaite refers to a number of researchers' findings to support his statement that 'as tax rates fall, compliance becomes economically rational for more individual taxpayers and voluntary compliance increases'.

However not all researchers consider the impact of tax rates as significant. Devos found the effect of tax rates to be inconclusive as to a motivation to tax evasion but points to research which indicates it may lead to perceptions of unfairness which may influence tax compliance. He confirmed these findings as to the strength of tax fairness in a further empirical study in 2011. Gruen concludes 'the behaviour of labour is relatively unresponsive to personal taxation rates, particularly at higher incomes'.[181] Wadhawan and Gray point to research as to the impact of marginal tax rates and conclude 'evidence on the impact of more quantifiable factors such as tax rates and personal income is ambiguous'.

The influence of income tax rates is coupled with, and leads to, other determinants. Barnett and Grown introduce the factor of gender into the

181 Nicholas Gruen, 'Tax Cuts to Compete: The Influence of Corporate Taxation on Australia's Economic Growth' (Information Paper No 85, Committee for Economic Development of Australia, 2006).

influence of income tax rates and indicate that females are very responsive to changes in the top marginal rates of personal income tax.

Allingham and Sandmo also note the correlation between income tax rates and evasion 'because an increased tax rate makes the tax payer less wealthy'. Christopher supports that finding and used the following example of the impact of effective marginal tax rates:

> Using pre-1979 Budget rates, a married man with two children who receives a gross weekly pay of £45 would have had spending power of £44 per week after paying tax and collecting benefits. A pay rise for him of £10 per week would have yielded an increase in real income of precisely £1. He needs gross pay of £75 a week to lift him and his family out of poverty.

Ilersic, Myddelton[182] and Seldon note the influence of taxation rates on tax avoision[183] as being elementary economics. Seldon states 'if the reward left to the labourer is reduced by taxes, he will labour less hard or less well'. He notes that:

> If the net earnings (price) are reduced by taxation, the supply of labour will fall; but if the labourer wishes to maintain an accustomed stream of income and standard of living he may work longer or better the lower the net price of each hour, week or month of labour. It has been found difficult to assemble evidence on the way individuals would react to changes in the rates of taxation of their efforts as measured by the tax on their final or 'marginal' hour, week or month.

Witte, Crane and Nourzad, Feldstein and Brown conclude that high marginal income tax rates greatly influence the marginal rate of substitution between income and leisure. Brown suggests an argument for a zero tax rate at high income levels.

Kirchler also states, '[m]ost empirical research shows ... that higher tax rates lead to less compliance'. This is despite economic modelling predictions that higher tax rates lead to higher compliance. He supports Brown in that he argues that the effect of high tax rates may serve as a disincentive to work and that '[h]igher tax rates lower the costs of leisure, and consequently people will reduce their work engagement'.

Potas considers 'that those who are in the higher income brackets can benefit handsomely by careful investment techniques, such as "negative gearing." This works extremely effectively where the taxpayer falls into the top marginal tax bracket.' He further states, '[i]t is unfair because only high income earners can take advantage of it'. This view is supported by Brooks and Head who consider the

---

182 David R Myddelton, 'Tax Avoision—Its Costs and Benefits' in Arthur Seldon (ed), Tax Avoision (1979).

183 Seldon's term for the amalgam of tax evasion and tax avoidance.

economic impact of the distortion of the supply of labour caused by progressive tax rates. As the wealthy enjoy a greater benefit by reducing the supply of labour, the burden to society from the reduced tax revenue contribution places an excess burden on lower income earners. This is not only by way of reduced tax savings but also the increased labour burden which has resulted from the shift from work to leisure choices by higher income earners.

Ginting states, '[o]ur [economic] simulations indicate that the reduction in the tax rates broadens the tax base'.[184] Of particular relevance to this research is his statement, '[t]he broadened tax base is sufficient to cover the loss of tax revenue from the reduction of the tax rates and hence increases the revenue collected by the government. At the tax rate of 50 per cent, which is the base case for the tax reform example above, the government is operating well beyond the value that maximises tax collections.'

An alternative view is that put by Agell and Persson. They consider the impact of high marginal income tax rates on tax avoidance behaviour and conclude that rather than being a disincentive leading to non-compliance, high marginal tax rates can be an 'ingenious way of reconciling incompatible political ambitions'. High marginal tax rates can be set in place to 'convey the message that politicians care about the less well off'. At the same time a generous attitude towards tax avoidance prevents the very same tax system from destroying the incentives of the rich and the highly educated.' Slemrod and Yitzhaki find that the impact of a marginal tax rate, in a progressive tax system, reduces the return of expenditure on avoidance or evasion as the marginal tax rate reduces and vice versa.

The findings of previous research pointing to tax rates having a significant influence on taxpayer compliance was further supported by the findings of Marriott, Randall and Holmes in their experiment conducted in 2009. Their behavioural simulation experiment found '[t]here is a higher level of tax evasion as tax rates increase'. Their review of the literature as to the influence of marginal tax rates, focussed on the findings of Graetz and Wilde, Vogel and Clotfelter.[185] Those findings ranged from no influence (Graetz and Wilde), to some influence (Vogel) and to a very significant influence (Clotfelter).

---

184 Edimon Ginting, 'Can Tax Reform Work in an Economy Where Tax Avoidance and Evasion are Endemic?' (Paper presented at the PhD Conference in Economics and Business, University of Western Australia, November 1997).

185 Michael J Graetz and Louis L Wilde, 'The Economics of Tax Compliance: Fact and Fantasy' (1985) 38 National Tax Journal ; Joachim Vogel, 'Taxation and Public Opinion in Sweden: An Interpretation of Recent Survey Data' (1974) 27(4) National Tax Journal .

Waincymer notes the discrepancy between personal income tax rates and the lower corporation tax rates in Australia. He refers to the use of private family companies being used as '"parking space" for income that would otherwise be taxed at a higher marginal tax rate'. However he does not comment as to whether high marginal tax rates are a cause of tax avoidance activity. His comments are significant to this research as they point to the discrepancy between personal income tax rates and company tax rates. That discrepancy is considered to be significant factor which influenced participation in mass-marketed tax avoidance schemes by blue-collar workers in the Pilbara region in the 1990s.

The differing rates between personal income tax and company income tax were also considered by Chand who found that:

> There is little need for harmonisation of tax rates on personal income to bring about arbitrage in after-tax returns; this being particularly true when franking of corporate income is permitted. A marginal tax rate on personal income being higher than on corporate income induces lower corporate savings when the corporate sector competes for funds across jurisdictions.[186]

The disparity of tax rates between personal income tax rates and company tax rates has encouraged the practice of interposing corporate entities between individuals and their income. In 2009 Deutsch commented that '[r]ecent case law (see for example, *Russell v Federal Commissioner of Taxation* (2009) FCA 1224) shows the extent to which some tax payers will go to attract a corporate tax rate even when it sits at the 30% level'.[187] It is noted that the court found in favour of the taxpayer.[188]

The practice is often referred to as 'tax arbitrage' and researchers have considered it from several differing aspects. Feldstein refers to the use of tax shelters to reduce marginal tax rates as a 'short term' response. He differentiates this activity from 'long term' responses which involve changes in education, occupation, location and so on. He uses the 1993 changes in marginal tax rates in the United States as an illustration of the influence of marginal tax rates on the use of tax arbitrage. He considers tax arbitrage to be a tax avoidance method and not a cause of tax avoidance.

---

186 Satish Chand, 'International Tax Arbitrage via Corporate Income Splitting' (Working Paper No 02-1, Australian National University Asia Pacific School of Economics and Government, 2002).

187 Robert L Deutsch, 'Tax Reform: The Never-ending Saga' (2009) 8 Atax Matters 5.

188 Russell v Federal Commissioner of Taxation (2009) FCA 1224.

Slemrod and Yitzhaki define tax arbitrage as an 'activity [which] takes advantage of inconsistencies in the tax law, featuring economically offsetting positions which have asymmetric tax treatments'. John Braithwaite argues 'a tax system that redistributes wealth from the rich to the poor is better than one that does the reverse'. He considers tax arbitrage, in particular international tax arbitrage, as a vice rather than a virtue.

On the other hand, Agell and Persson view tax arbitrage as an ingenious way of preventing the tax system from 'destroying the incentives of the rich and highly educated'. They suggest inconsistencies are deliberately placed within taxing systems 'as a means of blowing off some steam in order to save the engine from exploding'.

As examined in Chapter Two, the mass-marketed tax avoidance schemes of the 1990s often functioned as a system of tax arbitrage by using corporate entities interposed between income and individuals, or to offset losses from corporate entities such as agribusiness or film investments against ordinary personal income. Therefore to investigate the impact of the disparity (between company and personal income tax rates), respondents to this research were asked their opinion as to what they believed to be a fair tax rate. Their responses are considered in the following chapter.

Economic habits

A habit is 'a disposition or tendency, constantly shown to act in a certain way'. An economic habit is considered to be that part of human behaviour which disposes people to certain patterns of income earning and spending behaviour. The concept is exceptionally broad. However, in the context of this book, it relates to how individuals choose to maximise their disposable income, specifically how they react to changes in their disposable income and how they seek to maximise it by reducing their taxation burden—tax avoidance activity.

It is considered that economic habits have an influence on compliance but research to date is an insufficient basis for a reliable conclusion. Smith and Kinsey observe that 'acting according to habit affords relative certainty, taxpayers will be hesitant to move into new, uncertain areas for just a small gain'. Witte also suggests that '[t]axpayers are creatures of habit and starting them on the right taxpaying course could yield substantial compliance dividends'.

According to ATO statistics, shown in Chapter One, the years prior to 1994 reveal very little tax avoidance activity, as far as mass-marketed tax avoidance schemes deductions are concerned. There is no clear evidence that Pilbara taxpayers demonstrated tax avoidance activity prior to engaging in the mass-marketed tax avoidance schemes of the 1990s. However, as indicated in Chapter One, the economic habits of the Pilbara blue-collar workers are such that they tend to spend their increased income on consumer items and leisure.

Summary

Economic factors, particularly income levels, are significant to the examination of the Pilbara miners, among the highest paid blue-collar workers in Australia. Those income levels led to exposure to high income tax rates due to Australia's progressive tax system. The mass-marketed tax avoidance schemes offered a means of tax arbitrage to those employed blue-collar workers who had previously had little means of seeking relief from the high tax rates associated with the higher than average earnings of the Pilbara mining industry. Therefore the influence of high income tax rates is examined in detail in Chapter Four.

This review now moves to the final set of influencing factors—the group of legal and administrative factors influencing compliance.

3.5. Legal and administrative factors

This section examines the published literature on legal aspects of tax administration and how taxpayers respond to those influences. It will be used to examine the dynamics of the influence of compliance with the law and specifically taxation law on individuals within the groups of taxpayers considered in this research.

This section is divided into four sub-sections. They deal respectively with:

- The role of tax professionals,
- The impact of administrative delays,
- The impact of complexity of tax system and costs associated with increasing complexity, and
- How tax scheme designers interpret judicial decisions when designing new schemes.

Tax professionals

Research findings vary as to the degree of influence tax professionals have on tax avoidance activities, but most researchers conclude that their role is pivotal in scheme design. As to the promotion of tax avoidance schemes the position is not so clear. The view as to whether tax avoidance scheme promotion is, in economic terms, 'supply pushed' or 'demand pulled' is problematic.

Researchers such as John Braithwaite place considerable importance on the role of tax professionals in designing and promoting the mass-marketed tax avoidance schemes in the 1990s, finding that 'increased community demand for tax avoidance schemes was led by the supply of such schemes by promoters'.

Later evidence supports Braithwaite's statement. In 2008, the Organisation for Economic Co-operation and Development (OECD) study into the role of tax intermediaries found:

> The importance of the role of tax advisers play in a tax system can be tested by answering a simple question: would compliance with tax laws improve if tax advisers did not exist? The Study Team found no country where the answer to that question is yes.[189]

Stated simply, the OECD Study Team found that the presence of tax advisers has little effect on compliance. The study concludes '[s]ome taxpayers will continue to engage in aggressive tax planning and some tax intermediaries will continue to act as promoters of aggressive tax planning'. It notes, '[t]ax intermediaries are the supply side of a relationship in which taxpayers, their clients, form the demand side'.

However, McBarnet concludes that it is a fundamental attitude towards tax and law which affects policy and compliance. 'This is true not just for taxpayers, but for their professional advisers—the lawyers and accountants whose creative work lies at the heart of creative compliance'.[190]

---

189 Organisation for Economic Co-operation and Development, Study into the Role of Tax Intermediaries (2008).

190 Doreen McBarnet, 'When Compliance is Not the Solution but the Problem: From Changes in Law to Changes in Attitude' in Valerie Braithwaite (ed), Taxing Democracy: Understanding Tax Avoidance and Evasion (2003) 229.

Erard states:

> Tax practitioners undoubtedly fulfil a socially beneficial role in reducing many of the informational and computational barriers to compliance with the tax laws [they overcome the problems of complexity]. However, the results indicate that their use, most especially the use of CPAs and lawyers, is associated with a higher level of non-compliance, which can have negative consequences for both tax equity and tax efficiency.

Wallschutzky and Smith and Kinsey support his conclusion. However Hite and McGill conclude that they find no evidence to support taxpayer preference for aggressive tax advice. They suggest that client demand for tax minimisation arises from a misunderstanding of a client's wishes by the tax preparer but concede 'much remains to be done in the area of the relationship of taxpayers and their preparers'. Karlinsky and Bankman also conclude 'that [tax] preparers who aid and abet in their clients misreporting, or show their implicit acceptance of that misreporting, play a causal role in that misreporting'.

Houston and Tran find that while there was evidence 'that higher proportions of tax evasion are present among taxpayers who used the services of a tax agent to prepare their 1997 / 98 tax returns compared to those who did not use tax agents, ... the differences are not statistically significant'.

Devos, in 2005, found (albeit with a limited scope of research) that 42 per cent of respondents engaged the services of a tax agent to minimise the amount of tax they had to pay while a further 6 per cent gave the reason that it was to avoid paying tax.

Importantly Wadhawan and Gray find that the use of tax professionals increases the costs of compliance. Their finding indicates a further example of the influence of one factor affecting other factors of taxpayer compliance behaviour.

In summary, the degree of influence of tax professionals on tax compliance is problematic. Do tax professionals create non-compliance or, as Braithwaite suggested, merely facilitate it, the attitude of the taxpayer towards non-compliance being more strongly influenced by other factors? This issue is explored further in Chapter Four as the responses of interviewees to this research are examined.

Administrative delays

Administrative delays in responding to taxpayer engagement in aggressive tax planning may lead to an increase in taxpayer participation in tax evasion or avoidance activity as taxpayers perceive the lack of administrative action as tacit approval of the scheme. It is noted that the delay in detecting and addressing the mass-marketed tax avoidance schemes of the 1990s was considered by many participants as evidence of acceptance of the schemes by the ATO.

Considerable administrative delays are sometimes referred to as 'bureaucratic inertia'. Grabosky indicates that much of the cause for the proliferation of extremely artificial tax avoidance schemes in the 1970s was the encouragement of the legal and accounting professions. He further suggests that '[t]he medium in which these massive frauds on the revenue flourished was bureaucratic inertia'. Becker considers the time delay between commission and detection, apprehension and conviction as '[a]n important determinant' in the economic cost of crime. Smith and Kinsey also note that 'long lag times between filing and enforcement action may exacerbate tendencies toward non-compliance'.

Slemrod and Yitzhaki suggest that delays in administration of a tax system result in an economic decision to engage in tax evasion. Taxpayers calculate the profit and risk of non-compliance by assessing the value of tax saved, during the period of non-detection, to the tax and penalties payable when and if detected. Kirchler supports that view and hypothesises 'that taxpayers who experience a long delay between incorrect tax filing and tax authorities actions will be less likely to associate these actions with their behaviour, and thus, will be less likely to view that consequences in regard to their future filing behaviour'.

Torgler further reinforces Kirchler's hypothesis (and therefore Slemrod and Yitzhaki's) and also suggests that administrative delays, in detecting and dealing with tax evasion or avoidance, encourage taxpayers to engage in such activities from a purely economic perspective. Taxpayers assess the 'profit and risk' of evading or avoiding tax, in that the benefits of delaying the payment of tax can exceed the benefits of timely payment. The greater the administrative delay, the greater the benefit.

In this research, respondents were asked why they were attracted to the mass-marketed tax avoidance scheme(s). The purpose of the question is to establish whether administrative delays or bureaucratic inertia were a contributory factor in determining involvement in the mass-marketed tax avoidance schemes and, if so to assess the strength of the influence of those administrative delays. Secondly, it may indicate whether or not tax avoidance was the primary purpose of participating in the schemes. Further discussion of this aspect occurs in the following chapter.

Complexity of the tax system

There has been considerable research into the impact of the complexity of tax systems, and the associated costs of compliance, on taxpayer behaviour.

Murphy refers to numerous researchers when she states, 'For decades, taxpayers around the world have been concerned about the increasing complexity of tax systems.'[191] She uses the findings of researchers such as Cuccia and Carnes, McKerchar, Vogel, Collins and colleagues, Roth, Scholz and Witte, Inglis, Slemrod, Ahmed and colleagues, McGraw and Scholz, Schwartz and Orleans and Wenzel to support her findings that taxpayers often use complexity as a tool or excuse for disengaging with taxing authorities.

Murphy's findings are particularly relevant to this research in that not only does complexity of the tax system influence compliance, but it also reveals the influence of one factor on others. She finds that complexity was used as a tool to create social distance and to legitimise social influences such as guilt and shame.

These findings demonstrate that, in common with the other factors examined in this review, complexity of the tax system leads to, and is influenced by, other factors. Murphy suggests that 'taxpayers involved in aggressive tax planning are less likely to have a taxpaying conscience' and 'that taxpayers involved in aggressive tax planning are more likely to place more distance between themselves and a tax authority because they are more likely to be disengaged from the tax system'.

Shover, Job and Carroll support the concept of complexity being an excuse for aggressive avoidance behaviour rather than a cause of non-compliance. They give the example of a statement made by a plumber, who was interviewed with his business partner, to give an 'unusually clear representation of [cynicism of the ATO].'[192] He is quoted as saying, 'I mean it's all too hard; that something so simple is made so hard. On top of going to work and making a living, we're expected to work our tax out and everything else out, and it's that bloody complicated.'

---

191 Kristina Murphy, 'Aggressive Tax Planning: Differentiating Those Playing the Game from Those Who Don't' (2004) 25 Journal of Economic Psychology 307.

192 Neal Shover, Jenny Job and Anne Carroll, 'The ATO Compliance Model in Action: A Case Study of Building and Construction', in Valerie Braithwaite (ed), Taxing Democracy: Understanding Tax Avoidance and Evasion (2003) 159.

Other research is divided as to the impact of complexity of the tax system on compliance. Oxley and Elwela point to the cost of engaging tax advisers.[193] Engaging tax advisers in turn leads to another factor of influence—the influence of tax professionals. Christopher suggests that complexity is not a motivation for 'tax-dodging' but rather the opposite: 'Successful and lucrative dodging requires an appreciation of the intricacies of taxation which can be acquired only by assiduous study or by purchasing the ingenuity of those who have made such study.'

However, Witte states, '[c]omplexity and ambiguity in tax legislation increase the costs of compliance, increase the amount of non-compliance ... and decrease the chances that penalties will be imposed'.

Potas also points out that '[t]he fact remains that complexity and compliance are unhappy bedfellows'. He states, '[u]ncertainty, complexity and confusion provide the breeding-ground for tax avoidance and evasion'.

Richardson, who also refers to the impact of combinations of influencing factors, notes that whatever the prevailing tax rate 'some taxpayers will utilise the advantages of the [complexity of the] system so as to minimise the total tax paid in respect of their productive efforts'.[194]

Waincymer acknowledges that the complexity of legislative and administrative design of Australia's income tax laws and administration were necessary. However he concludes that '[i]t would be ... difficult to attempt to assert with any degree of certainty the relative causes of tax avoidance in Australia's history. It is simply not possible to prove the cause or connection to any clear degree.' Gammie also expresses doubts as to the influence of complexity. He states that '[m]any commercial arrangements are highly complex and are affected by taxes'.[195] He argues that a complex series of transactions or commercial structure may reflect a motive, purpose or intention to avoid or evade tax, but that it is not necessarily so.

Karlinsky and Bankman question 'underpayment of tax [as] a function of the taxpayer's attitude toward the government, complexity of the tax system or the tax that is evaded'. Their research focuses on the interactions between business

---

193 Prue Oxley and Darshana Elwela, 'Tax Compliance Costs of New Zealand Small Businesses, 2004: Designing the Survey for its Policy Purpose', in Margaret McKerchar and Michael Walpole (eds), Further Global Challenges in Tax Administration (2006) 435.

194 Sir Ivor Richardson, 'Reducing Tax Avoidance by Changing Structures, Processes and Drafting', in Graeme S Cooper (ed) Tax Avoidance and the Rule of Law (1997) 327.

195 Malcolm Gammie, 'Tax Avoidance and the Rule of Law: A Perspective from the United Kingdom', in Graeme S Cooper (ed) Tax Avoidance and the Rule of Law (1997) 181.

owners and their tax preparers and did not draw strong conclusions as to the relationship between complexity and underpayment of tax. However, they do 'find underreporting is primarily a function of ability to evade detection, rather than attitudes toward government or complexity'.

John Braithwaite also considers complexity of the tax system as a tool for non-compliant activity rather than an influencing factor. He identifies complexity as one of the deeper causes of the 'boom' in aggressive tax planning activity in Australia and the USA. He states:

> As rules were written to cover loopholes, they opened up new ones. The very complexity of the tax law expanded opportunities for arbitrage, a trend that was almost as bad in the US [as it was in Australia], but much worse in the US and Australia than in other developed economies.

He also suggests that:

> [N]o taxpayer can ever comprehend the complexity of the whole tax system. In fact, even the Commissioner for Taxation cannot comprehend anything like the vast totality of its flows and forms and systems and rules.

He further states that the influence of complexity on the behaviour of taxpayers may be explained by adding:

> If it is a simple pathway for a taxpayer with simple affairs; information packages can allow them to picture it on their own. If their affairs are more complex, they will need a tax preparer to help them see their pathway through the system.

Coleman, Hart and Sekhon suggest '[i]t is the failure to design a tax system in accordance with these criteria [efficiency, equity and simplicity] that leads to so many opportunities for minimisation of tax'.[196] In another approach, Krever suggests that complexity of legislation could arise from political expedience: 'Fuzzy drafting delegates the task of being the bad guys to Inland Revenue, leaving the politicians in the clear.'[197]

McBarnet looks at complexity as creating a means of tax avoidance activity through what she termed 'over-compliance'. She refers to creative compliance as 'that first cousin of tax avoidance'. She asserts that the essence of creative compliance is not in breaking or ignoring the law but rather in seeking ways to comply 'with the letter of the law while totally undermining the policy behind the

---

196 Cynthia Coleman, Geoffrey E Hart and Jas S Sekhon, Income Tax Analysis—Cases, Questions and Commercial Applications (2nd ed, 1997).

197 Richard Krever, 'Plain English Drafting, Purposive Drafting, Principle Drafting: Does Any of it Matter?' in Judith Freedman (ed), Beyond Boundaries: Developing Approaches to Tax Avoidance and Tax Risk Management (2008) 189.

words'. She suggests that 'creative compliance operates particularly effectively in the context of a rule-bound [complex] regime, where the words of the law can be treated as recipes for avoidance'. She concludes however that complexity, which leads to creative compliance, is not in itself a motivational incentive for tax avoidance activity but rather it influences taxpayers' attitudes towards the payment of taxes. She extends the necessity to foster a change in attitude not just to taxpayers but also to 'their professional advisers—the lawyers and accountants whose creative work lies at the heart of creative compliance'.

In summary, the impact of the influence of complexity of the tax system on compliance has been extensively researched. That research suggests that complexity may not necessarily be a causal factor of non-compliance but it certainly is a facilitator. Taxpayers and scheme designers often use complexity as a façade behind which tax avoidance schemes are structured and implemented. They also use complexity as an excuse for adopting tax avoidance schemes as part of their financial structures.

Costs of compliance

Generally the cost of compliance for individual taxpayers, in monetary terms, is that of a tax compiler[198] and can be less than a few hundred dollars per year. In addition a more significant compliance cost is the time taken by taxpayers to deal with their tax affairs. Time has to be allocated to compiling and collating tax documents, appointments with tax professionals arranging payments, dealing with tax authority queries and such other matters as may arise.

Evans and his fellow researchers find that:

> For individual taxpayers, the Australian studies show that despite the high use of tax agents, the costs of these agents are not the major component of compliance costs ... By far the largest component in the Australian studies of individual taxpayers (and, indeed, business taxpayers) is time cost.[199]

198 Generally a term used in the US to describe a person who compiles taxation returns. The common term applied to professional tax compilers in Australia is 'taxation agent', and these are registered as such. However, 'tax compiler' is a broader term and applies not only to taxation agents, but also to accounting and administrative staff employed by companies and incorporated bodies which are self-lodgers. Individual taxpayers often lodge their own income tax returns without engaging the services of a tax compiler such as a tax agent.

199 Chris Evans et al, A Report into the Taxpayer Costs of Compliance (1997).

The influence of the costs of compliance has a greater impact on business enterprises than on individual pay-as-you-go (PAYG) taxpayers that are the focus of this research. However, for both businesses and individuals, the general trend is that the higher the cost of compliance, the lower the compliance.

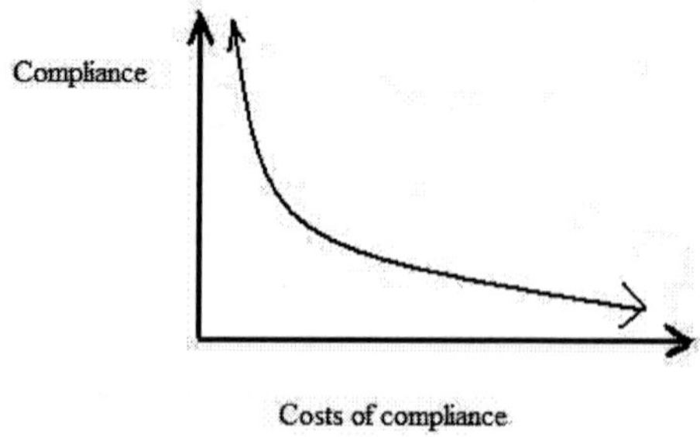

Figure 18 Effect of costs of compliance on tax compliance

Researchers in the US[200] also found that leisure time lost in filing tax returns influenced taxpayers' decisions to engage a professional tax compiler. Those findings are supported by Murphy and Byng's research, which revealed that 93 per cent of respondents engaged in the mass-marketed tax avoidance schemes had engaged a tax agent. The decision to engage a tax agent leads to the introduction of the factor of the influence of the tax professionals, which was examined earlier in this section.

Witte refers to Slemrod's earlier finding 'that higher taxpayer compliance cost[s] lead to lower level of compliance. However, to date [1989], there has been no empirical work to support this proposition.' Wadhawan and Gray also use the findings of Slemrod (1989) and Ekstrand (1980) to propose the view that '[h]igh compliance costs—time, effort and psychic energy—act as a barrier to compliance'. McKerchar also found that along with perception of fairness the cost of compliance influenced compliance to some extent and that '[t]he impact of upon compliance for non-personal taxpayers also offers scope for further research'.

Moody, Warcholik and Hodge view the costs of compliance from the perspective of time engaged by the taxpayer and the relationship with complexity. They note that '[w]hen examined by income level, compliance cost is found to be highly regressive, taking a larger toll on low-income taxpayers as a percentage of

200 J Scott Moody, Wendy P Warcholik and Scott A Hodge, 'The Rising Cost of Complying with the Federal Income Tax' (2005) 138 Special Report.

income than high-income taxpayers'. They also find that the cost, by way of time occupied in filing taxation returns, tends to influence taxpayers' decisions about whether to engage the services of professional tax preparers, which in turn introduces an additional factor of influence in tax compliance behaviour.

Evans[201] points to a raft of research into the costs of compliance over 20 years from the 1980s, however much of that research focuses on corporate and business taxes. He draws attention to the increasing costs of compliance and recommends that these rising costs be addressed by taxing authorities. That research also points to the regressive nature of compliance costs and that '[c]omplexity of legislative provisions together with the frequency of legislative change are identified as prime causes of high compliance costs'.

Woellner, and his fellow researchers, suggest there is a link between complexity and the psychological costs of compliance in their experimental research as to the use of the ITAA 1936 and the more simplified taxation legislation the ITAA 1997. They state '[our] findings provide reliable evidence that the simplified drafting style utilised in ITAA 1997 does provide benefits to both novice and experienced users in terms of reducing their psychological costs of compliance'.[202]

Evans later notes '[t]hree major themes emerge from the literature that has flourished in recent years: compliance costs are high and they are significant; compliance costs are regressive; and compliance costs are not reducing over time'.[203]

Of importance to this research is not the impact of the cost of compliance on individual taxpayer behaviour *per se*, but its impact on taxpayer compliance which may lead to other factors such as the perception of fairness, engaging tax professionals or complexity of the tax system. The importance of previous research into this factor is that it evidences a link between the factors influencing taxpayer compliance.

---

201 Chris Evans, 'Studying the Studies: An Overview of Recent Research into Taxation Operating Costs' (2003) 1 eJournal of Tax Research.

202 Robin Woellner et al, 'Can Simplified Legal Drafting Reduce the Psychological Costs of Tax Compliance? An Australian Perspective' (2007) British Tax Review 717, 733.

203 Chris Evans, 'Taxation Compliance and Administrative Costs: An Overview', in Michael Lang et al (eds), Tax Compliance Costs for Companies in an Enlarged European Community (2008) 447, 457.

Court interpretations

Scheme designers and promoters of the tax avoidance schemes rely heavily on court interpretations to structure new schemes and to validate their operations to participating taxpayers. Examination of the schemes under focus in this book reveals that many of the scheme promoters in the 1990s used 'legal opinions' as part of their promotional material.

McBarnet states that one significant factor contributing to 'creative compliance' is 'the nature and operation of law itself'. She further suggests 'it is in the nature of law that it is open to different interpretations, and that its meaning and application are arguable'. Waincymer also notes that different approaches to statutory interpretation and the varying judicial attitudes have fostered a situation in which 'taxpayers are encouraged to manipulate those criteria [set by judicial decisions] to maximise their after tax profit'. Their conclusions lead to the consideration of judicial decisions on tax planning activities.

Lapidoth supports the findings of McBarnet and Waincymer in his observation that 'the problem of tax avoidance may be related to the interpretation of taxing statutes'[204]. He indicates that 'literal' interpretation of statutes encourages tax avoidance schemes. Gammie also notes that 'the legal rules offer opportunities for manipulation. The outcome is equally arbitrary and unfair in allowing clever and well advised people to obtain the benefit of the relief [from taxation] where others cannot.'

Vanistendael points to examples where '[i]n some countries, the legislature has judged it necessary to take legislative action in the form of general or specific anti-abuse provisions to remedy the failure of the courts to cut off abuse'.[205] He concludes that there are different points of view as to the role of the courts acting in the role of legislators. 'Proponents of active political courts will argue that the courts should supplement the mistake made by the legislator and tax what has been left untaxed in the statute.' On the other hand the courts must impose the text of the law and 'there is no reason for the courts to legislate judicially'. Regardless of which point of view is adopted he points to the necessity of consistency in analysis of the 'relevant facts from a point of view of logic and efficiency for the taxpayer'.

---

204 Arye Lapidoth, 'New Legislative Measures in Israel to Counter "Aggressive Tax Planning"' (2006) 60 (6) Bulletin for International Taxation 255, 259.

205 Frans Vanistendael, 'Judicial Interpretation and the Role of Anti-Abuse Provisions in Tax Law', in Graeme S Cooper (ed) Tax Avoidance and the Rule of Law (1997) 131, 144.

Myers observes that '[o]ne should be under no illusions: personal character and social attitudes have a large influence on judicial decisions, as much as political decisions'. He observed varying statutory interpretative approaches of Australia's High Court between the years 1964 to 2005 to illustrate how those attitudes impact on the administration of income tax legislation. He concludes that 'an arid, literal construction of the statute [Pt IVA][206] ... will lead to uncertainty and unfairness in the administration of income tax legislation, to the disadvantage of individual taxpayers and the whole community'.

A global perspective is that of Pickup who states 'it was clear from our visits [to a number of countries] that a vital issue in the effectiveness of anti-avoidance measures was the approach of the judiciary to tax cases in general and avoidance in particular'.[207] He uses the example of the development of the 'bottom of the harbour' schemes in Australia in the 1970s to support, what he refers to as 'judicial castration' which encourages tax avoidance activity.

Commentators, such as Brooks, refer to policy analysts, legislative drafters, politicians, tax lawyers and law and accounting professors when he states '[a]ll of these folks deserve some blame for the sorry state of our tax laws'[208] which, they assert, leads to the creation of opportunities for tax avoidance activity.

It is not suggested that the judiciary should take part in designing or marketing tax avoidance schemes. However, judicial decisions, and in particular the reasons for findings, in tax cases may be closely examined by scheme designers to establish why a particular scheme succeeded or failed when designing new schemes. The influence of judicial decisions and legal opinion will be considered in this research when court transcripts and submissions to the Senate Inquiry are examined.

Summary

Administrative delays, the complexity of the tax system and the influence of tax professionals are arguably contributing factors which allowed the mass-marketed tax avoidance schemes to grow unchecked for a number of years. They were also

---

206 Part IVA of the ITAA 1936 (Australia's GAAR).

207 David Pickup, 'In Relation to General Anti-Avoidance Provisions: A Comparative Study of the Legal Frameworks Used by Different Countries to Protect Their Tax Revenues' in Judith Freedman (ed), Beyond Boundaries: Developing Approaches to Tax Avoidance and Tax Risk Management (2008) 9, 9.

208 Neil Brooks, 'The Responsibility of Judges in Interpreting Tax Legislation', in Graeme S Cooper (ed), Tax Avoidance and the Rule of Law (1997) 93.

found by Hobson to be reasons given by taxpayers for what was perceived to be approval of the tax arbitrage methods employed by the mass-marketed tax avoidance schemes. That perception may have given rise to the taxpayer resistance to ATO recovery action but this issue is beyond the scope of this book.

The impact of the influence of legal and institutional factors was common to all Australian taxpayers at the time of the mass-marketed tax avoidance schemes of the 1990s. Therefore this group of factors is not considered as a sufficient determinant to explain the disproportionate participation of the Pilbara blue-collar workers in the mass-marketed tax avoidance schemes in the 1990s. However their influence on participants in mass-marketed tax avoidance schemes is examined in Chapter Four.

3.6. Summary: The research gap

This chapter has reviewed research over a 40-year period from 1968 to 2008 on the factors that influence taxpayer compliance behaviour. For convenience, those factors were classified into four broad groups; demographic, socio-psychological, economic and legal and administrative factors.

It is noted that such classification is not necessarily discrete and some factors considered as part of one group could, arguably, be placed in another. However the adopted classification system permitted a review of the literature generally to follow the development from earlier research, which tended to consider influencing factors in isolation, to more recent research, which tends to consider them from a more holistic viewpoint. Later research also tends to consider the influencing factors and how they interact with each other. An example is the influence of perceptions of fairness. Taxpayers' perceptions of fairness are greatly influenced by a raft of other factors such as how their tax is spent and how connected they feel towards their government. Similarly taxpayers' attitudes towards risk aversion are greatly influenced by audit rates, penalties and the likelihood of amnesties. Peer influence, which is affected by social class and occupation, may also influence a taxpayer's attitude towards risk taking.

Over the 40-year period there has also been a transformation in research approaches. Earlier research tends to adopt objective quantitative statistical analysis approaches and focuses on quantifiable factors such as demographic and economic influences. Later research tends to adopt subjective qualitative research approaches and looks at the influences of socio-psychological and legal and administrative factors.

That transition does not indicate the creation of a hierarchy of research approaches, nor does it imply that one method is superior to another. Rather the evolution of research approaches has strengthened the concept of an interrelationship between single factors and groups of factors. That interrelationship among the groups of factors, initially shown in the figure showing the factors affecting tax compliance behaviour by individuals, at the beginning of the chapter as isolated groups, is illustrated in the following figure.

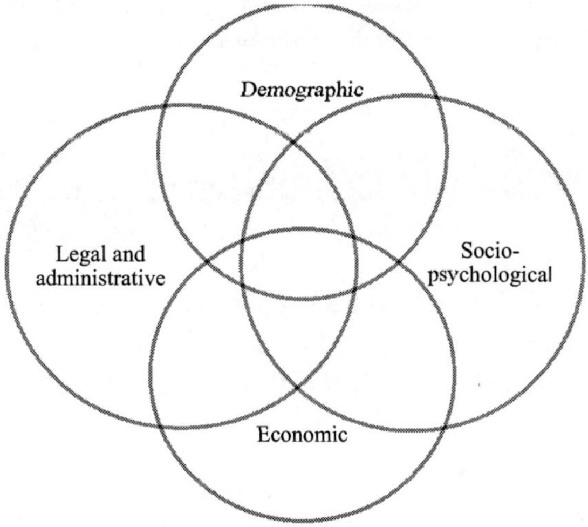

Figure 19 The interrelationship of factors affecting tax compliance behaviour

Generally research on the influence of demographic factors is extensive and well settled. Researchers have found that the strength of influence of demographic factors varies. Previous research suggests that some demographic factors, such as occupation and age, are quite strong and others, such as nationality and religion, are relatively weak. They further suggest that compliance tends to increase with age and education, though at some point education reduces compliance. They find that females tend to be more compliant than males and differing social groups, based on nationality or religion, demonstrate differing levels of compliance.

The focus group of this research is the taxpayers in the Pilbara in the 1990s. They are mostly engaged in the male-dominated mining industry. They tend to be younger, less educated and more secular than the broader Australian community. Therefore focus is on those demographic factors identified as particularly relevant to those taxpayers—gender, age, education and, to a lesser extent, religion.

Generally the literature suggests that the socio-psychological factor of the perception of fairness is one of the strongest influences on taxpayer compliance behaviour. It suggests that perceptions of fairness are greatly affected by social distance from government and peer influences. Researchers find that increased social distance strongly increases non-compliance behaviour. Therefore the physical isolation of the Pilbara taxpayers may have contributed to their participation rates in the mass-marketed tax avoidance schemes in the 1990s. In the next chapter, the responses of participants in this research are examined to assess their opinions on how fairly they were treated by taxing authorities and the tax system generally.

There is a high degree of interrelationship between economic factors. Generally levels of income relate closely to occupation. In turn, income levels directly affect income tax rates and economic habits. Also types of occupation closely relate to working conditions and leisure as hours spent at work or at leisure are mutually exclusive.

The income levels, and associated influencing factors experienced by the blue-collar workers in the Pilbara in the 1990s had a great disparity with income levels usually experienced by like occupations in the broader community. The economic factors considered significant to this research are examined in Chapter Four by examining the responses of participants to this research.

In addition administrative delays, complexity of the tax system and the influence of tax professionals, grouped as legal and administrative factors, may have had some impact on the growth and acceptance of the mass-marketed tax avoidance schemes. Administrative delays have been interpreted by respondents of previous research as indicators of 'acceptable tax planning' rather than 'unacceptable tax avoidance' activity. In the next chapter, this book compares findings of previous research with the responses of participants in this research in order to gauge the strength of legal and administrative factors on the decisions of blue-collar workers of the Pilbara to participate in the mass-marketed tax avoidance schemes of the 1990s.

4. CHAPTER FOUR: RESEARCH ANALYSIS AND OUTCOMES

'The only way to get your windows cleaned these days is to give the man cash and not ask if he is reporting it to the revenue.'

Sir Lawrence Airey, Chairman of the British Board of Inland Revenue (1926–71)

4.1. Introduction

This chapter examines the outcomes of the quantitative and qualitative approaches of this research. It looks at the influencing factors identified in the literature review in Chapter Three to highlight the most prominent factors which may have led to the disproportionate participation rates in mass-marketed tax avoidance schemes demonstrated by taxpayers of the Pilbara region in the 1990s.

John Braithwaite suggests that promoter supply and consumer demand forces act to create a marketplace. He concludes that, 'aggressive tax planning is more supply driven by promoters of shelters than demand driven.' He also finds that, 'supply-driven tax shelters pass a tipping point beyond which an aggressive tax planning contagion creates a demand-driven market.'

The analysis which is undertaken in this chapter is also based on the economic concepts of the free market forces of supply and demand. Following the approach taken by Braithwaite, who considers the marketing of aggressive tax planning schemes to be subject to those economic forces, this examination is also grouped into supply-driven (primarily legislative and administrative) factors and demand-driven (primarily demographic, socio-psychological and economic) factors.

This book submits that, in the mid to late 1990s, the marketing of mass-marketed tax avoidance schemes in the Pilbara took place after that 'tipping point' had been passed. It also suggests that the 1990s was a period of the tax scheme design and growth stage in the cyclical pattern of tax avoidance scheme development in Australia as illustrated in Chapter Two. As discussed in that chapter, the blue-collar workers of Western Australia's mining industry were responding to the closure of previous tax avoidance schemes by the ATO,[209] and were seeking new ways to reduce their taxation burden.

209 Chiefly the use of 'salary sacrifice' and 'interposed entity' schemes.

This chapter first considers the supply-driven factors—those grouped as legislative and administrative factors as illustrated in the illustration grouping the factors affecting tax compliance behaviour by individuals in Chapter Three. It then considers the demand-driven factors, which are the main focus of this book, to develop the examination of what may have influenced the blue-collar workers of the Pilbara region to engage in the mass-marketed tax avoidance schemes of the 1990s.

This analysis is primarily based on those semi-structured interviews with mass-marketed tax avoidance schemes participants from the Pilbara region and other taxpayers. It compares the attitudes and opinions expressed by taxpayers of Cohort One, who are blue-collar workers engaged in the Pilbara mining industry and who participated in the mass-marketed tax avoidance schemes, with those taxpayers of Cohort Two, taxpayers with similar occupations, and Cohort Three, taxpayers with similar incomes but from outside the Pilbara who did not engage in the mass-marketed tax avoidance schemes.

To give further insight into the manner in which the schemes were marketed and the blue-collar workers' attitudes towards participating in the schemes, the responses of Cohort One are also compared and contrasted with those of interviewees from an additional group of taxpayers. Cohort Four consists of Pilbara professionals who participated in the mass-marketed tax avoidance schemes and blue-collar workers from within the region who were not participants in the schemes.

In order to provide context to the analysis, and to place the population of blue-collar workers of the Pilbara region within the broader demographic, economic and social structure of the Western Australian and Australian populations, available statistical and survey data are examined to reveal prominent influencing factors which may have been present in that community at that time. The statistical data examined are those collated by ABS census data from 1991 to 2006, published ATO statistics for 1994 to 2000, the CTSI (2002) survey data and the ABC On-line (2007) survey.

Finally, this chapter suggests that the strength of factors that influence taxpayer compliance behaviour is greatly influenced by the interaction of those factors. It suggests that a trend emerges whereby the factor of high income tax rates was further compounded by harsh working and living conditions experienced by taxpayers in the Pilbara region in the 1990s. This combination of those factors may have led to an increase in a feeling of social distance and a perception of unfairness of their taxation burden, which in turn may have influenced those taxpayers to seek ways to reduce their tax.

4.2. Supply-driven factors

This section looks at the influencing factors which drive the supply side of the marketing of tax avoidance schemes. The factors considered in this section are grouped into influences that pertain to the interpretation and administration of tax law by law professionals, the courts and administrators. It looks at how tax scheme designers and promoters exploited weaknesses in taxation law and its administration to market their 'products' to the blue-collar workers of the Pilbara region in the 1990s.

The figure below illustrates the cycle of supply-driven factors examined in this research. Each cycle tends to add to the complexity of the taxation system as tax professionals begin to interpret the findings of litigated cases. In addition, the influence of each factor contributes to overall costs of compliance as increased complexity increases the requirement to engage tax professionals, which in turn creates further administrative burdens that can lead to further delays and increased references to the courts to settle disputes.

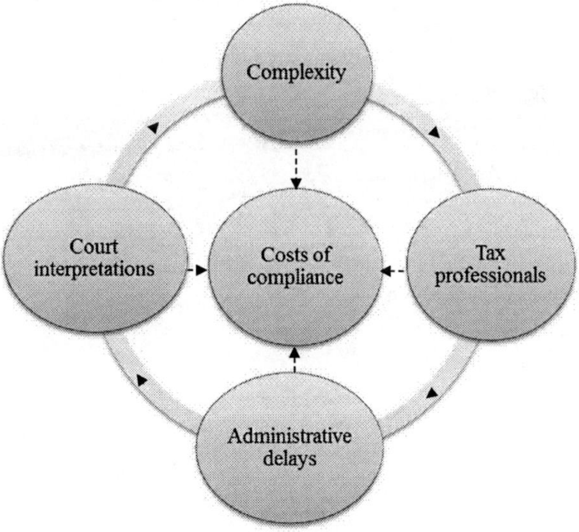

Figure 20 The cycle of supply-driven factors

For the purposes of this research, this cycle is considered primarily to lie within the scheme design and growth stage of the larger cyclical pattern of tax avoidance scheme development in Australia, illustrated in Chapter Two. For clarity, the position of the cycle of supply driven factors within the cyclical pattern of tax avoidance scheme development is illustrated in the following figure.

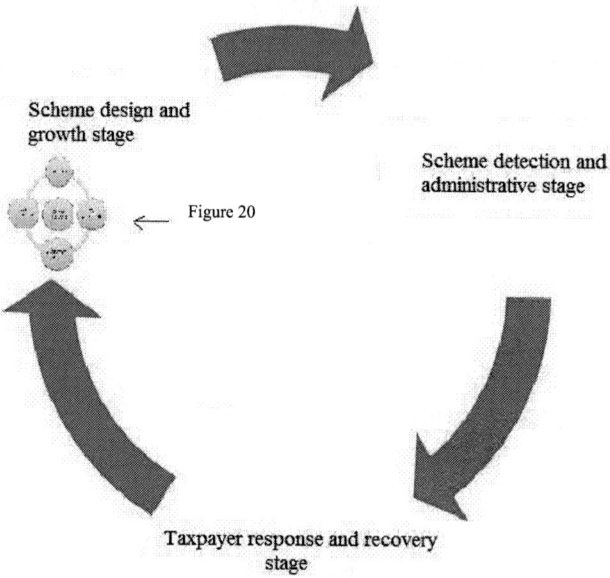

Figure 21 How the cycle of supply-driven factors relate to the cyclical pattern of tax avoidance scheme development in Australia

As costs of compliance are influenced by all of the other factors and appear at the 'hub' of the cycle, that factor will be examined first and the ensuing analysis will follow the factors clockwise, beginning with complexity of the tax system.

Costs of compliance

Taxpayers interviewed in this research were not specifically questioned as to their costs of compliance. However, it is noted that all interviewees had engaged the services of taxation agents and would therefore have incurred fees for those services as well as the other intrinsic costs discussed in this section.

Commonly, the fee for the taxation agent's service in the period in question was around $130 which would typically be deducted from the taxpayer's refund.

The system was thus relatively cheap and convenient. The commercial cost of $130 is trivial considering that the blue-collar workers' incomes were far in excess of $50,000 per annum. Moreover they did not have to deal directly with the ATO and a certain degree of stress in dealing with a large bureaucracy was avoided. The psychological cost of dealing with tax compliance is an influence which has to be taken into account when considering 'compliance costs'. As noted earlier, the blue-collar workers of the Pilbara region have little leisure time. They may also lack the desire to turn their minds to compiling tax returns when the services of a tax agent are available.

One interviewee expressed it simply: 'You look up to people that you think have the knowledge and the learning that you don't have, so that's why we go to the tax agent.' Another referred to the use of tax agents when he said, 'We don't use Tax Packs[210]. I haven't seen a Tax Pack in years.'

These opinions indicate that the 'costs of compliance' are not only considered by taxpayers as a financial cost but are also considered in terms of psychological costs (fear, complexity) and costs in terms of lost time (leisure or economic opportunity cost).

Respondents to the CTSI (2002) survey data, who were participants of mass-marketed tax avoidance schemes, gave the following reasons for engaging a taxation agent:

- Fear of making a mistake (47.5 per cent);
- To legitimately minimise the tax I had to pay (27.5 per cent);
- Insufficient time to prepare my own return (23.4 per cent);
- Too complex / don't have skills (1.2 per cent);
- To avoid paying tax (0.2 per cent);
- I am a tax agent (0.1 per cent);
- Don't need to talk to ATO (0.05 per cent)

Therefore it is suggested that the costs of compliance, including—but not exclusively—those of a financial nature, may have influenced the decisions of the blue-collar workers of the Pilbara to use the services of a taxation agent.

---

210 A TaxPack is a booklet that was issued by the ATO to assist an individual to lodge a taxation return. TaxPacks were introduced in 1990 and are issued each year. Previous year TaxPacks, which include the income tax return forms for each year, are now available from the ATO at <http://www.ato.gov.au/Individuals/Tax-return/2013/In-detail/Publications/Tax-return-for-individuals-2012-13/> at 17 August 2013.

As over 75 per cent of respondents to the CTSI (2002) survey referred to fear of making a mistake, and a desire to legitimately minimise their tax liability and complexity, complexity of the tax system is considered in the following section.

Complexity of the tax system

The complexity of the tax system may have been another factor which helped to create an environment in which the mass-marketed tax avoidance schemes were able to flourish. Complexity and a lack of understanding of the tax system by the blue-collar workers of the Pilbara provided the opportunity for the involvement of accountants and taxation agents in the affairs of these taxpayers. In turn, that involvement led to the increased impact of tax professionals in the marketing of the mass-marketed tax avoidance schemes as examined earlier.

Some comments were made by interviewees as to the complexity of the tax system, which have been noted. In particular one interviewee said:

> I think from a taxpayer's point of view it's excessively complex and it does make it hard to make sure that you're probably operating fairly within the system and its guidelines. Probably there are very few people who do really understand it and most people probably palm it off to [those] who do actually understand it. In the past I haven't done that so much, I've tried to do it myself but that's a bit too hard these days, the system is too complex for that.

Another said:

> I think that there are far too many complexities associated with taxation in Australia and I think that there are a lot of anomalies within the taxation system and I think that the bracket of income taxation helps to contribute to the distortion of taxpayer obligations.

Neither of those interviewees participated in the mass-marketed tax avoidance schemes of the 1990s. However, one interviewee who did was clear that complexity was a factor in the involvement of tax professionals marketing the mass-marketed tax avoidance schemes in the Pilbara region: 'We don't understand the tax system ... I don't understand finances ... we pay a lot of tax but we don't understand it. [That meant] we were pretty easy bloody targets for them eh, that's my opinion.'

It is suggested that the lack of understanding of the tax system expressed by the interviewees was, in part, brought about the complexity of the tax system and led to an increase in the costs of compliance for them. Given that complexity of the tax system appears to be a key factor in engaging the services of a tax professional for the blue-collar workers of the Pilbara region the role of tax professionals is addressed in the following section.

Tax professionals

This book suggests there are two basic reasons why taxpayers engage tax professionals:[211]

- First, in the case of the participants in mass-marketed tax avoidance schemes, compilation of the income tax returns by a tax agent was a procedural part of claiming the tax deductions generated by participating in the schemes; and

211 To provide clarity for the reader the terms used in this section are defined as follows: Tax professionals—all persons, holding tertiary qualifications, engaged in providing legal, accounting or financial advice and other services relating to compliance with taxation law. These include tax agents, as defined below, but are not necessarily registered as tax agents. Tax agents—those persons registered under legislative provisions to provide advice and to prepare and lodge tax returns for and on behalf of third parties for a fee. The liability of an unregistered tax agent is that he or she cannot legally charge a fee for his / her service. These may be, but are not necessarily, qualified legal practitioners or accountants. It is noted that formal qualification requirements began to be introduced in 1988 however transitional arrangements provide that 'unqualified' tax agents may remain registered in certain circumstances. These included providing a specified period to allow unqualified tax agents to gain the necessary qualifications or those with substantial relevant experience who were members of registered tax agent associations to remain registered, despite not having the requisite formal qualifications. The subsequent Tax Agent Services Act 2009 (Cth), and the elapse of time, may have reduced the current number of such persons, however during the period under review, the 1990s; the proportion of tax agents without formal qualifications was comparatively high. The following terms are also sometimes used interchangeably by tax professionals and the general public when describing those persons engaged in providing taxation law advice or services: tax (taxation) agent(s); tax (taxation) accountant(s); tax (taxation) consultant(s); tax (taxation) lawyer(s); tax (taxation) practitioner(s). Some of these terms have been used by interviewees to this research and have not been changed in their statements. In addition this research considers the role of financial advisers who are not necessarily qualified lawyers, accountants or registered tax agents. These are often 'para-professionals' such as insurance salespeople, stock and mortgage brokers or financial planners who assist clients in making financial decisions. Generally they are salespeople marketing financial 'products'.

- Second, generally the complexity of the Australian taxation system, coupled with the 14-day processing turnaround facilitated by the Electronic Lodgement Service (ELS) used by almost all taxation agents at the time,[212] encouraged over 76 per cent of individual Australian taxpayers to use the services of tax agents in 1997. In more recent times that figure has reduced slightly. However in 2010 it remained comparatively high (relative to other countries) at nearly 71 per cent.[213]

Seven out of the fourteen participants in the mass-marketed tax avoidance schemes interviewed had done so at the suggestion of their accountant and / or financial adviser. Only one had made the initial approach to the promoter. A further eleven of the twenty-three interviewees were made aware of the schemes by their financial advisers even though they had not participated.

The role and involvement of tax professionals is referred to in a number of judicial findings in cases involving the mass-marketed tax avoidance schemes of the 1990s. In *Federal Commissioner of Taxation v Sleight*, Hill J noted that:

> Mr Sleight was an investment adviser. Not much was asked in cross-examination as to his activities. However it would seem that, at least among other products, he sold what may neutrally be described as tax effective income tax schemes.

In *Vincent v Federal Commissioner of Taxation* it was noted that the scheme involved a number of cattle breeding projects operated by a number of companies associated with an accountant, Peter Jacobsen. It was also noted that '[t]he scheme was marketed by Mr Jacobsen to accountants and financial advisers'.

However the findings in *Howland-Rose v Commissioner of Taxation* show the degree of influence of legal opinions to be problematic. The taxation implications of the investment in the Budplan Company Syndicate (BPS) contained a legal opinion as to taxation issues relating to the investment. It was included in the prospectus produced by the BPS which contained a segment headed 'Taxation and Cashflow Aspects of years 1 and 2'.[214] However a disclaimer clearly states:

---

212 ATO, Taxation Statistics 1996-97 (1999) Table 8, show that 97.3 per cent of tax agent cases were lodged through the ELS.

213 ATO, Taxation Statistics 2009-10 (2012) Table 21C.

214 Howland-Rose and Ors v Federal Commissioner of Taxation [2002] FCA 246 [17].

> The following comments provide only a descriptive summary of the main taxation issues considered. They do not purport to be an exhaustive or definitive analysis of all potential tax issues relevant to participation in the business. The taxation consequences for an investor will depend upon the particular circumstances of each investor. Investors should not rely on this explanatory outline for taxation purposes, but should seek and reply on their own taxation advice.

Despite the clarity of the disclaimer, in giving evidence to the Court in *Howland-Rose v Commissioner of Taxation*, Ms Howland-Rose claimed she had ignored the disclaimer and said 'she ... felt these disclaimers would appear from anyone, irrespective of what opinion they were giving'. Further it is noted that:

> Ms Howland-Rose claimed that she did not take up her single unit or syndicate participation in the BPS, primarily because of the prospective availability of tax deductions, since she realised from the outset that there was a risk that the Australian Tax Office might not allow tax deductibility.

However it is noted that Ms Howland-Rose was introduced to the scheme by a financial adviser.

It was also found that in relation to the Second Applicant:

> Mr Harvey was attracted to the project because he saw it as a good opportunity to invest in an agriculturally based project which would produce products which added value to a raw material produced in Australia, and would have a better chance of success than the sale merely of the raw material.

However it was also found that '[n]evertheless Mr Harvey was at least partly motivated in taking up three units or syndicate participations in the BPS by the represented availability of income tax incentives.'

Another party to the case was Mr Braysich, who stated, 'I was not particularly interested in the tax, and it would not have made a significant difference in my position'. As a party to the litigation it is difficult to view Mr Braysich's statement as being truly independent or impartial.

Despite the close involvement of tax and legal professionals, the strength of influence of tax professionals may not have been as strong as indicated by some of the previous findings. It appears that the above parties in the *Howland-Rose* case relied more on the advice of financial advisers and promoters than qualified legal and taxation professionals.

It is suggested that the role of professional salesmen promoting the schemes is significant. An interviewee, who had participated in the schemes, commented:

> I was in [a Pilbara town] and [my employer] was introducing salary sacrificing, and I was in [a professional] role at the time and my manager asked me all sorts of things I'd like to salary sacrifice and did I have any comments on the sort of, as they were designing the scheme, that I might like to offer so where my interests would lie and I didn't really know. Then out of the blue I got a call from a, on spec in the evening, one night, I got a call from a financial consulting firm or accounting type firm and they asked me if I had any interest in, to hear what they were offering. But I said I am actually interested in talking to someone about salary sacrifice. It was new at the time to me.

He went on to say:

> So anyway they said 'oh sure, we'll send a fellow around to have a chat with you', and I thought fine. He came out and talked to me about what I thought was going to be salary sacrificing and it turned out to be a sandalwood plantation deal. Now despite it not being what I was interested in, I listened to what he had to say. And it sort of struck a chord for a number of reasons. Well it struck me that fitted that need if you like, and being sandalwood I don't know and a development based in a regional area that was leveraged.
>
> Australian government investment in the region; helped regional employment; Contributed to export industry, being sandalwood, you know, and a product that was well allegedly these people had a technological advantage in growing this stuff. They had done a lot of research, research that was based through CSIRO and WA Department of Agriculture. They were running the programs up at Kununurra at the time and anyway I guess, I finished up, signing up.
>
> The tax effectiveness of the deal was sweet and I probably could not have afforded to participate frankly in the upfront cash stakes if it hadn't been there. But it wasn't what motivated me to get into it.

Though the promoters were the chief facilitators in the marketing of the schemes they relied heavily on the opinions of legal and tax professionals to do so. The case of *Satcom* illustrates the significance of the use of those opinions as a marketing tool. In promotion of this scheme, a key aspect was the presentation of a 'legal opinion' given by a leading Western Australian legal practitioner.[215]

This aspect was evidenced in a speech given by the Second Commissioner of Taxation in October 2001. He used the following quote from extracts of a tape that recorded a briefing to salespeople on the sales pitch to be used when selling the franchise scheme:

> We took it to a guy called George he just happens to be the guy that went to university with a QC called Fred. Fred has written an opinion on this which I'll show you in a moment. When George found out that Fred had written an opinion George said you've got me. If Fred says it's ok it must be ok. We said, "why do you say that?". He said, "well I went to university with Fred ..."

---

215 Satcom Electronic Services Pty Ltd, Business Opportunity Disclosure Document (August 1997).

> Now be careful when you're talking about a QC, ask your audience do they know what a QC is. Don't assume that they know. And explain to them what a QC is and if you're involved in a big legal fight and please God that you're not—but if you ever get involved in one and you know you're in the right and you've got big heaps of money—if you're smart you'd be employing a QC to look after you. By the way, QCs are expensive, they cost anything from $2,000 to $30,000 a day to represent you in court. Fred's done an opinion on this because we still weren't happy and we said no, we want you to take this to a lawyer, preferably one of the better ones in Perth to tell us if this is ok.
>
> Well they went to Fred—and he says here on the last page, that the proposal makes good sense even without the tax benefits. When we read that we're staggered because I never thought I would see a lawyer use the words that the proposal makes good sense ... inaudible ... oh yes I usually open up the opinion and show them that bit ...

This legal opinion became a central marketing tool, even though it clearly disclaimed any loss or damage occurring to third parties through reliance on it. It further stated that each franchisee 'should seek advice and rely upon their own independent advice from their adviser'.[216] Despite containing the specific clause disclaiming liability to any third party, the written opinion was reprinted and bound in the promotional material used by the promoters.

In addition, *Satcom* added a further disclaimer to its promotional material. The further disclaimer of liability applied 'to any franchisee in relying whether wholly or partially, upon the whole or any part of the contents of this opinion'. However, as pointed out in the Senate Inquiry, the corporate structures of *Satcom* franchises were such that the ASIC requirements did not exist as they were a franchise arrangement and a formal prospectus was not required. Therefore the document had no legal value to the 'investor'. Its inclusion was purely to serve as an enticement to taxpayers to engage in the franchise.

216 Letter from Robert K O'Connor to Clayton Utz solicitors, 28 August 1997, in Satcom Electronic Services Franchise Business Opportunity Disclosure Document August 1997.

In his evidence to the Senate Committee, the Queen's Counsel involved said:

> In the early years I was not aware that that [circulating his legal opinion to the general public as promotional material] was happening. I was not told that that was happening. The managers were coming to me seeking advice as to what I considered the position was, and I was providing that information to them. When I became aware of the possibility that they [the legal opinions] would be distributed to other people, I included certain paragraphs in my opinions, which are on page 13 of the submission, telling people in the clearest of terms that they must seek their own particular advice. It is impossible for me to give an opinion for the great mass of taxpayers out there. These provisions depend on purpose. It is necessary for every individual's facts and circumstances to be considered by his or her own adviser so that they can get advice as to what their particular position is.[217]

The *Satcom* scheme involved a number of prominent national and Western Australian taxation and legal professionals in its design and promotion, and later, in dealing with objections to the Commissioner's decision to disallow the deductions in 2001, by way of establishing 'fighting funds'. The *Satcom* scheme highlights the indirect role that tax professionals played in the marketing and promotion of the mass-marketed tax avoidance schemes, albeit sometimes unwittingly.

Further, there appears to have been collusion between accountants, tax agents and legal practitioners in the operation of the schemes. As the schemes were detected and the ATO moved to close them in 2000, the scheme detection and administrative response stage of the illustration in Chapter Two, the tax professionals moved from designing and promoting the schemes to a new market—that of defending the taxpayers from ATO recovery action.

It is also suggested that tax professionals may have been sharing confidential client information with scheme designers and promoters. Evidence of that collusion appears in the establishment of 'fighting funds' to finance co-ordinated resistance to the ATO's recovery action. The organisers of the 'fighting funds' appear to have had access to information that was not in the public realm. A letter to one of the mass-marketed tax avoidance scheme participants, from the organisers of the 'fighting fund' for the Puzey appeal, refers to legal action by an investor in the Banalasta scheme. However, a search of the six 'test cases' of the ATO does not reveal reference to the Banalasta scheme. His particulars and details of his case had to have been either held by those practitioners, or provided by another without the knowledge of the taxpayer.

217 Commonwealth of Australia, Official Committee Hansard; Senate Inquiry Reference: Mass marketed tax effective schemes and investor protection, Canberra, 26 July 2001, E 736.

Further evidence of tax agents' involvement in the promotion of the schemes was given by an interviewee, who though not being a Pilbara blue-collar worker, clearly identified his tax consultant's involvement in promoting the mass-marketed tax avoidance schemes. He said, 'To an extent I relied on my then tax consultant or financial planner, who presented another reason to me why I should get involved.' To which he added the clear statement: 'He promoted those schemes'.

This research suggests that taxpayers of the Pilbara region of Western Australia were specifically 'targeted' by the promoters. Documents provided by participants of mass-marketed tax avoidance schemes support that suggestion. A letter from a scheme promoter, Serra and Company, to a prospective investor, evidences that the taxpayer was offered 'a number of ways ... to increase your wealth and reduce the tax you pay'.[218] It added 'We will in fact be in Paraburdoo over the next few weeks'.

Further, not only did individual designers market their own schemes, but there is evidence that promoters marketed the mass-marketed tax avoidance schemes as a range of 'products'. Documents provided by an interviewee, who participated in the mass-marketed tax avoidance schemes, provide further evidence that the promoters sold 'investments' in multiple schemes. Letters to that interviewee demonstrate the mass-marketing approach taken by the promoters: one contains exactly the same content but 'personalised' by a change to the name and address and town to that referred to above. It states:

> We will in fact be in South Hedland over the next few weeks, during which time you have a great opportunity to discuss with specialists the options open to you to reduce your tax and increase your wealth.[219]

The letter then lists the same twelve ways to 'increase your wealth and reduce the tax you pay'. Yet another interviewee states that the financial adviser who had introduced him to the *Satcom* scheme had 'canvassed the whole town of Wickham' in 1998.

The 'target marketing' activity partially explains the high participation rate of taxpayers in the Pilbara region in the mass-marketed tax avoidance schemes. However, this book suggests the promoters 'targeted' the regions where the propensity was highest, that is, in areas where heavy working conditions were

218 Letter from Serra & Company to a scheme participant, 20 May 1998.
219 Letter from Serra & Company to a scheme participant, 27 May 1997.

coupled with high taxation rates. It is suggested that at this point the promoters were responding to the market demand exhibited by the Pilbara taxpayers.

As indicated in Chapter One, South Hedland, Paraburdoo and Wickham are not the most pleasant places to conduct door-to-door sales. There had to be a demonstrated success rate of sales to motivate a salesman to walk the hot, dusty streets of the isolated Pilbara communities.

An interviewee from Pannawonica was in no doubt as to the reason why the blue-collar workers of the Pilbara were targeted. He described the promoters in the following terms:

> Yeah, because they are lower than sharks' bellies you know and they're really they're bloody they're like they play on people like us.
>
> People like me, an uneducated like average wage earning guy that earns a big enough income and pays a lot tax. You know like whereas you know like in the real world, and if I went back into the real world, out of the Pilbara and out of the iron ore industry, with my qualifications and education I would probably either working on a farm or I don't know bloody in a factory or something. I'm not am educated bloody I'm not a, I don't have any trade or anything like that basically.
>
> I'd be earning bloody probably $30 to 40 grand now you know like maybe as a labourer somewhere and you wouldn't have these blokes coming preying on me there would you?
>
> Like the reason they are preying on us here is because like we don't understand the tax system, we don't understand like. I don't understand finances and there is nowhere else in the country would you find as many average people who don't understand these systems and the way they money and stuff. Most people that earn a lot of money—understand money. Like up here we don't. When I say like up here like in this environment you know, we earn reasonable money, we pay a lot of tax but we don't understand it. You know like, and we were pretty easy bloody targets for them eh, that's my opinion.
>
> They probably weren't selling too many of these to doctors, lawyers and bloody financial advisers were they?

His statement considers many factors including education and social class. He suggests that better educated taxpayers such as doctors, lawyers and financial advisers would not be as susceptible to the marketing tactics of the promoters as the blue-collar workers of the Pilbara region. However, he focuses on the high incomes and accompanying high personal income tax rates experienced by the blue-collar workers of the Pilbara region.

Interestingly, the CTSI (2002) survey found that over three-quarters of participants in mass-marketed tax avoidance schemes held trade or tertiary qualifications. In addition, some Pilbara taxpayers with higher degrees had participated in the mass-marketed tax avoidance schemes. Further, the promoters had successfully marketed the schemes to many doctors, lawyers and financial advisers in the cities, though not at the same participation rates demonstrated by the blue-collar workers of the Pilbara region.

An interviewee of Cohort 3, who was resident in the extremely remote Pilbara community of Telfer[220] during the 1990s, but did not participate in a tax avoidance scheme, suggested the impact of promoters inducing taxpayers into the schemes was not significant. When asked if there were door-to-door salespeople involved in marketing the mass-marketed tax avoidance schemes in Telfer, the interviewee said:

> No. It was really word of mouth in a town like Telfer. The people flogging this stuff rarely came to town but because of the tax situation and the incomes they [the workers] had regular visits to Perth. People were seeing accountants and other financial advisers seeking advice.

Asked if it was common knowledge in Telfer that these schemes were available, he replied, 'Certainly and everybody they were telling, and it was that those who were participating were openly telling people that if they didn't get on board they were crazy'.

It is also noted that two of the promoters of mass-marketed tax avoidance schemes in the Pilbara were resident tax agents. They had a close knowledge of the taxpayers of the region and were able to exploit that relationship. Given that intimate knowledge and professional relationship to the taxpayers, those tax professionals may have had a significant impact on the acceptance of the mass-marketed tax avoidance schemes.

Evidence of the involvement of resident tax agents in promotion of the mass-marketed tax avoidance schemes came from an interviewee who participated in one of the schemes. He placed the blame for his involvement purely on his local accountant / tax agent. He indicated that, while he considered he was paying too much tax, he would not have participated in the schemes had his accountant not prevailed upon him to do so. In answer to the question: 'Who raised the subject

---

220 Telfer is a mine site in the East Pilbara about 250 km east north-east of Newman, postcode 6762. It has a transient population of around 460. In the 1990s it was a small settlement with a population of up to 1000 persons but is not on the ABS census statistics. It is one of the most remote locations in Australia. The town closed in 1996 and the entire workforce now works on a fly-in-fly-out basis. The CTSI survey indicates that one participant in a mass-marketed tax avoidance scheme who responded to the survey was a resident of Telfer. Given the proportion of respondents surveyed there could have been as many as 14 participants from that town. However that calculation has no statistical reliability.

[of participating in the mass-marketed tax avoidance schemes], you or he?' He replied: 'No, the accountant raised the subject. He suggested I go into these things. He suggested I was paying too much tax and he suggested that I should go into them to reduce my taxation.'

This section suggests that tax professionals designed the tax avoidance schemes to create financial products with the intent of mass-marketing those products for financial gain. As part of the promotional and marketing (supply) process they used legal opinions, based on past litigation, and the involvement of other tax professionals to support their marketing campaigns and to defray the concerns of taxpayers as to the validity of the schemes. During the marketing of the schemes, designers and promoters became aware of the enthusiastic demand which the blue-collar workers of Western Australia's mining industry exhibited for their tax avoidance schemes, and in particular the demand exhibited by those blue-collar workers in the particularly harsh and remote Pilbara region of Western Australia.

Administrative delays

Delays in dealing with matters of interpretation and / or processing of final taxation assessments by taxation administrators can create misunderstandings in the minds of taxpayers as to the validity of their actions. They may perceive that they are engaging in compliant taxation activities when in fact they are not. This factor may therefore have also been instrumental in the supply of mass-marketed tax avoidance schemes.

The facts outlined in the decision in *Vincent v Federal Commissioner of Taxation* illustrate the impact of administrative delays in dealing with taxpayers' assessments and the outcomes of taxation liability.

On 19 June 1995 Mrs Vincent entered into a cattle breeding venture. On 25 August 1995 and 30 July 1996 she received assessment notices for the respective years of income. The controller of the venture died in October 1998. On 8 December 1999 the ATO issued determinations to her disallowing deductions relating to the venture for the 1995 and 1996 income years. A further determination was made on 14 September 2001 and new amended assessments issued on 17 September 2001. The determination as to the allowable deductions of the venture was delivered by the Federal Court of Appeal on 16 September 2002.

Key consequences of the seven-year delay were:

- A key individual concerned in the design, implementation and operation of the venture had died four years prior to the final determination. Therefore it was not possible to examine him as to the details of the scheme;
- An amendment of the 1995 assessment was prevented due to the lapse of time. That limitation meant that the deductions claimed for that year, for the venture, could not be reversed and the tax revenue was lost; and
- The venture was wound up and a final dividend declared on 30 June 2000. That was before a final determination made as to the validity of the venture. The recovery of the 'over-refunds' therefore became problematic.

The Active Cattle Management Pty Ltd scheme had commenced, operated and been wound up before any action was taken by the ATO to disallow the deductions claimed by participants. All parties participated in the scheme with the honest, but mistaken, belief that all costs associated with, and deductions allowed, were genuine. Indeed the promoter may have died in that belief.

Administrative delays were referred to by a number of interviewees who were involved in the mass-marketed tax avoidance schemes. In particular, a number of interviewees expressed frustration at the time delay between 'investing' in the schemes and the ATO's apparent 'change of mind' as to the validity of the deductions. That led to a feeling that they had been 'cheated' by the ATO and the promoters.

However, the delay in action by the ATO in disallowing mass-marketed tax avoidance schemes deductions occurred after the schemes had been taken up by taxpayers. What is more likely to have occurred is that lack of action in determining the validity of the schemes may have provided an extended opportunity for promoters to market their schemes.

The following statements are consistent with reference to time delays. Frustration at administrative delays was expressed by a mass-marketed tax avoidance scheme participant of Cohort One who stated:

> For three years I wrote out cheques and I got those. The exact amount I wrote out the cheque for, I got back in my tax return and after three years it all, sort of, folded and I waited for my vessel to come to fruit and in the end it just went to shit and I had the trouble of a long and costly battle with the Taxation Department.

The implication from the above statement is that administrative delays encouraged him to continue to participate in the mass-marketed tax avoidance scheme and exacerbated his financial problems when the deductions were ultimately disallowed.

Another alluded to the time delay as being a deliberate action of the ATO when he said:

> I went in two in one year. I believe I went in two the following year, I think I was in about four schemes all up. Over four to five years, yeah. Then they went to court cases, the taxation department sent them broke and then they won the court case about 18 months later saying it was actually lawful but that didn't amount to hooey because everyone got in the shit for it over it anyway.
>
> I mean you had, they come up with these, what's names that had been stamped by ASIC. They had been you know, they had been approved by the ATO and had let them be put them out in the market.
>
> I believe they [the ATO] knew what they were going to do. They could have stopped it four or five years beforehand, they chose not to. I believe they let it run. The longer they let it run, the bigger fines and more money they were going to recoup off the people, which they did, at the cost of a lot of bloody things that should never have happened. But I believe, yeah I don't believe that there was a fair run by the tax department at all because they could have stopped it but they chose not to.

The five-year delay was raised by another mass-marketed tax avoidance schemes participant:

> Just cos some guy in the taxation department decides that these schemes aren't right. To me, we should have been warned. For five years or three years they were alright and then all of a sudden they are not and I believe the taxation office should have said, 'Ok the year 2000 that's the end of it and that's it stop. And anyone from there on in is going to get whacked'. But to get hold of you and take it back five years and then you have to bloody pay it back in five years.
>
> If they thought something was wrong they should have told you the first bloody year you were doing it. When the tax office paid you the money, they gave you the refund and they should have said this is not the right way to bloody do it. Crazy shit.

More colourful terms were used by another participant when he referred to the ATO's recovery action after a number of years of participating in the schemes:

> I personally think the whole thing was handled extremely poorly from the side of the taxation department goes. Like you know, it was just a shemozzle really you know like. I think from personally, to change a ruling like from the initial stages that's all good and well, but you know like not halfway through the proceedings.

From the above observations, it is suggested that administrative delays may have further encouraged participation in mass-marketed tax avoidance schemes as it appeared to participating taxpayers that the ATO had approved the deductions claimed. The success of taxpayers receiving refunds had a strong influence on encouraging others to take part in the mass-marketed tax avoidance schemes.

Court interpretations

As discussed in the section examining legal opinions and court interpretations, it appears that those opinions and interpretations were used extensively as a promotional tool by promoters to defray taxpayer concerns as to the validity of the mass-marketed tax avoidance schemes.

The legal opinion given to potential *Satcom* participants as to the deductibility of franchise fees relied heavily on a literal approach to statutory interpretation by the courts to support the opinion given, although it was supported by a number of cases which found to the benefit of the taxpayer.[221] The opinion also considered a case against the taxpayer[222] as 'authority for denying the deduction for the Initial Annual Franchise Fee' but decided 'the facts of that case are distinguishable from the present [facts]'.

The authorities that it relied upon were from the taxpayer-tolerant and literal interpretative Barwick High Court of the 1970s. The opinion also relied upon a literal approach to the general deduction provision of the tax law at the time, s 51(1) of the ITAA 1936. The case against was a 1996 case which had been decided under the provisions of s 15AA of the *Acts Interpretation Act (Cth)* and the general anti-avoidance provisions of Pt IVA. A more purposive interpretation would have, and later did, take the view that the franchises had the dominant purpose of avoiding tax, not actively pursuing business.[223]

It is noted that the ATO also relied on previous litigation to apply the general anti-avoidance provisions of Pt IVA to disallow the deductions claimed through the use of the mass-marketed tax avoidance schemes. However it relied on cases such as the *Spotless case*, which had been determined on the purposive interpretation of Pt IVA,[224] and not the literal approach previously used by the Barwick courts.

---

221 Fairway Estates Pty Ltd v Commissioner of Taxation (Cth) (1970) 123 CLR 153; Ferguson v Commissioner of Taxation (Cth) (1979) 79 ATC 4261; Hanlon v Commissioner of Taxation (Cth) (1970) 81 ATC 4617.

222 Labrilda Pty Ltd v Commissioner of Taxation Cth) 1996 96 ATC 4303.

223 Section 51 of the ITAA 1936 is the general deduction provision of the legislation. As discussed in Chapter Two, in the interpretation of a provision of an Act, a construction that would promote the purpose or object underlying the Act (whether that purpose or object is expressly stated in the Act or not) shall be preferred to a construction that would not promote that purpose or object. (Emphasis added) s 15AA (1) Acts Interpretation Act (1901) (Cth).

224 Australian Taxation Office, 'Test Case Litigation Program', <http://www.ato.gov.au/taxprofessionals/content.asp?doc=/content/57395.htm> at 12 July 2008.

However, other than referring to legal opinions presented to them in promotional material used by the promoters, no respondent or interviewee referred to previous litigation or court interpretations as an influencing factor in engaging in the mass-marketed tax avoidance schemes of the 1990s. It is possible at the time of interview that the interviewees knew of the cases, and as discussed above, some were involved in the 'fighting funds' supporting the defence of those cases. However the cases examined in this research were part of the scheme detection and response stage, and may not therefore have been influential in the blue-collar workers' decisions to participate in the mass-marketed tax avoidance schemes in the earlier stage.

Summary

It is submitted that the role of tax professionals in the design, implementation and promotion of tax avoidance schemes led to those schemes being marketed as mass produced financial packages. The promoters exploited many of the other influencing factors examined in this book to market their 'products'. Favourable, and arguably sometimes misleading, legal opinions and court decisions were used as promotional tools to convince the blue-collar workers to participate in the schemes.

In addition, the complexity of the taxation system and the associated influence of taxation agents and accountants, peer influence and social isolation created a marketing opportunity that promoters of mass-marketed tax avoidance schemes were quick to identify and exploit. In at least one case, that of *Satcom,* the promoters and designers used the complexity of the tax system to design and promote schemes to defraud taxpayers of their tax credits.

Administrative delays also arguably permitted tax professionals and scheme promoters to develop and market the mass-marketed tax avoidance schemes unchecked for a number of years. Those delays created an assumption of the validity of the schemes. The combination of administrative delays and the influence of tax professionals reduced blue-collar workers' concerns as to the illegitimacy of tax avoidance schemes.

Ultimately, the marketing of the schemes increased the desire of taxpayers to reduce their tax liability which in turn led to an increase in the marketing of the mass-marketed tax avoidance schemes of the 1990s. However, the schemes were initially marketed to *all* Australian taxpayers and were available to the entire population of Australian taxpayers.

Not all taxpayers demonstrated the same propensity to engage in them as did the blue-collar workers of the Pilbara region of Western Australia. The analysis therefore now looks at the influencing factors which drove the demand to participate in the mass-marketed tax avoidance schemes to examine the prominent factors influencing that particular community of taxpayers.

4.3. Demand-driven factors

Demographic factors

Demographic factors are personal characteristics which tend to place individual taxpayers within broader and categorised social groups. Generally the literature examined in Chapter Three indicates that taxpayer compliance behaviour is influenced by demographic factors. In particular that examination reveals that age and gender may have a strong influence. Education and religion have less influence than those and other demographic factors, such as marital status, race, nationality or ethnicity tend to have little influence.

The following examination using the ABS Census data for the years 1991–2006 places the Pilbara population in the 1990s within the context of the Western Australian and Australian populations generally.

Age

The literature suggests that age is a strong influence on compliance behaviour generally and taxpayer compliance behaviour in particular. It suggests that younger people are likely to be less compliant with the law than older people.

As illustrated in the following figure, the ABS census data for the period 1991–2006 shows that the median age of persons in the Pilbara region was younger than the general population of Western Australia and the overall Australian population. The age difference between the populations of the Pilbara, Western Australia and Australia ranged from four to six years in the period 1991–2006. For example, in 1991 the median ages were: the Pilbara region: 26 years; Western Australian: 31 years; and the entire Australia population: 32 years. In 2006 the median ages were 31 years, 36 years and 37 years respectively.

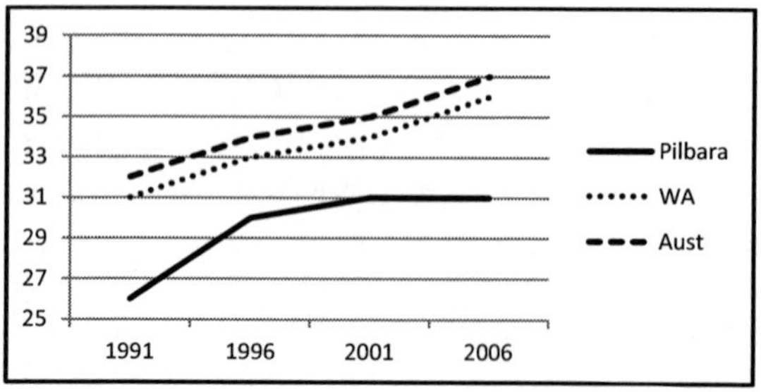

Figure 22 Median age of the populations of the Pilbara region, Western Australia and Australia

ATO statistics reveal that the median age of all Australian taxpayers between 1995 and 1999 was consistently 39 years. It is acknowledged that ABS census statistics cover the entire population from infants to the aged and ATO statistics focus on taxpayers only, however, the median age of taxpayers in the Pilbara region was likely to be well below the average age of Australian taxpayers generally. Therefore, as indicated by the previous research, the generally younger age of taxpayers in the Pilbara region may have been a strong influence in determining the compliance behaviour of those taxpayers in the 1990s.

Other data, however, reveal that participation in the mass-marketed tax avoidance schemes of the 1990s generally involved older taxpayers. For example, CTSI (2002) survey data indicate that the participants of mass-marketed tax avoidance schemes were older taxpayers. The median age of the respondents to the CTSI (2002) survey of mass-marketed tax avoidance schemes, was 46 years. Given that the CTSI survey was taken four years after the mass-marketed tax avoidance schemes were acted upon by the ATO, the median age when engaging in the mass-marketed tax avoidance schemes in the late 1990s would have been approximately 42 years of age. This may suggest that the younger age of the Pilbara population may be coincidental and not directly connected to the high participation rates of the Pilbara blue-collar workers in the mass-marketed tax avoidance schemes.

Additionally, data collected from the ABC On-line (2007) survey do not support the view that increasing age leads to increased compliance. The median age of those respondents was higher than the average revealed by the above statistical sources at 53 years of age (data not reported here). However, as shown in the table below their attitudes towards the fairness or unfairness of engaging in tax minimisation schemes were reasonably evenly distributed from very unfair to very fair.

Question 13. How fair is it for individuals to use tax minimisation schemes?						
Very unfair	Unfair	Neutral	Fair	Very fair	Unsure or no answer	Total
257	274	240	256	236	90	1353
19.0%	20.3%	17.7%	18.9%	17.4%	6.7%	100%

Table 8 The opinions of taxpayers relating to engagement in tax minimisation schemes

It is further noted that more than half of the respondents who considered engaging in tax minimisation schemes to be either fair or very fair were over 55 years of age (data not reported here). Therefore the ABC On-line (2007) survey data imply that the influence of increasing age may not significantly increase taxpayer compliance behaviour.

Torgler points to research which indicates that taxpayers' attitudes are tempered, or even changed entirely, by life's experiences. Those changes in attitudes or behaviour commensurate with increasing age appear statistically consistent. Therefore the apparent change in attitude towards compliance may lead to the assumption that people become more compliant as they grow older. However this research notes that this may not be the case. Rather this research suggests that a person's attitudes tend to be influenced by 'the age' or era in which they matured rather than by their age in years.

It may be the influence of social, economic and political conditions which prevail during a person's formative years which is significant, not simply the chronological development of a person. That process of transmitting the culture of a particular society during the modification from infancy of an individual's behaviour to conform to the demands of social life is termed 'socialization' and, as observed later in the examination of socio-psychological factors, can be a strong behavioural influence.

The following examples, drawn from the semi-structured interviews, suggest that social attitudes adopted in early life may continue into later life. These examples illustrate the influence of 'the age', or era, rather than age in years as a chronological demographic factor.

A consistent pattern of responses was found that indicates a negative attitude was held by blue-collar workers towards the Australian government of the 1990s. Both younger and older blue-collar workers expressed support for the ALP. However they gave differing reasons for doing so. Those reasons reflect the era in which they lived rather than their age in years though both concepts are mutually inclusive.

An older blue-collar worker interviewed gave his reflections of experiences during World War II, and the early days of the Australian Workers' Union, as reasons for opposing the government and his reluctance to pay it tax. On the other hand a younger interviewee was also opposed to the government of the day and resistant to pay it tax, but he gave different reasons, which were more contemporary.

In response as to what he considered was a fair rate of tax, the older (late 50s) interviewee considered that he should not have to pay tax to a government that he considered was biased and exploiting the worker in favour of multi-national industrialists. He said:

> I'm very cynical with governments; I'm very cynical with bureaucracy. My father was a paid up Communist. He was one of Sharkey's[225] right-hand men. He was a full-time paid official for the Communist party in Sydney. He went to gaol. It's pretty amazing that when Menzies got into power in '49 he used the preferences from the Communist Party, they gave 'em to him. Six months later he was trying to disband them. 'Lock them up!'

Consequently he felt betrayed by the Liberal Party and his attitude toward tax compliance reflected that feeling of social distance. His attitude towards tax compliance was formed from his life experiences at an earlier age. It is noted, however, that this interviewee was not a resident of the Pilbara, nor did he participate in a mass-marketed tax avoidance scheme.

On the other hand, a much younger (early 30s) interviewee, who was a resident of the Pilbara region and did participate in a mass-marketed tax avoidance scheme, also believed he was paying too much tax. He said he believed the government was ignoring the plight of those in the 'bush'. He gave the following response to the question, 'Do you think there should be some tax breaks for blokes in the bush?'

> Yes I do. Yeah we should be getting something to compensate for the harsh conditions and the isolation. As I said we are a bloody long way from nowhere and we have to deal with cyclones and that. Every now and again the road goes out and we are stuck here for weeks and that's not much fun I can tell you.

The above examples indicate that two people, of quite different ages in years, support their (negative) attitude towards tax compliance for two very different

225 Lawrence Louis Sharkey (1898–1967), prominent Australian Communist Party leader, 1929–1967.

reasons. Both are based on their life experiences of two very different eras. One formed in Sydney in the 1940s and the other in the Pilbara in the 1990s. Their experiences led them towards an attitude towards non-compliance regarding tax and were prompted by a feeling of social distance from government irrespective of their age in years but rather the age at which they had those experiences.

Despite the younger blue-collar worker participating in a mass-marketed tax avoidance scheme and the older blue-collar worker not participating, it is suggested that other factors, in particular living and working in the mining industry in the Pilbara, may have been a far stronger influencing factor. Therefore, despite the findings of previous researchers, it is suggested that age may not have been a strong factor in influencing the mass-marketed tax avoidance schemes participation rates demonstrated by Pilbara blue-collar workers in the 1990s.

Education

The literature examined in Chapter Three indicates that lower education levels tend to influence taxpayers towards non-compliant behaviour. The research also indicates that compliance generally tends to increase with education, and then reaches a point where the upward trend towards compliance begins to fall away towards non-compliance.

This research aligns with previous research as to the upward and then downward trends of education and compliance. It also suggests that a possible explanation is that social distance from government decreases with education. Perhaps a point is reached where, with higher levels of education, a person becomes more aware of, or familiar with, flaws in the political system generally and subsequent governance and administration. Consequently, at some point, social distance from government increases, the person feels alienated, and, as a taxpayer, his or her perception of the fairness of the taxation system decreases.

The following figure shows ABS census data from 1991 to 2006 and indicates that the population of tertiary qualified persons is consistently lower in the Pilbara region than the Western Australian and Australian populations. Further, at the beginning of the substantial rise in mass-marketed tax avoidance scheme participation in 1996, just over 9 per cent of the Pilbara population held tertiary qualification compared with the Western Australian population of 12.38 per cent and nearly 13 per cent for the nation generally.

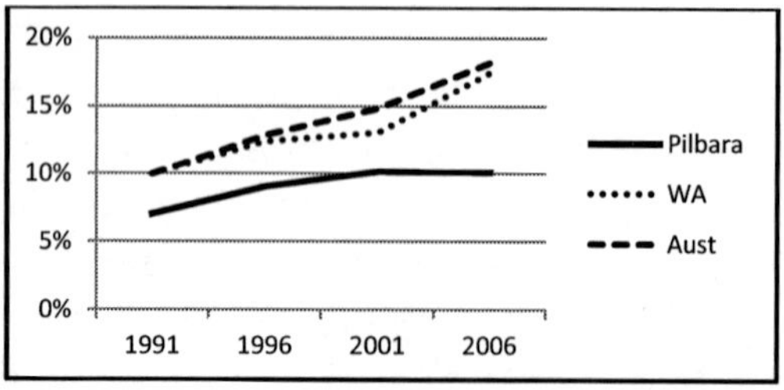

Figure 23 Percentage of the population holding tertiary qualifications in the Pilbara region, Western Australia and Australia.

It is also noted, below, that the population of tradespeople in the Pilbara region was consistently higher than the rest of Western Australia, and in 1996, nearly twice that of the Australian population. It may be that the predominance of tradespeople participating in the mass-marketed tax avoidance schemes in the Pilbara region is in part the result of the fact that tradespeople formed a higher proportion of the population of taxpayers in that region than in the general Western Australian and national populations.

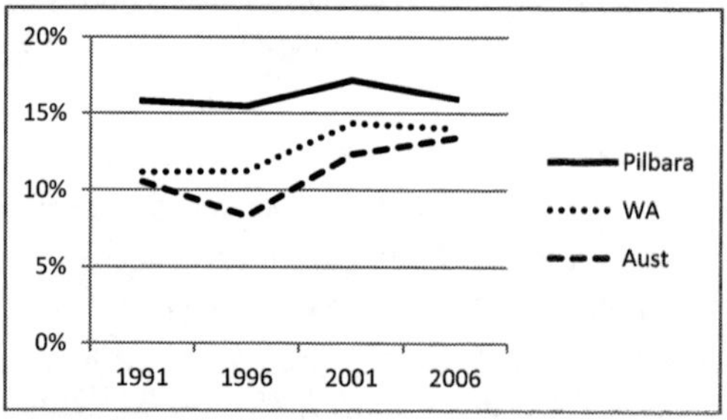

Figure 24 Percentage of the population holding trade qualifications in the Pilbara region, Western Australia and Australia.

Unfortunately, no corroborative information as to the education level of participants in mass-marketed tax avoidance schemes is available from the ATO as it does not keep records of taxpayer qualifications, nor did the ABC On-line (2007) survey include a question as to the education level of the respondents. Those data are therefore unhelpful in indicating the influence of education on participation rates in mass-marketed tax avoidance schemes.

The CTSI (2002) survey of participants in mass-marketed tax avoidance schemes indicates that nearly 17 per cent of respondents held trade certificates and almost 60 per cent held tertiary qualifications. Therefore, over three quarters of those participants in mass-marketed tax avoidance schemes held trade or tertiary qualifications. Given the findings of the CTSI (2002) survey, it would appear that despite the generally lower levels of education in the Pilbara community, education may have had a strong influence on the Pilbara taxpayers' decisions to engage in the mass-marketed tax avoidance schemes.

However, it is possible that taxpayers with educational qualifications exhibit a greater willingness to participate in research surveys and studies. In this research 28 of the 37 respondents interviewed, just over 75 per cent, held trade or tertiary qualifications. Of the 28 respondents who held trade or tertiary qualifications, eleven of them participated in mass-marketed tax avoidance schemes. Four of the participants held Master's degrees. Further, this research also notes that only three of the mass-marketed tax avoidance schemes participants interviewed did not hold trade or professional qualifications.

It is also noted that the professionals of Cohort 4, who shared the same working conditions, incomes and income tax rates with the blue-collar workers of Cohort 1, also participated in the mass-marketed tax avoidance schemes. The four interviewees with Master's degrees who participated in the mass-marketed tax avoidance schemes were very senior managers who were used to making high level management decisions. A high level of education did not make them more compliant, and willing to pay tax; rather, it only made those taxpayers more careful as to how to avoid it.

Some of the participants in mass-marketed tax avoidance schemes had investigated the 'investments' to a reasonably high level of due diligence before participating in the schemes. This was demonstrated by an interviewee who was one of participants in the mass-marketed tax avoidance schemes. He stated, 'It was a real investment. I went to the securities commission and they said he was a legitimate person.'

Another had carried out extensive research into his chosen investment including visiting the site where the project was carried out. He listed a number of criteria which he considered prior to investing in the scheme such as Australian government investment and research carried out by the Commonwealth Scientific and Industrial Research Organisation (CSIRO) and the Western Australian government into the establishment of sandalwood plantations.

It appears that those scheme participants may have taken the tax effectiveness aspect of the schemes at face value. In some cases, they based their judgements on research which was erroneous or, in the case of *Satcom*, deliberately contrived to mislead.

The income levels, and income tax rates, of the members of Cohort 1 and 3 are comparable. A key difference between the two groups of workers is education. Yet the CTSI (2002) survey data and the interviewees of Cohort 4 suggest that other influencing factors have a greater influence on the strength of tax compliance behaviour than education.

Gender

Gender was considered in the review in Chapter Three. It was found to be a significant factor in influencing taxpayer compliance behaviour. Previous researchers have found that males tend to be less compliant than females. Chapter One indicated that the Pilbara region is predominantly mining-based and ABS statistics support the concept that mining is a male dominated industry. Therefore gender bias could have been a significant factor in the high mass-marketed tax avoidance schemes participation rates demonstrated by the blue-collar workers in the Pilbara region in the 1990s.

The illustration of the ABS census data in the figure below shows that the bias of males to females in the population of the Pilbara region from 1991 to 2006 was nearly 6 per cent higher than that of Western Australia and the nation generally. In particular ABS census data for 2001 for Pannawonica, the community identified as having the highest participation rates in mass-marketed tax avoidance schemes, reveals that 62 per cent of the population were males.

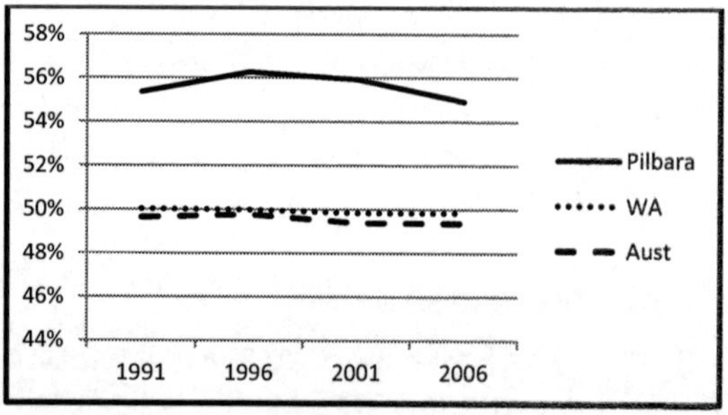

Figure 25 Percentage of males in the population of the Pilbara region, Western Australia and Australia.

The gender bias towards non-compliance appears to be supported by the CTSI (2002) survey data which shows that 82.5 per cent of participants in mass-marketed tax avoidance schemes were male.

Responses to the ABC On-line (2007) survey to the question 'How fair is it for individuals to use tax minimisation schemes?' are shown in the following table. The outcomes support the concept of gender bias found by previous researchers. Note that for the purposes of comparison respondents who are neutral (240) or unsure (90) have been excluded from the total population of respondents (1353).

Question 13. How fair is it for individuals to use tax minimisation schemes?	**Males**			**Females**			**Total** [226]		
	Unfair / Very Unfair	Fair / Very Fair	Proportion of respondents	Unfair / Very Unfair	Fair / Very Fair	Proportion of respondents	Unfair / Very Unfair	Fair / Very Fair	Total respondents
No. of respondents	333 (50.1%)	332 (49.9%)	665 (65%)	198 (55.3%)	160 (44.7%)	358 (35%)	531 (51.9%)	492 (48.1%)	1023 (100%)

Table 9 The opinions of taxpayers relating to engagement in tax minimisation schemes by gender

Just over half of the respondents who gave an opinion on the use of tax minimisation schemes to reduce tax consider their use to be unfair. However a slight gender bias is present given that 55.3 per cent of females consider the use of tax minimisation schemes to be unfair compared with the opinions of males, who are evenly divided.

These data suggest that gender may have had some influence on the disproportionate participation rates in the mass-marketed tax avoidance schemes by Pilbara taxpayers. It is certainly possible that the high proportion of blue-collar workers of the Pilbara engaged in the mass-marketed tax avoidance schemes may have been attributable to the high proportion of males in the mining-based industries of the Pilbara region.

226 Statistics are only provided for those who gave an opinion, 330 respondents answered 'neither fair nor unfair' or did not express an opinion.

Marital status

Despite the literature indicating that single people tend to be less compliant, data examined from the ABS statistics and the CTSI 2002 survey indicate that marital status may not have been significant in influencing taxpayer compliance behaviour demonstrated by the blue-collar workers of the Pilbara region in the 1990s.

ABS statistics show the proportion of married persons in the Pilbara region in the 1990s is generally consistent with Western Australian and Australian populations. In addition, data collected by the CTSI (2002) survey reveal that 94 per cent of respondents were, or had been, married.

Nationality

The examination in Chapter Three indicates that, unless people belonged to a minority group, race, nationality and ethnic origin have little impact on compliance behaviour. Minority groups can be affected by a feeling of social distance from the general community and the government which leads to non-compliant behaviour.

However, according to ABS census data, the taxpayers of Pilbara region, in the 1990s, were predominantly Australian born. According to ABS census data the proportion of Australian-born persons in the Pilbara region is only slightly lower than that of the entire Australian population. Also it is higher than the proportion of Australian-born persons in the general Western Australian population.

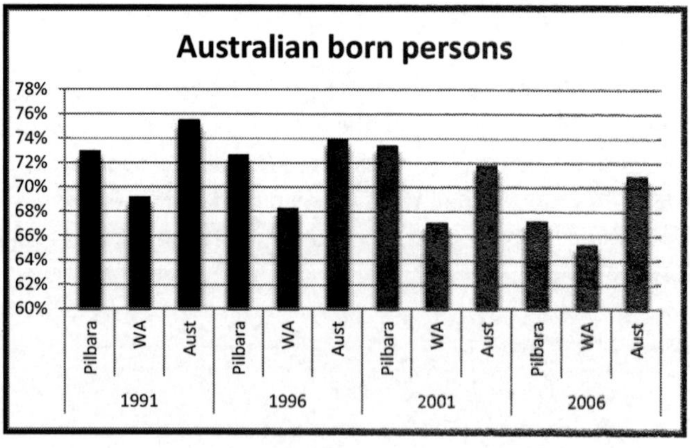

Figure 26 Proportion of Australian born persons

In 1991, the proportion of Australian-born persons in the Pilbara region was 73 per cent. When compared to the proportions of 69 per cent and 75.5 per cent for Western Australia and the overall Australian populations respectively, the higher proportion of Australian-born taxpayers of the Pilbara region should have demonstrated a propensity to engage in the mass-marketed tax avoidance schemes closer to that of the national average, shown in Chapter One, of less than 0.5 per cent and not the near 6 per cent.

In addition, the variation between the population of the Pilbara region and that of Australia decreased further in 1996 to just over 1 per cent. By 2006 the proportion of Australian-born persons in the Pilbara region exceeded that of the nation generally by nearly 2 per cent. This statistical examination indicates that if race, nationality or ethnicity was an influence, as indicated by the literature in Chapter Three, the taxpayers of the Pilbara region should have demonstrated a propensity to engage in the schemes less than that of all Australian taxpayers (less than 0.5 per cent); instead of a factor 15 to 18 times higher.

This suggestion is supported by the CTSI (2002) survey data that indicates that just over 72 per cent of the respondents were Australian born and do not generally represent ethnic minorities. This book notes the CTSI (2002) survey data and suggests that a high proportion of participants in mass-marketed tax avoidance schemes were Australian born. It suggests that race, nationality or ethnicity is not a sufficiently strong influence to explain the high rate of participation in mass-marketed tax avoidance schemes demonstrated by taxpayers of the Pilbara region in the 1990s.

ATO statistics are classified only by Australian resident and non-resident taxpayers and thus can provide no support to the suggestion as to the impact of race, nationality or ethnicity. Similarly, the ABC On-line (2007) survey does not include questions as to respondents' race, nationality or ethnicity and cannot support or refute the suggestion.

Religion

Illustrated below, the populations of the Pilbara and Western Australia are more secular than the overall Australian community. The ABS census data relates only to those who identify themselves as followers of a particular religion. Some segregation is made between Christians and non-Christians but their degree of devotion is not considered.

The figure indicates that the general trend of declared religion for the Pilbara population is downward, from nearly 65 per cent in 1991 to 46.5 per cent in 2006. In particular, in 1996 less than 60 per cent of the Pilbara population declared their religion on the census returns, compared with nearly 90 per cent in the Australian population.

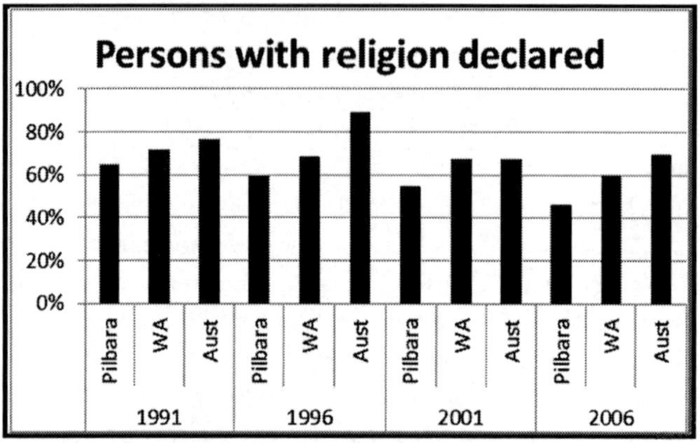

Figure 27 Percentage of persons with religion declared

Moreover ABS Census statistics for 2011 tend to indicate the trend has stabilised at just over 49 per cent.[227] If the factor of religion was a significant contributory influence on participation rates in mass-marketed tax avoidance schemes then participation in tax avoidance activity would have continued in the Pilbara and escalated throughout the broader communities of Western Australia and Australia after 2001. This was not the case. Therefore it would appear that secularism / religiosity[228] has little or no strength of influence as a factor in determining tax compliance.

There may be other factors which contribute to the higher rates of secularism in the Pilbara region. These may include a lack of established religious facilities and services in the more recently established towns and relatively transient communities of the Pilbara. It may also be possible that the lack of religious support, found in more established communities, leads to an increase in social distance and feelings of remoteness from the broader Western Australian and

227 Australian Bureau of Statistics, Basic Community Profile—Pilbara: 2011 Census of Population and Housing, (Catalogue 2001.0, 2012).

228 Term used by Torgler to describe the influence of religion on individual moral and social behaviour.

Australian populations. However the study of how religion affects social distance and perceptions of fairness is outside the scope of this book and is not investigated further.

Summary of demographic factors

The review in Chapter Three examined previous research into the influences of demographic factors on taxpayer compliance behaviour. Three key demographic factors—age, education and gender—were identified as potentially strong influences on taxpayer compliance behaviour. It indicates that younger, less educated and male-dominated communities may tend towards non-compliance with the law generally and tax compliance in particular.

In this section the examination of available statistics reveals that the Pilbara community in the 1990s demonstrated similar demographic characteristics of marital status and nationality or ethnicity to those of the wider Western Australian and Australian populations. Members of the Pilbara community in the 1990s tended to be married and Australian born in similar proportions to the wider Australian population. Those proportions were also present in the CTSI (2002) survey data of mass-marketed tax avoidance schemes participants.

The examination suggests that the population of the Pilbara region is significantly more secular than the wider Western and Australian population. However, previous research has not identified the factors of marital status, nationality or religion as being strong influences on taxpayer compliance behaviour therefore this book considers that none of those demographic factors appear to have caused the taxpayers of the Pilbara region to engage in mass-marketed tax avoidance schemes in the 1990s with the demonstrated disproportionate propensity shown in the table in Chapter One.

Statistical data examined in this section do indicate that the community of the Pilbara in the 1990s was generally younger, less educated and more male-dominated than the wider Western Australian and Australian populations during that decade. Therefore those factors—age, education and gender—may have had a strong influence on taxpayer compliance behaviour in the Pilbara in the 1990s. The demographic structure of the population of taxpayers of the Pilbara region in the 1990s indicates that they may have tended towards non-compliant tax behaviour as observed.

Despite the findings of previous research this examination of statistical data indicates that increasing age does not tend to increase taxpayer attitudes towards tax compliance. This section also finds that education is not a strong influence towards compliance behaviour. The statistical data examined in this section indicate that a high level of education does not lead to greater compliance but rather it makes taxpayers more careful in how they choose to avoid paying tax. These findings are supported by data from the CTSI (2002) survey which shows that the participants of mass-marketed tax avoidance schemes were typically older, educated taxpayers.

This section also considers that the apparent influence of gender may be due to the over-representation of males engaged in mining activities in the Pilbara region rather than a gender bias towards non-compliant behaviour. While 82.5 per cent of participants in mass-marketed tax avoidance schemes in the 1990s were males, attitudes towards tax avoidance activity revealed in this research show that acceptance of tax minimisation schemes by females is only marginally less than that of males. Therefore it is submitted that the demographic factors examined in this chapter do not satisfactorily explain the research question of this book as to why a high proportion of blue-collar workers from the mining region of the Pilbara engaged in the mass-marketed tax avoidance schemes of the 1990s.

In addition, analysis of responses to the semi-structured interviews conducted in this research suggest that, despite previous research which indicates that demographic factors influence taxpayer compliance behaviour, this may not have been the case in the context of the taxpayers that are the subject of this research.

Therefore, this book now considers those other factors that may have influenced the tax compliance attitudes of the blue-collar workers of the Pilbara in the 1990s. Against this background, the following sections look at socio-psychological and economic factors that may have intensified the non-compliant taxpayer behavioural postures demonstrated by those taxpayers.

Socio-psychological factors

The influencing factors considered in this section as socio-psychological factors are perceptions of fairness, risk aversion and peer influence. Contained within those broad headings are: social distance from government, audit rates, penalties, amnesties and social class (as depicted in Chapter Three).

Perceptions of fairness

This section looks specifically at the perceptions of taxpayers as to the fairness of the tax rates they pay and their perceptions of how they view the rates of tax paid by others.

The literature examined in Chapter Three indicates that a taxpayer's perception of fairness is greatly influenced by other factors. Previous researchers are also divided as to the significance of 'fairness' as an influence on taxpayer compliance behaviour and willingness to pay tax. Most researchers suggest that perceptions of fairness have a strong influence on taxpayer compliance behaviour, while some find that perceptions of fairness have little or no influence on taxpayers' decisions to pay tax.

The perception of what is 'fair and reasonable' is inevitably subjective. This research uses a combination of approaches to examine the impact of the perception of fairness and how it relates to other factors. The ABC On-line (2007) survey contains three questions on this issue: what the respondents think of how fair their tax rate is, what is a fair rate of tax, and if it is fair to use tax minimisation schemes. They were also asked for their comments as to a fair rate of tax and the use of tax minimisation schemes.

Those interviewed by way of the semi-structured interviews were also asked their opinions as to the fairness of their tax rate, what a fair tax rate is and if they think others are paying a fair tax rate. They were also asked if they feel they are fairly paid and if they are treated fairly by the ATO. The interviews also investigate if a relationship exists between tax rates and the manner in which taxpayers earn their income by asking interviewees if they feel they work hard for their income.

The following section initially considers the outcome of the ABC On-line (2007) research survey, followed by a detailed analysis of the outcomes of the semi-structured interviews.

In addition to their opinions on their preferred and actual tax rates, and how hard they work for their money, respondents to the ABC On-line (2007) survey were asked the question, 'How fair is it for individuals to enter into tax minimisation schemes?'.

The table showing the ABC On-line (2007) survey respondents' opinions on the fairness of using tax minimisation schemes to be relatively evenly distributed. The table indicates that respondents were only slightly biased towards a belief that using tax minimisation schemes was unfair: 39.3 per cent thought it was unfair for individuals to use tax minimisation schemes and 36.3 per cent thought it fair.

However, this is not a clear guide to how determined respondents may be on the use of tax minimisation systems. A person may consider an action fair and reasonable but not engage in the activity themselves. Further investigation is required to determine the strength of influence of the perception of fairness towards tax avoidance activity.

Respondents to the ABC On-line (2007) survey were asked to give their opinions to the question 'How fair is the tax rate that you pay?'. Their responses are shown below.

Question 10. How fair is the tax rate that you pay?						
Very unfair	Unfair	Neutral	Fair	Very fair	Unsure or no answer	Total
141	269	282	420	182	59	1353
10.4%	19.9%	20.8%	31.0%	13.5%	4.4%	100%

Table 10 ABC On-line (2007) survey respondents' perception of fairness of their current personal tax rate

The table shows that 44.5 per cent of respondents thought that the tax rate they paid was 'fair' or 'very fair', while 30.3 per cent thought the tax rate they paid was 'unfair' or 'very unfair'.

To provide context to the respondents' viewpoints they were also asked to give their opinions to the question 'What do you think is a fair rate of tax?'. This aspect (which is examined in more detail under the sub-heading 'Income tax rates') is shown later.

A significant number of respondents to the survey referred to government and government services when giving reasons for their choice of a 'fair' tax rate. Of the respondents, 218 (16.1 per cent) considered that the government acted indifferently to their wishes. These data suggest that taxpayers associate how their taxes are being spent with what they consider they are willing to pay in tax. A number of respondents supported their opinion of the use of tax minimisation schemes by suggesting that the use of schemes is fair if they feel their tax is being wasted, applied inefficiently or spent on frivolous projects.

Many researchers—including Smith and Kinsey, Witte, Wadhawan and Gray, Webley, Adams and Elffers, John Braithwaite, Valerie Braithwaite[229] and Rawlings—suggest that the correlation between taxpaying and the running of government and services is too tenuous to affect taxpayers' compliance decisions. However this research suggests that taxpayers consider how their taxes are spent when considering fairness of tax rates.

This suggestion is supported by the findings of a review of tax compliance by small business owners by Kamleitner, Korunka, Kirchler. [230] They suggested that 'fairness is an important consideration in tax decision making. Lack of trust in the fairness of a tax system and the legitimacy of tax authorities increases the likelihood of tax evasion among small business owners.' While their research focussed on small business owners, they noted that this phenomenon is not specific to small business.

The supporting comments of the ABC On-line (2007) survey respondents show that taxpayers relate the degree of government services they receive to their perception of a 'fair' rate of tax. Typically one respondent put it as follows: 'Tax is necessary but governments are often inefficient and frivolous in the use of it so a high tax rate seems like money down the drain.' Another suggested the reason for 'high taxes' as: 'I believe Australia has too many levels of government which is why current tax rates are so high—there is a huge amount of duplication'.

In an attempt to quantify a 'fair' rate of tax, one respondent stated, 'The average worker would not mind providing 20 cents from his dollar earned for the things governments are required to provide'. Another suggested, 'I would prefer to pay slightly more tax and receive high quality government services (education, health) than pay less tax and leave everything to the private industry. At the end of the day my disposable income will still be similar.'

Participants in the semi-structured interviews were also asked if they thought others were paying a fair rate of tax and what they thought was a fair rate of tax. To the question, 'Do you believe you pay a fair rate of tax?', one interviewee simply commented 'for the benefits we get out of it—no'. This interviewee also related his perception of fairness of taxation to government spending.

---

229 Valerie Braithwaite, 'Games of Engagement. Postures within the Regulatory Community' (1995) 17 Law and Policy 225.

230 Bernadette Kamleitner, Christian Korunka, Erich Kirchler, 'Tax compliance of small business owners: A review' (2012) 18(3) International Journal of Entrepreneurial Behaviour & Research, 330.

Further, the perception of fairness also appears to extend to other areas of social spending and taxation. One interviewee made the connection to his child support liability. He felt his tax liability should take into account his liability to pay child support.

One participant in mass-marketed tax avoidance schemes felt that he was paying more than the company tax rate of 30 per cent and that that was unfair. Another stated that even though he was paying 40 cents in the dollar, his tax rate was 'a little fairer now but it is a little over what it should be'. The interviewee colourfully made a connection between tax liability and living conditions. He commented on the impact of zone taxation rebates intended as recompense for the uncongenial climate, isolation and high cost of living in prescribed remote areas of Australia.

> It's a load of bullshit. It's a load of wank. It's not even it's just the difference of a tank of fuel. Put it this way, for the amount of tax I was putting into the big bucket, I don't think that our concessions in the North West matched those of people who had the benefits they had down south or anywhere.

Comments like this suggest that the perception of fairness manifests itself in such a way that it influences taxpayer behaviour towards tax minimisation activity when taxpayers perceive tax rates to be unfair.

This research was unable to assess the strength of the perception of fairness or whether it acted as a catalyst towards the strength of influence of other factors. This examination is inconclusive as to the degree of the impact of the perception of fairness. However, it does illustrate that a relationship exists between factors. What is deemed to be 'fair' by a taxpayer is likely to be determined by the influence of a number of other factors. A dominant factor influencing the blue-collar workers of the Pilbara in the 1990s appears to be the relationship between their living conditions and their perceptions of a 'fair' rate of tax.

If the physically and socially isolated blue-collar workers in the Pilbara region felt they were being taxed unfairly they may have been drawn to mass-marketed tax avoidance schemes. In the particularly physically and socially isolated community of Pannawonica that feeling of unfairness may have been very strong indeed. In addition to being asked if they were being taxed fairly the mass-marketed tax avoidance schemes participants were asked if they thought they had been treated fairly by the ATO. The discussion of taxpayers' perceptions of fairness and the relationship of social distance from government is developed further in the next section.

Social distance

Jary and Jary consider social distance as being an 'aloofness and inapproachability' between the people and their government. While none of the Pilbara blue-collar workers interviewed made specific reference to feelings of social distance from government bodies, they did make a connection between their physical 'isolation' and their perceptions of fairness. All of them referred to their physical isolation and made a connection between that and their feelings that their rates of tax were unfairly high.

Social distance from 'mainstream' society, and not just government services, was given as a strong justification for participating in the mass-marketed tax avoidance schemes by scheme participants in Cohort 1 and by non-participants in Cohort 2.

Four interviewees made specific reference to 'isolation' from 'mainstream' society in a physical sense. Two of them were participants in mass-marketed tax avoidance schemes who considered 'isolation' as a factor influencing their decision to enter into the schemes. The others did not participate, but considered the influence of 'isolation' as reasonable grounds for trying to reduce tax.

The following extract of an interview with one of the interviewees of Cohort 1 illustrates the general feeling of 'isolation' and reflects the attitudes to tax compliance generated by that feeling of being left out of 'mainstream' society.

> Interviewer: Do you see a difference between the 'city' and the 'bush', do you?
>
> Interviewee: Well yeah. I mean we get paid a lot more than the guys down there in the city but they get all the schools and that and pay a lot less tax. It seems we do the paying but they get all the amenities and that.
>
> And how does that influence your tax?
>
> Well I reckon we could get a lot more tax breaks than we do for being up here. We don't get any of the things they do. It's a 300 kilometre round trip just to go to Karratha. You think of McDonald's, just a Hungry Jacks, and that.
>
> I take it they're things you don't have rather than things you do have?
>
> Yeah. I mean I don't know if that's a fact or not but it's just the way I see it.
>
> It doesn't matter whether anything is true it's your opinion we are looking for. Just on that 'city and bush' rate of tax, do you think there should be some tax breaks for blokes in the bush?
>
> Yes I do. Yeah we should be getting something to compensate for the harsh conditions and the isolation. As I said we are a bloody long way from nowhere and we have to deal with cyclones and that.

> Every now and again the road goes out and we are stuck here for weeks and that's not much fun I can tell you.
>
> So Pannawonica would be particularly isolated?
>
> I think that they should give us a bit of a break for the isolation, you know?

However, social distance was not expressed by interviewees in Cohort 3 – Western Australia's professionals. That group of professionals did not feel 'isolated' or distant from 'mainstream' society. It is suggested that as professionals, resident in the capital city of Perth, they feel part of and empowered as members of 'mainstream' society.

It appears that the physical isolation felt by taxpayers in the Pilbara region led to feelings of being 'left out' of mainstream society. Similarly, the blue-collar workers in Cohort 2, though not participants in mass-marketed tax avoidance schemes, were able to sympathise with those who did. On the other hand, the city dwelling, better educated, professionals of Cohort 3 did not feel isolated from mainstream society.

This suggests that the heavy working conditions experienced by the blue-collar workers living in the Pilbara region were exacerbated by their physical isolation from mainstream society. That social distance prompted increased perceptions that their high tax rates were unfair and contributed to their attraction to the mass-marketed tax avoidance schemes of the 1990s.

Risk aversion

As indicated by previous research examined in Chapter Three, important factors which shape attitudes to risk aversion are: audit rates (the chances of being caught), penalties (what happens if you are caught) and amnesties (the chances of being forgiven). Those three factors are considered later under their own sub-headings.

Generally respondents to the ABC On-line (2007) survey did not consider risk as a significant factor influencing their attitudes towards the use of tax minimisation schemes. When giving reasons as to why they considered the fairness of using tax minimisation schemes to be fair or unfair, only 11 (0.81 per cent) of the 1,353 respondents to the ABC On-line (2007) survey considered risk as an influencing factor.

Those that did consider risk associated it with rewards and tax rates. One respondent suggested: 'If the schemes are legal OK, but they take a risk—it's up to the government to close unfair loopholes'. Two referred to their right to take risk.

Eight referred to the relationship between risk and reward. Three of those considered that high income tax rates reduced rewards and increased the tax benefits of entering into tax minimisation schemes.

Another respondent suggested that a fair tax spread risk to the community whereas tax minimisation schemes focused risk away from those involved in the schemes, stating:

> Tax keeps the country running—only if the government actually spends it to build [and] repair. Hoarding it does nothing. By minimising tax, you are not paying to improve the country. We all benefit when the country is improved. User-pays is useless—the risk is not spread.

As to the interviewees in this research, half of those in Cohort 3 referred to risk aversion as a decisive factor in their consideration for not participating in tax avoidance activity. One interviewee summed up the general attitude of that group to tax avoidance schemes by saying:

> Anything that provides a return greater than the current market value has risks, so therefore it only has a risk for a particular reason. Anything that is into implying that you are getting a greater benefit than the money you are putting in—dodgy.

On the other hand, only one interviewee in Cohort 2 referred to risk as a consideration for participating in tax avoidance schemes. He considered risk as part of his job and had learned to accept it. However, when referring to tax avoidance schemes, he said 'I would not have participated in something I thought was illegal or high risk'. It is noted that this interviewee did not participate in the mass-marketed tax avoidance schemes.

Three of the six interviewees in Cohort 4 were professionals resident in the Pilbara who participated in the mass-marketed tax avoidance schemes of the 1990s. In reference to participating in the schemes, one said:

> There certainly was an awareness, at that stage, that there was a risk but there were a lot of such arrangements in place I gather. I learned afterwards, but not at the time, and you know, I just would have stayed away from it, full stop.
>
> I just wasn't interested in anything dodgy or risky. When you're a single parent like that and you are constrained income and the only way, you know, you can't even make more money by working longer, you look to sort of create wealth, risk can't be too big a part of it.

In this interviewee's case it appears risk was considered in his decision to enter into the schemes but he was unaware of the degree of the risk. The factor of risk was also referred to by another mass-marketed tax avoidance schemes participant who said his accountant 'wouldn't do it himself. He had fears that because the ATO hadn't approved it in writing that it was a risk.'

When questioned as to why he ignored the advice of his accountant he said:

> Because at the same time he would have most likely said to me, 'I mean we have got a verbal approval from the ATO', but he would have said, 'I can't guarantee that the written approval you know, I mean it's 99 per cent but yeah I can't guarantee that one per cent'.
>
> And he, you know, left the investment up to me whether I wanted to make it or not but if I did, I did it on the advice of my financial adviser.

It is noted that while both interviewees considered risk in their decisions to enter into the schemes, they ignored it. Their fears were either allayed as they were unaware of the true degree of risk or it was overcome by other factors.

Two of the Pilbara blue-collar workers, who participated in mass-marketed tax avoidance schemes, referred to the influence of risk being weakened other factors. One referred to risk in the context that the agricultural trial that he was investing into could fail. He commented, 'Yeah well he [the promoter] didn't have that much information about the whole scheme itself but he was talking about it being possible that the trees might not grow in Kununurra. The trials were promising but he would not guarantee it 100 per cent.' He was clearly appreciative of the possibility his investment could fail and accepted the risk. However he was not appreciative of the risk that the 'investment' could be considered a tax avoidance scheme and therefore any arising tax benefits could be disallowed.

The other interviewee who referred to risk had other reasons for accepting it. He said:

> Well it was a little risky. I've never actually taken risks with money before. I mean I don't go stock market or any of that stuff. So this was a big—this was a huge risk for me this was a huge step forward for me to do this.

When questioned as to why this type of investment and why not some other investment, such as Wesfarmers shares, he responded:

> Well I think this was sold to me. I think this was sold to me in a fairly, in a bit of a pressure situation where you got to have a look at what you could get. But at the end of the day, but in the end of the day you get fuck-all. I guess what my comment is that when you sit back at the end of the day and I wonder why I ever done it. But at the time I did.

When asked if it had been for the tax benefit, he replied, 'It was the tax saving yeah and the fact that I could roll it through to my kids' education. That was the whole, sole purpose of my doing it.'

It appears some taxpayers are willing to accept higher levels of risk than others. This examination suggests that risk may be considered as a factor influencing taxpayer compliance behaviour but the degree of influence is affected by other factors which override that risk. In the case of the above interviewee, it was tax savings. In the case of another, the influence of tax professionals and promoters overrode the influence of risk aversion.

Comparisons of responses between interviewees of the groups of blue-collar workers and professionals indicate that the professionals interviewed tended to exhibit a higher degree of risk aversion than the blue-collar workers. The professionals, in Cohort 3, were more aware of, and averse to, risk taking than interviewees in other cohorts. Interviewees from the cohorts of blue-collar workers appeared to be less aware, and some even dismissive, of risk. This book suggests that risk appears to have been either ignored or accepted by the blue-collar workers as part of their everyday living and working conditions.

Audit rates

The influence of audit rates is not specifically considered in this research. However, participants in the mass-marketed tax avoidance schemes generally believed that the schemes had been 'audited' and were approved by the ATO. Two interviewees specifically referred to the schemes having been 'audited'. Their statements indicate that some consideration was given to the schemes as having been 'audited' in influencing their decisions to participate in the mass-marketed tax avoidance schemes.

One said:

> I mean I had been told by my financial adviser that the scheme had been audited if you like by Coopers and Lybrand and their written opinion which I think I had a copy of, and probably still do somewhere, was that the scheme was valid just pending written approval from the ATO.

The other stated:

> I mean you know I've seen them [the ATO] change their minds on things at the drop of a hat and it would appear to be that they [the ATO] were self-auditing. I mean you know, they make up their own rules as they go along and they can change them tomorrow if they feel like it.

These statements do not indicate a fear of being audited but rather reveal a desire to be audited, to ensure compliance. They also reflect an assumption that the ATO was auditing the mass-marketed tax avoidance schemes as the promoters claimed, but the situation was subject to change. This may have been a principle used by designers and promoters of the schemes to market their 'products.'

This discussion suggests that risk aversion may have been a factor in deterring taxpayers from engaging in the mass-marketed tax avoidance schemes, but it does not appear to be relevant to the blue-collar workers in the Pilbara in the 1990s. Further research is required to form a satisfactory conclusion as to the influence of audit rates on taxpayer compliance as these statements have no empirical evidence to support them.

Penalties

Previous research, examined in Chapter Three, indicates there is a strong relationship between audit rates and penalties. Both relate closely to the influence of risk.

Penalties may have some influence in affecting taxpayer compliance behaviour. In this research, however, a comment on penalties was made by only one interviewee. That interviewee, who did not participate in the mass-marketed tax avoidance schemes, expressed that he had:

> Not gone after perhaps, claims, that I was probably legitimately entitled to, because of not understanding what I was or wasn't entitled to, and being concerned that if I did claim bits that I wasn't entitled to, there would be penalties to follow.

Asked if he would rather overpay tax than have contact with the tax office, he replied simply 'yes'. No other interviewees (whether participants in mass-marketed tax avoidance schemes or not) made reference to a caution, or fear, of penalties.

In addition only one of the 1,353 ABC On-line (2007) survey respondents expressed the opinion that engaging in tax avoidance activity was 'legal avoidance of social responsibility and should incur heavy financial penalties'.

The matter of penalties was also included in the CTSI (2002) survey, however that was specifically in response to the penalties levied as part of the ATO's recovery action. Therefore the influence of penalties may not have been in the minds of those taxpayers at the time of participating in the mass-marketed tax avoidance schemes as:

- It appears they were of the belief that the mass-marketed tax avoidance schemes were valid projects with authorised tax minimisation benefits;
- The penalties were levied well after the decision was made to enter into the mass-marketed tax avoidance schemes; and

- As a result of public pressure and political intervention penalties were not applied to the mass-marketed tax avoidance schemes deduction claims.

Therefore the fear of penalties appears to have little or no influence on taxpayers' decisions to participate in the mass-marketed tax avoidance schemes of the 1990s.

In contrast, the experience of engaging in the mass-marketed tax avoidance schemes, and the subsequent recovery action by the ATO, resulted in a strong response by those participants interviewed. Not one of them stated that they would re-engage in any tax minimisation scheme, although two said that they might consider 'having a look'. One interviewee put it colourfully, 'No bloody way mate. This thing has cost me plenty. There is no way I would do it again. I had a gutful. I would not go near anything like this again.' His sentiments were supported by another respondent who said:

> Never in my wildest dreams. I consider myself an honest, working, taxpaying citizen of this country and have always paid my dues. I would never knowingly go into any such schemes like that. Even though I believe they were legally and morally correct.

From the above observations it appears that a negative experience of contact with the taxing authority has greater influence on taxpayer compliance than the fear of potential penalties.

Amnesties

The influence of amnesties was found to be insignificant, if considered at all, by mass-marketed tax avoidance schemes participants in the 1990s. No interviewees or respondents in this research referred to amnesties as a consideration for participating in the mass-marketed tax avoidance schemes or for involvement in tax avoidance activity generally. Neither the ABC On-line (2007) survey nor the CTSI (2002) survey included questions on the influence of amnesties.

However, Torgler refers to the anticipation of future tax amnesties as a crowding out of tax compliance and it is possible that some taxpayers may have thought that if the scheme deductions were to be disallowed they would be able to settle the problem during the next amnesty.

Though Australia has held few taxation amnesties, the ATO conducted an amnesty in 1988 for taxpayers who had failed to lodge tax returns.[231] It is important to note that, in 1994, that amnesty had taken place only six years

231 ATO, The Commissioner of Taxation—Annual Report 2009-10.

before. It may have been fresh in the minds of taxpayers and it is suggested that some taxpayers in the early 1990s may have held the opinion that there would be further amnesties. It was noted by the author, who was in private practice at that time, that some taxpayers who had missed the amnesty, expressed the opinion, 'Oh well, never mind, there will be others. I will lodge then.'

The subsequent relief of penalties and interest granted to mass-marketed tax avoidance schemes participants in 2002 could be interpreted as an amnesty. Therefore despite not being evidenced in this research, if the belief existed that there would be further amnesties, it may have had some impact on the decisions of mass-marketed tax avoidance schemes participants.

It is noted that since 1 July 2000 the ATO has had a practice of encouraging voluntary disclosures of tax avoidance activity by reducing penalties.[232] The policy may be viewed as an ongoing amnesty. Penalty reductions vary from 20 per cent of that which would otherwise apply to 100 per cent of the penalty. This practice has occurred in the period subsequent to that of this research and further consideration is therefore outside the scope of this book.

Peer influence

The strength of peer influence is difficult to establish with certainty. However, previous research, examined in Chapter Three, indicates that work colleagues may be a strong influence on taxpayer compliance behaviour. That research also indicates that the strength influence of work colleagues may be closely linked to the varying types of occupation.

This research considered, inter alia, how family, friends and work colleagues influenced the blue-collar workers of the Pilbara region to participate in the mass-marketed tax avoidance schemes.

Part of the sociological concept of enculturation (referred to as 'socialization' by Parsons and Bales),[233] the influence of friends and family may be significant in determining taxpayer compliance behaviour. The CTSI (2002) survey data shows just over 28 per cent of those surveyed had been introduced to the mass-marketed tax avoidance schemes by family, friends or work colleagues. Further, six of the 15 interviewees who were mass-marketed tax avoidance schemes participants, stated that they had been introduced to the schemes by friends.

232 ATO, Miscellaneous Tax Ruling MT 2012/3, 4 June 2010.

233 Talcott Parsons and Robert Freed Bales, Family, Socialization and Interaction Process (1955).

However, they stated that they had not relied exclusively on the involvement of friends in the mass-marketed tax avoidance schemes.

One interviewee said:

> Our friend had a small business and he had a financial adviser that he used to use to do his tax and his investments and all that for him. Through him and word of mouth through our friends we went on their, you know, recommendations, that he was a good, you know, reputable sort of person and to follow his advice and we did.

However he went on to say:

> They [the promoters] approached us but at the same time we had heard our friends discussing all of this and you know, the investment that we were going to go into wasn't going to mature you know, for years, or pay dividends, for another six to eight years which is when we were looking at retiring so that matched and looked pretty good to us.

None of those interviewed placed the blame for their participation in the mass-marketed tax avoidance schemes on their family, friends or acquaintances. It is noted that those participants interviewed in this research expressed that they had ultimately relied on other advice and not the influence of friends. Perhaps a sense of loyalty to one's friends, and a reluctance to blame them in the place of less socially familiar persons such as the promoters or financial advisers, may pervade taxpayers' attitudes or opinions. The fact that friends were participating in the mass-marketed tax avoidance schemes may have had some influence, at least, in facilitating the introduction to the promoters.

Another interviewee referred to a friend in Brisbane having the same problems as he was with the ATO's recovery action, but that friend had nothing to do with his decision to participate. Yet another specifically referred to friends as not being influential in his decision: 'Friends had said to us that they had been into it but I don't know if that was after we made contact or before'.

Despite those examples which indicate a lack of influence of peers, other cases were found which indicate a strong influence. One interviewee stated:

> [I was introduced to the scheme by] a very good friend of mine who was working on the tugs up at Dampier. He got hold of the scheme and we went down to his accountant's office and met the promoters of the scheme in the accountant's office and discussed it there and they assured us that it was cleared by the taxation department and they showed paper work from the taxation department or on taxation department letterheads and yeah I bought one and my friend bought two of the schemes.

In the case of *Vincent v Federal Commissioner of Taxation*, it appears that Mrs Vincent had relied on the opinion of family and friends, rather than seeking independent professional advice. When questioned as to her investigations of the commercial viability of the scheme she stated that she had:

> discussed [the income projections] with her father. They both were of the view that the projections were realistic. She also discussed them with her partner and his father. She thought she would get the projected return. However, she did not make any external checks of the figures.

This book suggests that the social closeness of small, isolated communities, such as those found in the mining towns of the Pilbara, and in particular characterised by the very small and extremely isolated mining community of Pannawonica, serves to strengthen the influence of peer opinion. Despite some participants' statements to the contrary (that they were not influenced by their friends and work colleagues), peer influence may have had some influence in their decisions to participate in the mass-marketed tax avoidance schemes of the 1990s.

Social class

Though social class, as defined by Jary and Jary, was not specifically researched in the book, some comparisons and distinctions were observed between Cohorts 1 and 2, blue-collar workers, and Cohort 3, those in the professions. Cohort 3 held formal university qualifications and generally the others did not, though most held trade qualifications.

It is noted that one of the other distinctions related to social class is that of income and wealth. However in the case of the blue-collar workers of the Pilbara, the labourers and tradespeople often receive higher incomes than those of their salaried professional 'bosses'. It is suggested that the economic factors of income or wealth, generally connected to social class, do not satisfactorily explain the difference of attitude towards tax compliance behaviour between the 'working' and 'professional' classes as interviewees in Cohort 1 had incomes and wealth commensurate with those of Cohort 3.

However, there are many other socio-psychological influences which characterise social class. Educational opportunities, family history and generational social attitudes, as well as peer influence in formative years, are also strong determinants. In Australia social class is not fixed by ancestry, but children tend to follow their parent's class. Transition between classes, referred to as 'social mobility',[234] is possible in Australia, and often occurs, between generations.

---

234 Nicholas Abercrombie, Stephen Hill and Bryan S Turner, The Penguin Dictionary of Sociology (3rd ed, 1994).

As described in Chapter One, there is an apparent lack of communication or socialising between the tradespeople and the professionals in the Pilbara. A general distrust between the two groups tends to manifest itself as a 'them' and 'us' attitude. However social class appears to have no more than a weak influence upon tax compliance behaviour. The professionals based in the Pilbara appear to have demonstrated the same willingness to participate in the mass-marketed tax avoidance schemes of the 1990s as the blue-collar workers. They also gave similar reasons for doing so.

Notwithstanding, this research is unable to reach a reliable conclusion as to the strength of influence of the factor of social class and further research is recommended.

Summary of socio-psychological factors

Socio-psychological factors tend to interact to affect the strength of influence of other factors. For example, the influence of peers may negate risk aversion. A person who may normally be fearful of detection and subsequent penalties may be encouraged by his / her peers to overcome that fear and participate in tax avoidance activities.

Risk aversion may be affected by other social influences. Social class, brought about by demographic and / or economic factors, appears to play a dominant role in determining the influence of risk aversion. The blue-collar workers of the Pilbara region appear to be more accepting of risk than the professional class. Perhaps day-to-day exposure to working hazards or peer influence of friends and workmates alters taxpayers' perceptions and acceptance of risk. That peer influence, in the remote and isolated communities of the Pilbara, may have been able to overshadow other socio-psychological factors which lead towards tax compliance.

Similarly the strength of the influence of risk aversion which moves taxpayers towards compliant behaviour may also have been reduced by social isolation from government. It appears that 'social isolation' was also a contributing factor which influenced the decisions of the blue-collar workers of the Pilbara in the 1990s. Their decisions to participate in the mass-marketed tax avoidance schemes were brought about in part by their perceptions of unfairness in the tax system.

The interaction of socio-psychological factors tends to reinforce the concept of the interrelatedness of factors that may affect compliance behaviour generally.

The following section looks at the group of economic factors which influence taxpayer compliance behaviour.

Economic factors

This section follows the pattern of previous sections, and examines available statistics from external sources and findings from the semi-structured interviews undertaken as part of this research to highlight the main economic factors which may have influenced taxpayer compliance behaviour in the Pilbara in the 1990s. Broadly, it looks at how the blue-collar workers of the Pilbara earn their incomes, how much they earn and the tax rates they pay, their economic habits or how they spend their earnings, and relates these factors to their engagement in the mass-marketed tax avoidance schemes of the Pilbara in the 1990s.

The factors examined are:

- occupation and associated working conditions;
- income and associated income tax rates; and
- the economic habits of the blue-collar workers of the Pilbara in the 1990s.

Occupation

Previous research, examined in Chapter Three, indicates that occupation is a significant influencing factor on compliance behaviour. However it was difficult to determine from the examination of statistical information used in this research, if occupation in isolation was strong enough to cause the blue-collar workers of the Pilbara to participate in the mass-marketed tax avoidance schemes of the 1990s as illustrated in Chapter One.

The predominance of tradespeople in the mass-marketed tax avoidance schemes was more likely due to the high density of tradespeople in the population of the Pilbara rather than a factor contributing to the strength of influence of occupation in isolation. ABS statistics, illustrated earlier, show the proportion of tradespeople in the Pilbara region in the 1990s to be nearly twice that of the Western Australian and Australian populations. A partial explanation may be the manner by which the modern mining industry operates. The modern mining industry requires specialisation and trade skills to carry out work that once was the realm of large gangs of manual workers. Therefore functions which were once carried out by unskilled labourers now require workers with trade qualifications.

This book suggests that the occupations of the Pilbara taxpayers may have had a significant impact in contributing to their increased participation in mass-marketed tax avoidance schemes. This section considers other influencing factors that often relate to occupation, those of working conditions and the antithesis of work—leisure. Further, occupation is often related to a person's income, and accompanying income tax rates, as well as the influence of work colleagues, social class and economic habits.

The following table illustrating the distribution of ABS census, CTSI (2002) survey and ABC On-line (2007) survey respondents by occupation is provided to examine the statistical data considered in this research. It is a comparison of statistical data of the ABS census of Population and Housing for 2006, the CTSI (2002) survey and ABC On-line (2007) survey. Though the three data sources are from the overall Australian population there are discrepancies between them. According to the ABS 2006 census data, tradespeople and other blue-collar workers comprise just over 10 per cent of the Australian workforce. In the CTSI (2002) survey tradespeople made up nearly 13 per cent of respondents, close to the wider Australian population. However, in the ABC On-line (2007) survey the population of tradespeople was just 2.5 per cent.

It is also noted that the classification of occupations varies slightly between the three types of surveys. The ABS 2006 census used the 2006 Australian and New Zealand Standard Classification of Occupations which has 474 categories of occupation. This replaced the 1996 Australian Standard Classification of Occupations (second edition) (ASCO2) used in the CTSI (2002) survey which had 258 categories. The ABC On-line survey (2007) only had 34 categories. Therefore the ABS census and the CTSI categories were aggregated into those of the ABC On-line survey (2007) categories for consistency. Further statistics for business proprietors, homemakers, retirees and students from the ABS 2006 census were added to the table to permit comparative examination with ABC On-line survey (2007) data. The CTSI (2002) survey did not include categories for business proprietors, homemakers, retirees and students.

The ABS 2006 census shows that the professions comprise just over 8 per cent of the Australian workforce. However, the CTSI (2002) and the ABC On-line (2007) survey data show the professional occupations to comprise nearly one quarter of all respondents. A possible explanation for the differences is that taxpayers with formal educational qualifications, required by the professions, exhibit a greater willingness to participate in research surveys and studies. Therefore the opinions presented by examination of data from the CTSI (2002) and ABC On-line (2007) surveys must be considered biased in favour of the opinions of professionals and may not truly reflect the opinions of Australia's blue-collar workers.

Occupation	ASCO 2 Code [235]	ABS Australia 2006 census (count)	(%)	CTSI (2002) survey (count)	(%)	ABC On-line (2007) survey (count)	(%)
Professionals							
Accountant / auditor	2210	123 690	0.95	73	3.17	20	1.48
Analyst	2231	63 453	0.49	59	2.56	17	1.26
Architect	2121	19 307	0.15	6	0.26	1	0.07
Computer professional	1224	142 311	1.10	34	1.48	42	3.10
Doctor	2310	49 286	0.38	71	3.09	11	0.81
Educator / Teacher / Professor	2400	362 598	2.79	73	3.17	142	10.50
Engineer	2120	125 932	0.97	41	1.78	20	1.48
Health care worker	2380	80 827	0.62	89	3.87	48	3.55
Lawyer / Judge	2712	60 767	0.47	0	0.00	13	0.96
Military officer	1294	7 824	0.06	5	0.22	4	0.30
Researcher	2290	3762	0.03	57	2.48	28	2.07
Scientist	2110	45 199	0.35	33	1.43	18	1.33
Sub-total		**1 084 956**	**8.36**	**541**	**23.51**	**364**	**26.91**
Trades							
Skilled Labourer	4000	1 100 170	8.48	232	10.08	16	1.18
Technician	3120	209 085	1.61	62	2.69	18	1.33
Sub-total		**1 309 255**	**10.09**	**294**	**12.77**	**34**	**2.51**

235 Australian Bureau of Statistics, 1220.0 – Australian Standard of Classification of Occupations (2nd ed 1997).

Occupation	ASCO 2 Code [236]	ABS Australia 2006 census (count)	(%)	CTSI (2002) survey (count)	(%)	ABC On-line (2007) survey (count)	(%)
Others							
Administrative Assistant	5111	106 892	0.82	14	0.61	34	2.51
Artist / Musician	2530	16 827	0.13	13	0.56	5	0.37
Associate	3100	0	0.00	70	3.04	1	0.07
Broker / trader / adviser	2222	19 998	0.15	13	0.56	11	0.81
CEO / President / Chairman	1112	46 766	0.36	103	4.48	32	2.37
Clerical Worker	6100	550 733	4.24	57	2.48	35	2.59
Clergy	2515	14 783	0.11	0	0.00	22	1.63
Consultant	2294	3 579	0.03	30	1.30	56	4.14
Government Official	1111	1 314 252	10.12	2	0.09	72	5.32
Homemaker / housekeeper		1 869 702	14.40	0	0.00	26	1.92
Manager	1100	1 202 262	9.26	330	14.34	64	4.73
Partner / Principal / Owner		1 434 982	11.05	0	0.00	38	2.81
Retired		3 020 877	23.27	0	0.00	280	20.69
Sales manager / Account executive	3300	87 321	0.67	72	3.13	17	1.26
Service provider	5900	7 913	0.06	34	1.48	19	1.40
Student		680 113	5.24	0	0.00	30	2.22
Supervisor	3390	21 865	0.17	36	1.56	6	0.44
Writer / editor	2534	22 507	0.17	5	0.22	27	2.00
Other		90 681	0.70	44	1.91	150	11.09
no answer		74 911	0.58	121	5.26	30	2.22
Sub-total		**10 586 964**	**81.53**	**944**	**41.02**	**955**	**70.59**
Total		**12 981 175**	**100.00**	**2 301**	**100.00**	**1 353**	**100.00**

Table 11 Distribution of ABS census, CTSI (2002) survey and ABC On-line (2007) survey respondents by occupation

236 Australian Bureau of Statistics, 1220.0 – Australian Standard of Classification of Occupations (2nd ed 1997).

The table is provided to illustrate the relationship of data from the three sources and gives context as well as an indicator of reliability of the ABC On-line (2007) survey data when comparing those data to the other surveys.

Despite the bias noted above, the next table is presented to compare the opinions of respondents to the ABC On-line (2007) survey in order to allow for the bias, and to examine the influence of occupation on taxpayer attitudes towards the use of tax minimisation schemes. It specifically compares the opinions of the general groups of tradespeople and professionals shown in the previous table. It does not include those respondents who were unsure or did not answer (330).

Question 13. How fair is it for individuals to use tax minimisation schemes?	Tradespeople			Professionals			Total of all respondents[237]		
	Unfair / Very Unfair	Fair / Very Fair	Proportion of respondents	Unfair / Very Unfair	Fair / Very Fair	Proportion of respondents	Unfair / Very Unfair	Fair / Very Fair	Total
No. of respondents	16 (51.6%)	15 (48.4%)	31 (3.0%)	157 (53.8%)	135 (46.2%)	292 (28.5%)	531 (51.9%)	492 (48.1%)	1023 (100%)

Table 12 The opinions of taxpayers relating to engagement in tax minimisation schemes by occupational groups

Despite the comparatively small percentage of tradespeople who responded to the survey, their opinions as to the fairness of engaging in tax minimisation schemes are distributed similarly to opinions of the overall population of respondents shown earlier—slightly opposed to the use of tax minimisation schemes.

On the other hand, professionals were slightly more opposed to the use of tax minimisation schemes. Of the professional group, 53.8 per cent were opposed to the use of tax minimisation schemes while 46.2 per cent considered the use of such schemes to be fair or very fair. It is noted that the ABC On-line (2007) survey data indicates a bias by professionals away from engaging in tax minimisation schemes in contrast with the CTSI (2002) survey data, which indicates a bias by professionals towards them.

ATO statistics do not provide a breakdown of occupations by postcode, and are therefore not useful in determining the population of Pilbara tradespeople

237 Statistics are only provided for those who gave an opinion, 330 respondents answered 'neither fair nor unfair' or did not express an opinion.

engaged in the mass-marketed tax avoidance schemes of the 1990s. However, 1997-98 ATO statistics indicate that nearly half of the taxable individuals involved in the mining industry resided in Western Australia. When combined with the ABS statistics of the same period it is likely that the principal occupation of taxpayers in the Pilbara region, in the 1990s, was that of tradespeople engaged in the mining industry.

The following section examines a factor closely related to occupation, namely working conditions.

Working conditions

The examination of the influence of occupation suggests that, in isolation, it may not be a strong factor in influencing taxpayer compliance behaviour. However occupation, which is often associated with taxpayer incomes and associated income tax rates, usually determines a taxpayer's working conditions. Bosco and Mittone found that 'heavy workers' had a tax evasion rate 50 per cent higher than that of 'light workers', and these conclusions may be significant in the current research.

This section therefore considers the impact of the working environment in the Pilbara on the decisions made by the blue-collar workers to engage in the mass-marketed tax avoidance schemes of the 1990s. It suggests that working conditions may have been a significant influence on those taxpayers' perceptions of fairness and their attitudes to tax compliance behaviour. Generally the work of blue-collar workers is carried out 'in the field' or in open workshops. Those workers are often not only subject to the harsh environmental conditions and dangers of their workplace, but also those of the climatic and geographical environment in which they are working. In particular, the blue-collar workers of the Pilbara are subject to extremes of heat and cold experienced in the climate of the region. It is suggested that the harshness of the working conditions of the Pilbara blue-collar workers had a significant influence in their decisions to seek methods to reduce their taxation liabilities.

Attitudes affecting taxpayers' compliance behaviour are not only affected by a physically harsh living environment and heavy working conditions but may be strengthened by working long hours. In the Pilbara, in the 1990s, the blue-collar workers were subject to both physically harsh environmental working conditions and a significant loss of leisure.

Long working hours lead to a loss of leisure time which may be viewed by taxpayers as increasing the harshness of working conditions. This book suggests there is a relationship between long working hours and taxpayers' attitudes towards the perception of a fair tax rate.

An ABS survey conducted in 2008 indicates that the hours worked by the interviewed participants in mass-marketed tax avoidance schemes were excessive when compared with the average number of hours worked by other employees. Western Australian employees generally worked 41.4 hours per week and the average for the mining industry was a little higher at 43.9 hours per week.[238] A number of respondents to the ABC On-line (2007) survey referred to long hours worked when expressing their opinion as to the fairness of tax rates.

The next table shows the percentage of respondents to the ABC On-line (2007) survey respondents who responded to the question: 'How hard do you work for your money?', on a scale of 1–5, where 5 equals 'very hard' and 1 equals 'not hard at all'.

Scale	Number	Percentage
5 (very hard)	392	29.0
4	437	32.3
3 (moderately hard)	255	18.8
2	99	7.3
1 (not hard at all)	169	12.5

Table 13 ABC On-line (2007) survey respondents' perception of their work

Just over 80 per cent of respondents to the ABC On-line (2007) survey considered they worked moderately hard to very hard for their money. Less than one in eight considered they did not work hard at all. Supporting comments made by the survey respondents to the question show that the number who related hard work with their choice of tax rate was comparatively small. However, an opinion expressed by one respondent was straight forward and simple: 'The harder I work for my money the less I am inclined to share it.'

Unfortunately, neither the ATO statistics nor the CTSI (2002) survey include questions as to hours worked or leisure time and data from those sources are not available for examination.

238 Australian Bureau of Statistics, 6306.0 – Employee Earnings and Hours, Australia Aug 2008, (2009).

Examination of the available statistical data suggests that heavy working conditions in terms of long working hours may have had a significant influence on the decisions of blue-collar workers of the Pilbara to engage in the mass-marketed tax avoidance schemes of the 1990s. The remainder of this section examines the strength of that influencing factor through analysis of semi-structured interviews with members of Cohort 1 – blue-collar workers of the Pilbara region who participated in the schemes. Their responses are also compared to interviewees of the other three cohorts of interviewees.

It is notable that all interviewees in Cohort 1 said they worked hard for their money. Further, all of them pointed to long hours at work to support that opinion. Most of them claimed to work long hours, as many as 84 hours a week. By comparison the fewer hours worked by the interviewees of Cohort 2 (those in similar occupations) and Cohort 3 (those who earn similar remunerations) strongly aligns with the findings of Bosco and Mittone who compared the tax compliance behaviour of 'light' workers with 'heavy' workers based on the amount of hours input for similar remuneration.

As an example, one interviewee stated:

> At that stage, in the 90s and that I was on call 24 / 7 and I was putting in something like about 15 hours a day maybe, 17 hours a day sometimes. I was on the go all the time, physically and mentally. I was reasonably stressed and during holidays you were contacted. So even on holidays, if you had a phone—you were still contacted.

When asked to clarify the number of hours a week worked the interviewee replied:

> Then 84 probably, yeah no that might be a bit of an exaggeration. Maybe not that great, but in excess of 70 hours a week.

Given there are only 168 hours in a week and time taken by the physiological demands of eating and sleeping must be considered, there can be little or no time allocated to leisure by these interviewees. Brown noted the equilibrium of hours of leisure and works hours and attempted to measure the relationship. Though the influence of leisure was not specifically researched in this study, it is the converse of working hours and therefore is considered in this examination of working conditions. A lack of leisure time appeared as a consistent factor with all mass-marketed tax avoidance schemes participants interviewed.

A typical work regime in the Pilbara was illustrated by one of those interviewees:

> We were on 12 hour shifts so you are on two days, maybe three days and change over to maybe three or four nights and the following week you might do four days three nights and then a bit of a break and you were on 12 hour days and nights.

The impact of long working hours was further detailed by another interviewee who said:

> It's not so bad for me but the other blokes can't see their kids or anything. The way that we work, three days are on nights. You take off around 5.30 and you're home at daybreak for breakfast. You have a shower something to eat and you go to bed. You wake up at 4.30 and you start all over again. Then you have three days on day shift and you start at 5.30 in the morning and it's after half past seven when you get home. Same thing then you have a shower, grab something to eat and go to bed cos you've got to get up at half past four the next morning.

Their working hours are virtually double that of the average Australian worker and significantly more than ABS reports for the mining industry generally.[239] By working up to twice the length of time of the average Australian worker, the blue-collar workers of the Pilbara region earn more than twice as much as their counterparts in other regions and industries. However the progressive Australian taxation rates result in those workers paying far more taxation than their counterparts.

A statement by a blue-collar worker in the Pilbara region illustrates his view of a relationship between working conditions and his perception of a fair income tax rate. When questioned as to what he was considered to be a fair rate of tax, he included his working conditions in his response. He replied, 'A lot less than that [48 per cent], we work a lot of hours in the heat and shit. We vote, so why should we have to pay more tax for where we work?'

Three interviewees referred to the climatic extremes of the Pilbara region and a further two specifically considered a lack of social amenities when forming their opinions of 'hard work'. A typical statement outlining the attitude of blue-collar workers in the Pilbara is as follows:

> I mean you know you're working out in the outskirts not in the metropolis of Perth or anything and you work hard and the conditions are a lot harder there. The hours are usually longer and I suppose you haven't got the hospital and medical schemes and facilities that they have in Perth or a major city.

---

239 Reported as 43.9 hours per week for the mining industry in August 2008.

The combination of the long hours, harsh climatic conditions, isolation and lack of social amenities in influencing tax compliance attitudes was crystallised by an interviewee who said:

> In the 1990s I did a bit of blast crew where you're out with drills and stuff on the ground and you work in 48 degrees some days. Yeah, a lot of it sometimes I'd be in a machine with an air-conditioned cab but you're in and out of the machine sort of on a fairly regular basis. Yeah in summertime up here, we get up to, I think the record up here was 49.5 degrees and we didn't knock off for that. Yeah no it gets quite hot, very dry, yeah dust, very dusty, like our iron ore dust. Yep it is by no means, a bloody, a cushy number.
>
> But yeah if I suppose, you came from the city or to be honest with myself I grew up in similar environments and stuff and that and it's been my life like, the bush and a little bit of going without stuff has always been my life and I quite enjoy harsh conditions but yeah it's not sitting in an air-conditioned office no. If that Is where you are coming from?
>
> But it's not like and yeah but I'm not sure that it's not so much the job and the environment of the work, but it is the fact that it's also part of the job is living here like in the Pilbara you know like? And my family are living here with me in similar conditions. Not that we go without a great deal but it is definitely not like living in the city. You know like, my family has gone without stuff no doubt from living out here.

Another interviewee, from Pannawonica, summed up the response to the question 'Do you think you work hard for your money?' by saying: 'Yeah I do. We put in bloody long days and nights. In the summer it's stinking hot and it's freezing cold in the winter and we can't go nowhere if you could knock off.'

Yet another interviewee from Cohort 1 referred to his working conditions in elaborating on why he considered he worked hard for his money, said:

> Oh we were out in the open. Sometimes un-air-conditioned. Sometimes working in air-conditioned space, going from one air-conditioned space to another. In some instances so you are looking at 40 plus, 45 plus out in the open, depending on the jobs you were doing.

However, when asked if his working conditions had any influence on his participation in the mass-marketed tax avoidance schemes he replied, 'probably not'.

Generally all of the interviewees of Cohort 1 considered the tax concessions granted for harsh climatic conditions, isolation and lack of social amenities as being inadequate to the point of being irrelevant. An example of how they felt about the adequacy of tax concessions is the following statement:

> It's [the Remote Area Taxation Allowance] not even it's just the difference of a tank of fuel. Put it this way, for the amount of tax I was putting into the big bucket, I don't think that our concessions in the North West matched those of people who had the benefits they had down south or anywhere.

All interviewees in Cohort 2 expressed the opinion that they worked hard for their money and also pointed to long hours as the cause. However they didn't feel that they worked especially hard in the physical sense. One interviewee suggested a fair exchange of work to remuneration: 'Yeah well I feel I do an honest day's work for what I get. It's certainly not hard work, not hard physical work but I yeah I do an honest day for what I get.'

There were other factors considered by interviewees in Cohort 2. These included inherent dangers in the job. An interviewee pointed to the dangers of working with fast moving machinery:

> There are virtually things that I don't go near, that I don't touch, particularly rotating machinery and squirrel-caged alternators and stuff that you can stick your hands in and get very killed, very quickly.

Another interviewee, who considered he worked moderately hard for his money, referred to others who, in his opinion, worked even harder. In reference to high income earning tradespeople he said:

> Because people who, employees who, earn that much money work very hard for it. They don't get it for nothing, they work longer hours and that sort of thing, you know? Well let's say people working in the outback. Outback—rural Australia.

Nine of the 10 interviewees comprising Cohort 3 considered they worked hard for their money and pointed to hours of work as the reason. It is noted that their hours worked were between 37.5 and 50 hours per week, around half of those stated by the interviewees in Cohort 1. The comparison of hours worked by the two cohorts for around the same remuneration strongly supports the findings of Bosco and Mittone's research which compared 'light' workers to 'heavy' workers based on the amount of hours input for the same remuneration.

One interviewee of Cohort 3 referred to extreme climatic conditions as influencing his opinion as to hard work. He worked within the mining industry however he was not based in the Pilbara region. Two referred to high levels of stress relating to senior management positions.

Five of the six interviewees of Cohort 4 (Other Taxpayers) were participants in mass-marketed tax avoidance schemes. The sixth said he was not, however he said that was due to him having a low Australian income in the 1990s. He said he would have participated in the schemes if he had had to pay Australian income

tax. They all referred to long working hours as the reason influencing their decision to engage in the schemes and one added climatic conditions as a factor. It is also noted that four of the six were professionals working in the Pilbara in the 1990s and were closely associated with the blue-collar workers engaged in the mining industry at the time. They had worked the same hours as the interviewees of Cohort 1, though in slightly better physical conditions.

The examination of opinions supports the findings of available statistical data and points strongly to a correlation between working conditions and tax compliance behaviour. The general view of all of those respondents to the ABC On-line (2007) survey, and interviewees in this research, was that those who work hard for their money should pay a lesser tax rate.

It appears that this sentiment applies not only to the taxpayers themselves, but extends to others. The sole interviewee of Cohort 3 who considered he did not work hard for his money said, 'My Dad probably pays too much, but Alan Bond[240] probably doesn't pay enough'. He implied that his father worked 'hard' but Alan Bond didn't.

This examination suggests there is a strong correlation between working conditions and taxpayers' attitudes towards the perception of a fair tax rate. Attitudes affecting taxpayer compliance behaviour are not only affected by a physically harsh environment and heavy working conditions but are further strengthened by long working hours. Long working hours lead to a loss of leisure which is viewed by taxpayers as increasing the harshness of their working conditions.

In the Pilbara, in the 1990s, the blue-collar workers were subject to both a physically harsh living environment, coupled with heavy working conditions, and a significant loss of leisure. It is suggested that the physical harshness of the working conditions of the Pilbara blue-collar workers was a significant influence in their decisions to seek out methods to reduce their taxation liabilities.

Income

Previous research explored in Chapter Three indicates that high incomes have a negative influence on tax compliance. The table showing average income comparisons of taxpayers examined in the research compares the incomes of

240 An Australian entrepreneur of the 1980s. Despite his achievements of fame and fortune, from beginning as an immigrant sign writer to becoming one of Australia's richest men and winner of the America's Cup, Alan Bond was ultimately jailed for fraud.

interviewees with data from available statistics. It is not intended as a statistical analysis, as used to support scientific research, but it is provided in this book to give background and context to the research groups studied in this book.

Taxpayer group	Mean average annual income
MMTAS participants	
Cohort 1 (1990s)[241]	$ 94 750
Cohort 4 (1990s)[242]	$ 87 600
CTSI survey (2002)	$ 72 870
Non-participants	
ATO Pilbara (2002)	$ 55 295
ATO Western Australia (2002)	$ 38 330
ATO Australia (2002)	$ 39 254
ABS Pilbara (2001)	$ 30 368
ABS Western Australia (2001)	$ 19 500
ABS Australia (2001)	$ 19 500
ABC On-line (2007) survey	$ 44 930
Cohort 2 (1990s)	$ 51 000
Cohort 3 (1990s)	$ 73 400

Table 14 Average income comparisons of taxpayers examined in the research

Not only did the Pilbara blue-collar workers who engaged in avoidance activities (Cohort 1) have incomes over 85 per cent higher than their counterparts who did not (Cohort 2 non-mining industry tradespeople) but the table indicates they earned 30 per cent more than the participants in mass-marketed tax avoidance

241 As estimated by interviewees. No independent audit of interviewees incomes were conducted but the estimated annual gross incomes for the years 1996–1999 appeared to be in line with their rank and occupations for Pilbara workers at that time. For example, a maritime officer on a tug in Dampier estimated that he was paid between $80 000 and $84 000; a maintenance supervisor suggested his gross annual income was between $95 000 and $100 000; and a plant operator working 84 hours a week was certain his gross income was just over $100 000.

242 Four of the six interviewees were participants in mass-marketed tax avoidance schemes. Their average annual income was $ 103 000.

schemes who were surveyed by CTSI in 2002. It also indicates that professionals in the Pilbara who participated in mass-marketed tax avoidance schemes (Cohort 4) earned more than the other professionals of Cohort 3 who were not.

Income tax rates

Australia has progressive individual income tax rates where taxpayers pay higher tax rates on higher incomes. This book suggests that the strength of the influence of income is determined, in part, by that relationship to income tax rates.

To assess the impact of income tax rates, taxpayers' opinions as to what constitutes a 'fair' tax rate will presently be examined. It is suggested that the further a taxpayer's actual tax rate strays from his or her perception of a 'fair' tax rate, then the less likely the taxpayer is to comply with taxing authorities and to pay tax.

The general tax rate for individual Australian residents from 1994 to 2000 is shown in the table below to provide appropriate context.

Taxable income **$**	**Tax payable** **$**
0–5 400	Nil
5 401–20 700	Nil + 20% of excess over 5 400
20 701–38 000	3 060 + 34% of excess over 20 700
38 001–50 000	8 942 + 43% of excess over 38 000
50 001 +	14 102 + 47% of excess over 50 000

Table 15 General income tax rates for individual Australian taxpayers 1994–2000

A levy of 1.5 per cent for the Medicare health insurance system is added to the tax on incomes over $14 649, which takes the effective highest tax rate for a resident individual to 48.5 per cent in this period.

However, the manner in which progressive tax rates are applied means that a taxpayer with an income in excess of $38 000 has an average tax rate of less than 43 per cent. For example, from 1994 to 2000, the 'average' Australian taxpayer, with an assessable income of $39,254, would have incurred an income tax liability of $9,481.[243] His or her average tax rate is therefore only 24.2 per cent. It is noted that that tax rate is within the preferred income tax rates for nearly two-thirds of

243 Excluding the Medicare levy of 1.5 per cent and assuming no rebates.

respondents to the ABC On-line (2007) survey shown in the table showing ABC On-line (2007) survey respondents' perception of a fair tax rate.

To assess how taxpayers feel about their tax rates, respondents to the ABC On-line (2007) survey were asked 'How fair is the tax rate that you pay?'. Their responses are shown in the table showing ABC On-line (2007) survey respondents' perception of fairness of their current personal tax rate in the previous section dealing with perceptions of fairness.

The responses reveal a bias of opinion towards their personal tax rates being fair. The responses indicate 44.5 per cent of respondents considered their tax rate as fair or very fair whereas only 30.3 per cent believed their tax rate to be unfair or very unfair.

Respondents to the ABC On-line (2007) survey were then asked 'What do you think is a fair rate of tax?'. The following table shows the distribution of their answers.

Question 11. What do you think is a fair tax rate?		
Fair tax rate	**Number of respondents**	**Respondents (%)**
Less than10 %	174	12.86
11 to 20%	304	22.47
21 to 30%	406	30.01
31 to 40%	158	11.68
41 to 50%	30	2.22
51 to 60%	10	0.74
61 to 70%	1	0.07
71 to 80%	0	0.00
81 to 90%	1	0.07
Greater than 91%	0	0.00
No answer	269	19.88
Total	**1353**	**100.00**

Table 16 ABC On-line (2007) survey respondents' perception of a fair tax rate

The table indicates that just over 77 per cent of the respondents chose a 'fair' tax rate of less than 40 per cent. Further, 65.34 per cent of respondents preferred a rate of less than 30 per cent, which was the company tax rate at the time.

From a comparison of the ABC On-line (2007) survey, respondents' opinions of a fair tax rate shown in the table above, and the Australian tax rates shown in the previous table, it may be assumed that most Australian taxpayers with incomes over $38,000, and therefore with marginal tax rates in excess of 43 per cent, may not have been happy with their marginal tax rates in the 1990s.

Further, based on the same opinions expressed by respondents to the ABC On-line (2007) survey, the blue-collar workers of the Pilbara region, with average incomes of $94,750 and their associated personal tax rates being 47 per cent, may have been extremely dissatisfied with their marginal tax rate and influenced toward non-compliant tax behaviour.

This book looks further to investigate if there is a relationship between taxpayers' opinions of 'working hard' and their preferred rates of income tax. Therefore respondents to the ABC On-line (2007) survey were asked to elaborate on their particular choice of tax rate.

However, it appears from the ABC On-line (2007) survey data that taxpayers do not necessarily relate hard work to their preferred tax rate. Eight of the 169 respondents who considered they did not work hard at all considered their tax rate very unfair and chose a preferred tax rate of less than 20 per cent.

The table showing ABC On-line (2007) survey respondents' perception of their work reveals that only 392 of the 1,353 respondents (29.0 per cent) considered they worked very hard for their money. Further, of those 392, 38 thought the rate of tax they were paying was very fair. In addition only 93 of the 1,353 (6.9 per cent) of them identified 'working hard' as their reason for their choice of tax rate.

This book looks further at the opinions of those 93 and the table below shows the distribution of tax rates chosen by them.

Preferred tax rate	Number of respondents	Percentage
31–40 %	6	6.5
21–30 %	20	21.5
11–20 %	40	43.0
0–10 %	27	29.0
Total	**93**	**100.0**

Table 17 ABC On-line (2007) survey 'hard workers' choice of personal tax rate

This examination indicates that taxpayers do not necessarily relate physically harsh working conditions to their preferred personal tax rates. It is also reasonable to assume that some taxpayers simply do not wish to pay tax regardless of the rate or the manner in which they earn their income. However, heavy working conditions combined with high incomes and associated high personal tax rates, may have had some impact in mass-marketed tax avoidance schemes participation rates demonstrated by the blue-collar workers of the Pilbara region in the 1990s.

The data provided from the ABC On-line (2007) survey are now compared to the opinions expressed by interviewees to the semi-structured interviews conducted in this research. The next table shows the responses by those interviewees who were also asked if they thought they were paying a fair rate of tax.

Do you believe you are paying a fair rate of tax?				
Cohort	Number	Yes	No	Maybe
1	11	2	8	1
2	10	5	5	
3	10	3	6	1
4	6	1	5	

Table 18 Interviewees' perception of fairness of their personal tax rate

The responses of Cohort 2 are reasonably consistent with the ABC On-line (2007) survey results. The taxpayers of this group, from the general population of taxpayers, are evenly divided in their opinions. The interviewees in Cohort 3 are high income earners and their responses are also reasonably consistent with the ABC On-line (2007) survey results which suggest that high personal tax rates influence the perception of a 'fair tax rate'. However Cohort 1, which consists entirely of mass-marketed tax avoidance schemes participants, shows a strong bias towards the view that they were paying an unfair personal tax rate. Interviewees in Cohort 4, most of whom participated in mass-marketed tax avoidance schemes, also indicate the bias shown by Cohort 1.

The following table shows Taxpayer income, tax rate and mass-marketed tax avoidance scheme participation rates of the groups of taxpayers examined in this research. It compares the tax rates of the taxpayer groups in this research. By calculating the 'average' tax rates of the groups of taxpayers considered in the table of ABC On-line (2007) survey respondents' perception of their work,[244] those

244 ABS census data is not included in this table as not all respondents to the census are taxpayers. In addition the census does not include questions as to tax compliance therefore the number of participants in mass-marketed tax avoidance schemes cannot be ascertained using census data.

taxpayers are placed in order of an actual tax rate[245] and can be compared with the 'preferred' tax rates in the table of ABC On-line (2007) survey respondents' perception of a fair tax rate above.

Taxpayer group	Mean average annual income ($)	Average tax ($)	Average tax rate %	MMTAS participants %
Cohort 4 MMTAS[246]	103 000	40 557	39.37	100
Cohort 1 (1990s)[247]	94 750	36 555	38.58	100
Cohort 3 (1990s)[248]	73 400	26 201	35.70	nil
CTSI survey (2002)	72 870	25 944	35.60	100
ATO Pilbara (2002)	55 295	17 420	31.50	6
Cohort 2 (1990s)[249]	51 000	14 572	30.00	nil
ABC On-line (2007) survey[250]	44 930	12 596	28.03	n / a
ATO Australia (2002)	39 254	10 785	27.47	0.39
ATO Western Australia (2002)	38 330	9 659	25.20	1.64
Cohort 4 Non-MMTAS	25 000	4 897	19.59	nil

Table 19 Taxpayer income, tax rate and mass-marketed tax avoidance scheme participation rates of the groups of taxpayers examined in this research.

The typical Pilbara taxpayer during that time with an income of $55,295 incurred an income tax liability of $17,420 or 31.5 per cent, which approaches the level of dissatisfaction indicated in the table showing taxpayers' preferred tax rate. According to the CTSI (2002) data, the tax rate of mass-marketed tax avoidance schemes participants was 35.6 per cent. The average tax rate of the blue-collar workers who participated in the mass-marketed tax avoidance schemes and were

245 Calculated using the schedule of general income tax rates for individual Australian taxpayers, 1994–2000.

246 Cohort 4 has been broken down into schemes participants and non-participants. Four of the six interviewees were participants in mass-marketed tax avoidance schemes and their average annual income was $ 103 000. The remaining two were not mass-marketed tax avoidance schemes participants and their average annual income was $ 25 000.

247 As estimated by interviewees.

248 As estimated by interviewees.

249 As estimated by interviewees.

250 Of those who indicated their personal weekly income (1151: missing 202).

interviewed in this research was 38.6 per cent and almost at the limit of the 'preferred' tax rate. The table above suggests that the relationship of income tax rates to tax compliance behaviour may be quite strong. The blue-collar workers of the Pilbara region in the 1990s were certainly within the ranges of income and income tax rates which this research indicates may lead to non-compliant behaviour.

However, they may not be the only influencing factors. It is noted that the professional group in Cohort 3, whose incomes and income tax rates were marginally below those of the participants in mass-marketed tax avoidance schemes of the Pilbara region, did not participate in the schemes. Further their average incomes and income tax rates are above that of the participants, according to CTSI survey (2002) data.

It is therefore suggested that a number of factors combined to influence the decisions of the blue-collar workers of the Pilbara region to participate in the mass-marketed tax avoidance schemes. The interaction of the influence of high incomes and their associated income tax rates together with a physically harsh living environment and heavy working conditions is further explored in the concluding Chapter Five.

Economic habits

The ethnographic narrative contained in Chapter One describes the lifestyles and economic habits of the permanent Pilbara population. It indicates that the blue-collar workers in the Pilbara tend to direct their high disposable income towards increased spending on consumer goods and leisure activities rather than savings and investment. Their economic choices are unlike the spending habits of their occupational peers, who do not have the same levels of disposable income, or the professional groups, who tend to invest their 'excess' disposable incomes in long-term financial securities or real property.

Many of the blue-collar workers interviewed in Cohort 1 indicated that, despite living in the Pilbara for over 20 years and earning higher than average incomes, they had little or no extra financial security in the longer term. As they had adopted the economic habits described and spent their 'excess' income, the only additional source of revenue for investment was by way of diverting taxation liabilities.

It is noted that eleven of the fifteen interviewees who had participated in mass-marketed tax avoidance schemes referred to their participation in the schemes as 'investments'. A typical answer to the question 'Why did you enter the scheme?' was, 'Well it did reduce tax but it was also an investment as well. You know we got a portfolio and all the rest of the shit that came with it.' However, another interviewee ignored the taxation perspective when he said:

> Well basically I had money for the first time in my life. I had money that I called investing money. It was money that I didn't need to live or survive on and so at the time I was looking around for good investments to get into.

Two of the six professionals in Cohort 4 who had participated in mass-marketed tax avoidance schemes also referred to the schemes as 'investments'. One commented he was investigating investment opportunities when he was approached by a promoter. He said 'the tax effectiveness made the investment "sweeter" but was not a motivating factor. The approach from the promoter came at a merely convenient time.'

Therefore despite the Pilbara blue-collar workers having higher than average incomes, their high consumer spending habits left little for long-term investments. The Pilbara blue-collar workers spent their 'excess' income on higher costs of living and recreational pursuits and therefore had no further funds for 'investing'. Reducing their tax liability was their only remaining source of funds for investments. This suggests that the economic habits of the Pilbara blue-collar workers may also have had an influence on their decisions to engage in the mass-marketed tax avoidance schemes of the 1990s. The impact of economic habits was a factor which the promoters of the schemes exploited.

Summary of economic factors

This book suggests that a key economic factor which may determine the strength of influence of all other economic factors is that of occupation. Not only does occupation often determine a person's working conditions, income, and in Australia, income tax rates and economic habits, but it is often closely associated with many socio-psychological factors such as peer influence, risk aversion, social class and social distance. It is submitted that those factors act to influence a taxpayer's perceptions of fairness of the taxation system and willingness to pay tax.

The attitudes of taxpayers from a range of occupations have been examined in this section. In particular, comparisons have been made between those of the professional class of worker and the blue-collar workers (tradespeople) who are the focus of this research. Survey data examined in this research indicated that the perception of fairness of using tax minimisation schemes is generally evenly distributed between those who consider it fair and those who consider using the schemes unfair.

It is noted that while the ABC On-line (2007) survey data indicated that professionals show a slight bias away from the use of tax minimisation schemes, the CTSI (2002) data indicated a bias by professionals towards participating in the mass-marketed tax avoidance schemes of the 1990s.

No occupational group of taxpayers surveyed indicated a bias towards the participating tax minimisation schemes to the same extent as that exhibited by the blue-collar workers of the Pilbara in the 1990s. This is despite some of those groups, and in particular the professional workers, being at similar levels of income and subject to the same rates of personal income tax as the blue-collar workers of the Pilbara region.

The key influencing factor, which was also influenced by their occupation, is that of the working environment experienced by the blue-collar workers living in the Pilbara in the 1990s. This book suggests that the extreme physically harsh living environment and heavy working conditions led to the blue-collar workers adopting economic habits which eroded their significantly higher than average incomes. Despite enduring those harsh conditions for many years the blue-collar workers had little economic benefit to compensate for those privations.

It is suggested that the economic factors of working as blue-collar tradespeople in the Pilbara in the 1990s led to them receiving incomes significantly higher than their counterparts in the wider Australian community. However, those incomes required them to live and work in an extremely harsh physical and social environment. In turn the blue-collar workers developed economic habits which led to them having very little improvement in their economic status despite long-term employment in the mining industry of the Pilbara region.

The mass-marketed tax avoidance schemes of the 1990s proffered an opportunity to increase or establish their wealth, and to provide for a 'better' future for their families. Income tax was the only economic expenditure that had not been exploited as a revenue source for those 'investments'. The opportunity to 'invest' rather than endure their taxation burden provided a very susceptible market to the designers and promoters of the mass-marketed tax avoidance schemes.

4.4. Summary

This book has suggested that a range of factors may have influenced the tax compliance attitudes of the blue-collar workers of the Pilbara in the 1990s. The figure illustrating the pattern of tax scheme development in Chapter Two was provided to suggest the cyclical pattern of tax avoidance scheme development in Australia. It is further suggested that in the 1990s Australia was in a period of tax scheme design and growth in that cycle.

This chapter examined the factors influencing taxpayer compliance behaviour as shown in the review conducted in Chapter Three. To conduct the examination this chapter broadly grouped the influencing factors into the economic market force drivers of supply and demand.

Firstly, the section that dealt with the supply drivers (principally legal and administrative factors) suggested that the taxpayers of the Pilbara were subjected to considerable marketing activity conducted by the designers and promoters of the tax avoidance schemes. In particular it looked at the activities of promoters and tax professionals. It is suggested that the promoters exploited many of the other influencing factors examined in this book to market their 'products'. In particular favourable, and arguably sometimes misleading, legal opinions were used extensively as promotional tools to attract the blue-collar workers to participate in the schemes.

The complexity of the taxation system, which increased the influence of tax professionals, peer influence and a high level of social and physical isolation created a market that mass-marketed tax avoidance schemes promoters were quick to identify and exploit. The complexity of the taxation system was further exploited in at least one case for the promoters and designers to design and promote schemes which defrauded taxpayers of their tax credits.

Administrative delays facilitated an opportunity for tax professionals and scheme promoters to develop and market the mass-marketed tax avoidance schemes unimpeded for a number of years. The apparent lack of administrative action to close the schemes may have created an assumption on the part of the blue-collar workers that the mass-marketed tax avoidance schemes were valid. Therefore the combination of the influence of tax professionals and the administrative delays served to reduce their concerns as to the illegitimacy of tax avoidance schemes.

Examination of ATO statistics, as illustrated in Figure 5 in Chapter One, appear to indicate that, in the mid 1990s, the supply-driven market forces reached a 'tipping point'. It appears that those market forces were overtaken by taxpayer (consumer) demand forces and the resulting 'surge' in the schemes was detected by the ATO. Accordingly this chapter then looked at those demand-driven (demographic, socio-psychological and economic) factors that may have intensified the non-compliant taxpayer behavioural posture demonstrated by those taxpayers.

The sections which considered the demand-driven factors commenced with an examination of available statistical data of demographic factors. Previous research indicated that comparatively younger, less educated and male-dominated communities as found in the Pilbara region tend towards non-compliant behaviour generally and tax non-compliance in particular. Therefore it examined those factors identified as being significant to the population of blue-collar workers of the Pilbara region in the 1990s.

This examination of ABS census data suggested that the demographic factors of age, education and gender may have been factors in influencing taxpayer compliance behaviour in the Pilbara in the 1990s. Generally the demographic structure of the population of taxpayers of the Pilbara region in the 1990s implied that they would have tended towards non-compliant tax behaviour.

However, statistical data provided by the CTSI (2002) survey was also examined. That data indicated that generally the participants in mass-marketed tax avoidance schemes tended to be older and more educated taxpayers. Further while a high proportion of the participants in 1990s mass-marketed tax avoidance schemes in the Pilbara region were male, attitudes towards tax avoidance activity shown by respondents to the ABC On-line (2007) survey revealed that acceptance of tax minimisation schemes by females is only marginally less than by males. This book suggested that the over-representation of males engaged in mining activities in the Pilbara region and the high participation rates of males in the mass-marketed tax avoidance schemes was more a coincidence than an indication of gender bias towards non-compliant behaviour. It is also found that taxpayers tend to be evenly divided in their opinion as to the fairness of the use of tax minimisation schemes to reduce tax.

This chapter moved from examining available statistical data to asking taxpayers, by way of semi-structured interviews, their opinions on the operations of the mass-marketed tax avoidance schemes. Analysis of responses by participants in the semi-structured interviews conducted in this research suggested that demographic factors may not have been central to the behaviour of the blue-collar workers of the Pilbara in the 1990s. It is therefore considered that the influence of demographic factors by themselves did not satisfactorily explain the phenomenon that this book investigates.

Further, in addition to considering the influence of demographic factors, the attitudes and opinions expressed by interviewees who participated in mass-marketed tax avoidance schemes were compared with those of other taxpayers of similar occupations and incomes from outside the Pilbara. The interviews considered a range of matters which included questions as to why the interviewees participated in the schemes, and if not, why not.

This chapter suggests that the perception of fairness is an overarching factor and is central to influencing taxpayer compliance behaviour. Perceptions of fairness are greatly influenced by socio-psychological factors such as social distance and peer influence, which are in turn influenced by social class and occupation. It also suggests that the impacts of risk aversion, penalties and audit rates alone may have little strength of influence but may be greatly affected by peer influence.

Groups of influencing people may be occupational (work colleagues) or social (family and friends). The influence of work colleagues, particularly in the case of the isolated communities of blue-collar workers of the Pilbara, acted to increase social distance and exacerbated the feeling of isolation from mainstream Australian society and arguably led to a resistance to paying tax.

It appears that working and living conditions may have been a significant influence on taxpayers' attitudes to perceptions of fairness and in particular their view of a 'fair' tax rate. The research found that the blue-collar workers of the Pilbara region work considerably longer than the average blue-collar worker and in very harsh climatic and social conditions.

However, it appeared that heavy working conditions, considered in isolation, may not have been a significant influence contributing towards tax avoidance behaviour. Social distance from government, in particular in the isolated and remote community of Pannawonica, appears to have strengthened the influence of taxpayers' perceptions of fairness.

In addition to the examination of the demand-driven demographic and socio-psychological factors, economic factors that influence taxpayer compliance behaviour have been examined in this chapter. This chapter considered how high income tax rates experienced by the blue-collar workers of the Pilbara could have been a significant influencing factor in their decisions to engage in mass-marketed tax avoidance schemes in the 1990s. It was found, perhaps unsurprisingly, that as income tax rates rose, taxpayer compliance fell.

Another impact of the physically harsh climatic and heavy working conditions experienced by the blue-collar workers of the Pilbara region was that they arguably encouraged the blue-collar workers to spend most of their additional disposable income on consumer goods and leisure activities to compensate for the privations of those conditions. That increased consumer spending resulted in the taxpayers of the Pilbara having reduced funds for long-term savings and investment, despite their higher than average incomes.

Therefore, to provide a source of funds for savings and investment as compensation for long-term residency in the Pilbara, the blue-collar workers were encouraged to participate in financial schemes designed to divert taxation payments to those 'investments'. Many taxpayers, and not only blue-collar workers but also professionals, in the Pilbara region in the 1990s, actively sought methods to reduce their tax liability and therefore engaged in the mass-marketed tax avoidance schemes. This tax avoidance activity was considerably evident in the extremely remote and inhospitable community of Pannawonica where the blue-collar workers demonstrated the highest propensity to engage in the mass-marketed tax avoidance schemes of the 1990s of any particular community in Australia.

The conclusions of this book are now presented in the final chapter. Chapter Six concludes the book by looking at the impact of the phenomenon of the mass-marketed tax avoidance schemes in the Pilbara region of the 1990s on taxpayer compliance behaviour, identifies limitations of the current research and suggests areas for further research into taxpayer compliance behaviour.

5. CHAPTER FIVE: REVIEW, ACADEMIC CONTRIBUTION AND SUGGESTED AREAS FOR FURTHER RESEARCH

'I consider in a Christian country it is an immoral and outrageous act to tax me because I am living in holy matrimony instead of as my husband's mistress.'

Marie Charlotte Carmichael Stopes,
British scientist and birth-control campaigner (1880–1958)

5.1. Introduction

This book has investigated the phenomenon, described in Chapter One, of the exceptionally high participation rates of the blue-collar workers of the Pilbara region in Western Australia in the mass-marketed tax avoidance schemes of the 1990s. It has focused on the narratives of a range of taxpayers to establish an understanding of their tax compliance behaviour.

The findings of Chapter Four suggest that a combination of taxpayer compliance behavioural factors influenced those taxpayers to participate in tax avoidance activity. Specifically, it concluded that the physically harsh living environment and heavy working conditions, combined with high personal income tax rates were the chief drivers which may have caused blue-collar workers of the Pilbara region to enthusiastically participate in the mass-marketed tax avoidance schemes.

This chapter concludes the book. It begins by reviewing the book and then describes its contribution to the literature before acknowledging the limitations of the research and providing suggested areas for further research.

5.2. Review

Chapter One examined the participation rates of the blue-collar workers of the Pilbara region of Western Australia in the mass-marketed tax avoidance schemes of the 1990s. As well as outlining the design and conduct of the research, it included an ethnographic study of the taxpayers of the Pilbara region to provide the necessary context and to assist with the understanding of the social, physical and economic influences present within the taxpayer community at that time.

It was demonstrated that the population of taxpayers in the region lived and worked in an inhospitable physical and social environment at a time when mass-marketed tax avoidance schemes were being promoted in the region. In particular, it revealed that the taxpayers of the remote mining community of Pannawonica were subject to an extremely harsh, physical and socially isolated living environment as well as heavy working conditions. It was those taxpayers who had the highest participation rates in the mass-marketed tax avoidance schemes of the communities examined in this research.

Chapter One also highlighted the fact that the mining industry offered remuneration to workers which was significantly higher than that usually paid for skilled and unskilled labour, in order to compensate for the privations of the Pilbara region. It suggested that, while the higher levels of remuneration attracted a significant workforce to the mining industry of the region, the blue-collar workers were also confronted with the highest personal income tax rates in the Australian tax system.

As a result of these high taxation rates, disposable income was considerably lower than the income levels that the high pre-tax remunerations promised. Therefore, despite earning much higher-than-average incomes for many years, being resident in such a remote and inhospitable environment resulted in many blue-collar workers of the Pilbara region apparently being no better off after tax than their colleagues who lived and worked in more clement regions of Australia.

In **Chapter Two,** a conceptual framework was developed and a distinction was made between the concepts of tax evasion, tax avoidance and tax planning. Those concepts were examined in some detail. This showed how tax avoidance scheme designers, administrators and taxpayers reacted to the changing legislative, social and economic circumstances and revealed an emerging cyclical pattern in the development and promotion of tax avoidance schemes.

That cyclical pattern was revealed that with each cycle, tax avoidance schemes evolved in accordance with changing economic, social and legislative boundaries. This also indicated a trend towards increasing complexity of the tax system with each cycle.

A history of tax avoidance schemes in Australia over a thirty year period from 1970 to 2000 was then presented, which traced the cycles of the development of tax avoidance schemes, from individually crafted financial arrangements tailored for high wealth individuals in the 1970s to the mass-produced tax avoidance schemes which were mass-marketed and available to all Australian taxpayers in the 1990s.

Chapter Three identified, from the extant literature, the taxpayer compliance behavioural factors which were investigated in this book. These factors were categorised into four major groups: demographic; socio-psychological; economic; and legal and administrative, in order to provide a structure for the research. A broad range of factors which influenced taxpayer compliance behaviour was covered. The discussion highlighted the factors most likely to have been significant in motivating the blue-collar workers of the Pilbara region to engage in the mass-marketed tax avoidance schemes of the 1990s.

Chapter Four considered the influencing factors identified in Chapter Three in the context of two broad economic categories—those factors which drive the **supply** of mass-marketed tax avoidance schemes and those factors that drive taxpayer **demand** to participate in tax avoidance activity.

In a similar way to the analysis of the findings in Chapter Two, Chapter Four suggested that supply-driven factors also emanated from a cycle directed towards complexity and subsequent increases in costs of compliance. It placed that cycle of supply-driven factors within the scheme design and growth stage, depicted in Chapter Two. It found that, at some point, supply-driven factors can 'tip' towards demand-driven factors. As noted by Braithwaite, 'what started out as supply driven has become demand driven.'

Chapter Four found that, despite the scheme, promoters marketed their 'products' very aggressively in the Pilbara region, but those marketing campaigns did not, of themselves, satisfactorily explain why the demand to participate in the schemes was markedly higher in the Pilbara communities than in the broader taxpayer population. Instead, it suggested that the 'target marketing' was a response to the high level of demand for the schemes and did not satisfactorily explain why the blue-collar workers were attracted to the schemes, as revealed in Chapter One. Therefore, after looking at the supply-driven factors, Chapter Four examined the demand-driven factors—demographic, socio-psychological and economic factors.

Firstly it examined the demographic structure of the Pilbara communities. Previous research had suggested that three particular key demographic factors—age, education and gender—may have influenced the population towards the non-compliant tax behaviour exhibited by the blue-collar workers in the 1990s. Therefore those factors were examined in detail. However, despite the suggestions in the previous research, this book suggested that those demographic factors had no identifiable influence on the mass-marketed tax avoidance schemes and participation rates exhibited by the Pilbara region's blue-collar workers.

The examination of socio-psychological factors found that those factors may have had an influence on the tax compliance attitudes adopted by the blue-collar workers of the Pilbara in the 1990s. In particular, feelings of social isolation and the peer influence of work colleagues may have been strong influences contributing towards participation in the schemes. It was also found that these issues combined with economic factors may have had the strongest influence of all of the factors on the participation rates of the blue-collar workers of the Pilbara region in the mass-marketed tax avoidance schemes of the 1990s.

It was suggested that the physically harsh living environment and heavy working conditions of the Pilbara region may have influenced the blue-collar workers' perceptions that their income tax rates were excessive and 'unfair'. Their physical isolation may have led to an increased perception of social distance, which in turn may have led to an increased resistance to paying tax. This may have promoted their desire to seek out ways "to reduce [their] tax and increase [their] wealth."

The relationship between incomes and the associated tax rates, and working and climatic conditions to participation rates in the mass-marketed tax avoidance schemes is depicted in the table below. This indicates that a trend exists which suggests that when high incomes, and their associated high income tax rates, are coupled with a physically harsh living environment and heavy working conditions, taxpayers may be inclined towards non-compliant tax behaviour. This combines the findings of the ethnographic narrative in Chapter One and the examination of available statistical information in Chapter Four.

Taxpayer group		Period	Mean average income	Average tax rate %	Working conditions	Climatic conditions	MMTAS participants %
1	Cohort 4 MMTAS[251]	1990s	$ 103 000	39.37	Very heavy	Very harsh	100
2	Cohort 1	1990s	$ 94 750[252]	38.58	Very heavy	Very harsh	100
3	Cohort 3	1990s	$ 73 400[253]	35.70	Moderate	Moderate	nil
4	CTSI survey	2002	$ 72 870	35.60	n / a	Harsh / Very harsh	100
5	ATO Pilbara	2002	$ 55 295	31.50	n / a	Very harsh	6
6	Cohort 2	1990s	$ 51 000[254]	30.00	Moderate	Moderate	nil
7	ABC On-line (2007) survey[255]	2007	$ 44 930	28.03	Moderate / Very heavy	n / a	n / a
8	ATO Australia	2002	$ 39 254	27.47	n / a	n / a	0.39
9	ATO WA	2002	$ 38 330	25.20	n / a	n / a	1.64
10	Cohort 4 Non-MMTAS	1990s	$ 25 000	19.59	Moderate	Moderate	nil

Table 20 Comparisons of income, income tax rates and working and climatic conditions to mass-marketed tax avoidance scheme participation rates

To provide a clearer depiction of the data, the following figure provides a graphic representation of the relationships depicted in the above table. In order to illustrate the position of each taxpayer group the group is represented by its number in the table.

251 Cohort 4 has been broken down into scheme participants (taxpayer group 1 in the table) and non-participants (taxpayer group 10 in the table). Four of the six interviewees were participants in mass-marketed tax avoidance schemes and their average annual income was $103,000. The remaining two were not mass-marketed tax avoidance schemes participants and their average annual income was $25,000.

252 As estimated by interviewees.

253 As estimated by interviewees.

254 As estimated by interviewees.

255 Of those who indicated their personal weekly income (1151: missing 202).

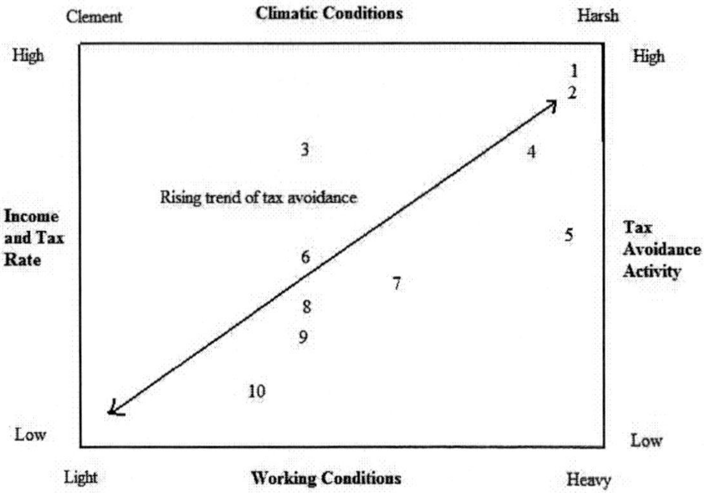

Figure 28 Tax avoidance activity trends

A trend emerges that suggests that when high incomes and associated high income tax rates are coupled with a physically harsh living environment and heavy working conditions, taxpayers may be influenced towards non-compliant tax behaviour (depicted by a position in the top right-hand part of the diagram). It also indicates that those factors may have been very strong influences on the tax compliance posture adopted by the blue-collar workers in the Pilbara region in the 1990s.

The trend indicated in the figure shows that taxpayers subjected to the combined influences of a physically harsh living environment and heavy working conditions, and high income and associated high income tax rates, exhibited the highest propensity toward mass-marketed tax avoidance schemes with regard to the participation of the groups of taxpayers surveyed in this research. In contrast, it also shows that those taxpayers in group 10, who were relatively poorly paid and who consequently paid lower tax rates, and who were carrying out light work in moderate climatic conditions showed little tendency toward tax avoidance activity.

The trend indicated by the examination of the available statistical data is supported by the analysis of the semi-structured interviews. That analysis led to the suggestion that the blue-collar workers of the Pilbara region were driven to engage in the mass-marketed tax avoidance schemes of the 1990s by the combination of two key motivational factors: high personal income tax rates and inhospitable living and tough, and sometimes heavy, working conditions.

Therefore, the combination of high personal income tax rates and harsh living and working conditions may have led to a perception by taxpayers that their levels of taxation were unfair, so accordingly they sought methods to reduce or eliminate their taxation burden.

This book extends the groups of taxpayers examined in the previous research to include the group of taxpayers being surveyed here—the blue-collar workers in Western Australia's mining regions. Taxpayers implicitly demonstrated their tax compliance behaviour as follows: "The harder taxpayers work for their income, the less willing they are to pay tax."

As indicated in Chapter One, a connection appears to exist between the physical and social environments of the remote communities of the Pilbara region and participation rates in mass-marketed tax avoidance schemes. When the tax avoidance scheme designers and promoters of the 1990s marketed their 'products' in the remote and harsh mining-based communities of the Pilbara region of Western Australia, they encountered a very enthusiastic demand.

5.3. Contribution to the literature

The findings of this book provide a contribution to the literature by way of adding four key understandings of taxpayer compliance behavioural influences.

Firstly, this book introduces the concept of the cyclical pattern of tax avoidance scheme development in Australia, illustrated in Chapter Two. It also suggests that this cycle of development is initially driven by the supply-driven factors examined in Chapter Four. It suggests that the 'hub' of mass-marketed tax avoidance schemes creation is located within the cyclical pattern of tax avoidance schemes at the scheme design and promotion stage, as illustrated in Chapter Four.

The incorporation of those concepts should assist taxation administrators in better understanding the formation and development of tax avoidance schemes and the likely level of tax avoidance activity within the economy at any given point in time.

Secondly, through an examination of the physical, social and economic environments of the taxpayers engaged in the mining industry of the Pilbara region of Western Australia, this book has provided a practical illustration of the theoretical principles developed by Bosco and Mittone. This book provides support for Bosco and Mittone's 1972 laboratory based findings that 'heavy workers' are more likely to evade tax than 'light workers'. It also supports Smith and Kinsey's 1980 findings that taxpayers are less willing to pay tax on income which involves 'extra effort'.

Thirdly, by examining the cases of individual taxpayers who participated in the mass-marketed tax avoidance schemes of the 1990s, and comparing their statements to those who did not, the book highlights how social factors strengthen taxpayer compliance attitudes. In the taxpayer population examined in this research, the overarching social factors of a physically harsh living environment and heavy working conditions, combined with the economic factor of high personal income tax rates, resulted in extremely high taxpayer resistance to paying tax.

Fourthly, and most importantly, this book enhances the manner by which research is conducted to improve our understanding of taxpayer compliance behaviour. It provides an insight into the transition of research methodology from an objective, scientific, empirical based data analysis to a subjective, sociological study of human behaviour.

This research represents a transition from a scientifically based, empirical study of taxpayer attitudes towards tax compliance and the payment of taxes to that of a sociological study of human behaviour and the influence of social networks. It demonstrates the value of sociological studies of human behaviour and the influence of social networks in trying to understand taxpayer compliance behaviour.

There is an examination in this research of how the combinations of factors affecting taxpayer compliance behaviour interrelate. In particular there is an analysis of the interrelationships between the influencing factors that vary with the physical, social and economic environments of taxpayers. Variations in taxpayers' environments provide a challenge to taxation administrators who may be tempted to attempt to establish uniformity in applying compliance rules within their jurisdictions. This book highlights the difficulties associated with applying uniform taxation rules in a jurisdiction as broad and as varied as Australia and its population. It therefore provides taxation administrators with an illustration of the impact of variations in the physical, social and economic micro-environments within the broader taxpayer community.

5.4. Research limitations

This book cautions that the proposition that the combination of high tax rates with a physically harsh living environment and heavy working conditions is an 'apparently' rational explanation for the phenomenon examined in this research. It does not suggest that it is the *only* explanation for the compliance behaviour exhibited by the blue-collar workers of the Pilbara region in the 1990s. A key problem in rationalising exhibited social behaviour is that there are many pathways and decision processes which had taken place before that behaviour was exhibited. Watts[256] suggests that it is only once an event has occurred that the circumstances leading to that event can be examined and rationalised.

The complexity of the network of possible decisions has led to the conclusions in this research that while it is suggested that the combination of influencing factors may have led to the high proportion of blue-collar workers in the Pilbara region who engaged in the mass-marketed tax avoidance schemes of the 1990s, that model cannot be relied on to predict future taxpayer compliance behaviour. Future events will be governed by the influence of future combinations of tax compliance factors. The decisions of future groups and individual taxpayers may lead in many directions. It is the unpredictability of the future that condemns tax administrators to be reactive rather than proactive in their responses to tax avoidance activity. It is impossible to address all possible outcomes of tax avoidance scheme designs and promotions.

It is suggested that the cyclical development of tax avoidance schemes, as illustrated in Chapter Two, introduces further complexity to the tax system as tax administrators attempt to predict and counter future tax avoidance schemes. This book suggests that the measures taken to counter tax avoidance scheme design and promotion by Australian tax administrators since 2000 are therefore likely to be circumvented by future scheme designers.

At some point, practicality requires research boundaries and limitations to be set. This study includes a discussion of possible significant taxpayer compliance behavioural influences which may have caused the blue-collar workers of the Pilbara region of Western Australia to enthusiastically participate in the mass-marketed tax avoidance schemes of the 1990s. This has been carried out by means of a series of interviews with the blue-collar workers of the mining-based

256 Duncan J Watts, Everything is Obvious: How Common Sense Fails, (2011).

industry in the 1990s who participated in mass-marketed tax avoidance schemes and groups of taxpayers in similar occupations or income streams who did not.

While this book has examined the available statistical data in order to provide corroborations and a background to its findings, a 'scientific approach' has not been the focus of this book. It has not used a scientific approach to the empirical study of reliable, randomly selected data that may be extrapolated to the attitudes and behaviour of the wider Australian population of taxpayers in a scientific manner. The statements and opinions expressed by interviewees are not intended to be extrapolated to the behavioural patterns exhibited by the wider community. For example, of the 42,000 participants who engaged in mass-marketed tax avoidance schemes, only 11 were interviewed here. It can also be acknowledged that the taxpayers interviewed in this research may have sought to present rational post-hoc explanations. Rather than admit that they had simply been caught up by the appeal of the mass-marketed tax avoidance schemes pedalled by the promoters, and enthusiastically supported by members of their social and economic groups, they may have looked for more rational explanations by referring to their high income tax rates and harsh working conditions.

There is no assertion here that the phenomenon being researched did not occur elsewhere in other taxing jurisdictions and or at other times. Similar experiences and tax compliance behavioural patterns were more than likely have occurred in other parts of Australia and the world in general. The examination of the available statistical data was provided only to give some background and context to the phenomenon of mass-marketed tax avoidance scheme participation rates by the blue-collar workers of the Pilbara region in the 1990s. Therefore, despite a thorough search of ATO statistics, indicating that participation in the mass-marketed tax avoidance schemes of the 1990s was highly focussed in the Pilbara region, it is possible that other communities may have exhibited similar tax compliance behavioural attitudes.

One further limitation is that the researcher's personal biases in conducting and examining transcripts of the semi-structured interviewees may have also created avenues for alternative interpretations of interviewee responses and attitudes.

Ultimately, it is suggested that this book has sought to ascertain a rational explanation for what might have been irrational behaviour. However, logic can never satisfactorily explain behaviour which is influenced primarily by emotion.

5.5. Suggestions for further research

The findings of this book and the identification of the limitations of the scope of its research highlight seven principal areas for further research. Firstly, much of the previous research indicates that there is a gender bias demonstrated by females towards compliance behaviour compared to that by males, which tends to veer away from compliant behaviour. That finding is not supported in this book, where it is established that demographic factors did not have any significant or meaningful influence on the participation rates in the mass-marketed tax avoidance schemes by Pilbara taxpayers.

However, there is an acknowledgement here that there was a predominance of males in the mining industry generally and in the Pilbara region in particular. Since 2000 females have been encouraged into the mining workforce as tradespeople. That change in demographic structure may provide a basis for future research into the influence of the demographic factor of gender through the examination of the same taxpayer population researched in this book at a later date.

Secondly, the peer influence of work colleagues on tax compliance behaviour could be further examined. The influence of work colleagues was illustrated in a comment made by a taxpayer who was outside of the groups of taxpayers interviewed here. He made an observation about the influence of age and a relationship with the influence of older work colleagues. He related his experiences as a military officer in the 1970s and 80s, observing that:

> Generally it struck me that the younger 'defaulters' may have been 'ignorant' in the true sense of the word (or naive). Schools do not teach anything about workplace employment and taxation etc to students (which I find incredible!!). My own experience of joining the RAAF was one of total ignorance regarding 'allotments' and such. I relied entirely upon advice from the Flight Sergeant etc.
>
> Single, young males geographically isolated from their familial support structures etc may be more susceptible to 'advice' from slick financial tax consultants trying to earn a commission. Consequently, they are more ignorant rather than deliberately avoiding tax. They received advice, and thought it was from a bona fide source and 'would save them tax'. One would be mad not to be involved (especially if everyone else is involved at work!). Almost the domino effect following on from Chinese whispers about the camp!

It is interesting to note that a person of 'junior' rank, who was actually older than those who were classified as being of 'senior' rank had a greater influence on attitudes towards conditions of employment than superior officers through the use of formal administrative channels. The use of informal administrative channels has long been a reality in management hierarchies.[257] That combination of influences could usefully be further investigated in terms of the influence on taxpayer compliance behaviour.

Thirdly, it is suggested that further research could be conducted into the impact of living conditions on taxpayer compliance behaviour. After 2000, living conditions for workers' families changed. To alleviate the impact of inhospitable living conditions of workers' families, a significant number of workers relocated their homes to Perth and other cities. To accommodate the desire of workers' families to live away from the Pilbara, the mining industry moved its workforce from being chiefly resident in the Pilbara, to being resident in Australia's major cities. 'Fly-in-fly-out' (FIFO) working patterns had been adopted by some employers in parts of the Pilbara and other mining regions in the early 1980s, but this has since become the principal working pattern for workers engaged in the remote mining regions of Australia, particularly since 2000.

This has resulted in a significant increase in the number of FIFO workers in the Pilbara and Goldfields regions of Western Australia. FIFO workers commute not only from the state capital of Perth but also from other major cities, including Melbourne, Sydney and Brisbane. International tourist destinations such as Indonesia, Malaysia and Thailand are also frequently visited during the periods of extended stand downs. Demand for travel to international destinations caused the town of Port Hedland to establish an international airport in 1999. Direct flights to destinations to Asia, and in particular Bali, have operated from Karratha for a number of years.

The introduction of FIFO working patterns has reduced the physical problems faced by families of workers living in harsh environments. It has reduced the impact of other factors which lead to social isolation and perceived distance from the government. It has also affected the significance of peer influence as workers' social groups are no longer confined to the isolated community groups as much as they were in the 1990s.

However, the long periods of absence from families have led to other social problems. A Federal parliamentary inquiry[258] into the social and economic impacts of FIFO work practices was held in 2012 in response to concerns raised by the

---

257 Charles R Milton, Lanny Entrekin and Bruce R Stening Organizational Behaviour in Australia (1984).

258 House Standing Committee on Regional Australia, Parliament of Australia, Inquiry into the use of 'fly-in, fly-out' (FIFO) workforce practices in regional Australia (2011).

Western Australian government and community health and social organisations. The committee reported to Parliament in 2013. It is suggested that the findings of the report may also lead to the need for further research in this area.

Interestingly, the working conditions which the blue-collar workers of the Pilbara endure have deteriorated due to the FIFO shift rotation systems. To facilitate the temporary nature of residence on site, longer hours are worked by those on shift and 14 hour days are 'normal' working hours. Therefore further research on the impact that FIFO working patterns may have on taxpayer compliance behaviour would be useful.

Fourthly, it is suggested that further research could be undertaken into other tax reducing activities or schemes. The apparent lack of tax avoidance activity by way of mass-marketed tax avoidance schemes in the 2000s suggests that the two major factors leading to high participation rates in tax avoidance activity by the class of taxpayer examined in this research appear to have diminished. However it may be that the cycle of tax avoidance scheme development, illustrated in Chapter Two, is in the 'design and growth' stage. If historical evidence is to be relied on, the next 'outbreak' will begin in the next few years and remain undetected for a few years after that. This may still occur despite attempts by tax administrators to improve detection of tax avoidance activity and the implementation of anti-avoidance measures. This study may provide a useful foundation for the further development of a grounded theory to support or refute the principle that harsh living and working conditions coupled with high personal income tax rates greatly increase taxpayers' propensity to reduce tax liabilities.

Once the tax schemes were closed down by the ATO in 2000 the blue-collar workers of the Pilbara region turned to other methods of reducing their tax, in particular the use of 'negatively geared' real estate investments. Though this is really beyond the scope of this research, the following table presents statistics which indicate that investment in negatively geared rental properties has sharply increased since 2000.

Town	Region	Postcode	Annual net rental losses ($)		
			1999	2001	2004
Kalgoorlie	Goldfields	6430	1 068	1 857	2 077
Dampier	Pilbara	6713	1 931	3 176	2 530
Pannawonica	Pilbara	6716	2 891	4 106	4 163
WA			150	1 260	2 226

Table 21 Negative income from rental properties in the Pilbara and Goldfields compared to all Western Australian taxpayers 1999-2004

The involvement of blue-collar workers in the real estate market was identified by a report published by Wizard Home Loans. Wizard chairman Mark Bouris said '[p]rofessionals are actually declining in numbers while blue-collar workers are on the rise, especially in WA and Queensland'.[259]

While it is recognised that there are many other social and economic factors which influenced Western Australia's growth in the real estate market in the early 2000s, the sharp growth of real estate investment by the mining communities of the Goldfields and Pilbara may not be regarded as merely being coincidental. This may reflect a switch from mass-marketed tax avoidance schemes (which were under intense ATO scrutiny at the time) to other tax-effective investment strategies.

Further research may reveal consistencies in taxpayer behaviour of the 1990s to enter into future tax avoidance activities influenced by high personal income tax rates coupled with heavy working and harsh living conditions in other regions and at other times. This book has suggested that tax avoidance activity simply crossed another boundary from unacceptable to acceptable activities. The primary motivational drivers continue to exist and so too does the potential for tax avoidance activity.

Therefore, whatever the primary influencing factors were for the participation in the mass-marketed tax avoidance schemes of the 1990s, those causes continue to exist. Personal income tax rates have been marginally reduced but remain comparatively high for relatively highly paid workers in the mining industry compared to other blue-collar workers. The blue-collar workers continue to carry out heavy work in a physically harsh environment, though they may no longer live there.

259 Mark Bouris, 'Blue-collar workers keen to invest', The West Australian (Perth) 2 September 2006, Real Estate.

Fifthly, this book has focused on the tax compliance behavioural attitudes of blue-collar workers in the mining and associated industries in the Pilbara region of Western Australia. It is suggested that other classes of workers in other industries and regions could be researched to investigate relationships between the factors examined in this book and other taxpayer behavioural attitudes.

Sixthly, and related to the preceding point, future research could further investigate the relationships between occupations, their related working conditions and perceptions of a fair tax rate to indicate taxpayer compliance behaviour focussed on occupation. In order to do this, the impact of occupation on attitudes towards tax avoidance activity could be further investigated.

The findings in Chapter Four indicated that professionals tend to be opposed to the use of tax minimisation schemes.[260] However, a more detailed examination of data from the ABC On-line (2007) survey, shown in Appendix C, revealed variations of opinion regarding the use of tax minimisation schemes by differing groups of professionals.

That examination, which indicates that the general opposition of professionals towards the use of tax minimisation schemes is not evenly distributed across professions, is outside the scope of this research. It is therefore suggested that the attitudes of professional groups could be further examined to provide a foundation for research into taxpayer compliance behaviour and the broader influences of occupation.

Finally, Chapter Four suggested that the perception of fairness is an overarching factor influencing taxpayer compliance behaviour and that is in turn is influenced by social, as well as occupational, peer groups. Thus, further research could be conducted into the strength of influence of social groups and in particular how they act to increase social distance from government and the resistance to paying tax.

5.6. Conclusion

In the 1990s, tax avoidance scheme designers and promoters began marketing their products in the remote and physically harsh environments of Western Australia's mining regions. They discovered a population of taxpayers who demonstrated an extremely high demand for their products. This research

260 ABC On-line (2007) survey; Table 12—53.8 per cent opposed as to 46.2 per cent in favour.

investigates why those taxpayers demonstrated an extremely high propensity to engage in the mass-marketed tax avoidance schemes.

During the course of conducting interviews with taxpayers, it became evident that a relationship existed between the degree of isolation and harshness of the physical environment, and their desire to engage in the mass-marketed tax avoidance schemes. Almost all of those taxpayers interviewed referred to high tax rates as justification for engaging in the mass-marketed tax avoidance schemes. Even some of those taxpayers interviewed, who were on lower incomes and associated income tax rates, expressed the opinion that it was fair for others to engage in the schemes. It also became evident that increased physical isolation and heavy working conditions exacerbated a feeling of social distance and increased the influence of work colleagues towards engaging in the mass-marketed tax avoidance schemes.

One of the blue-collar workers, who participated in the mass-marketed tax avoidance schemes, summed up what he saw as the overall reason for him and his workmates participating in the schemes. He put forward this observation:

> Most people that earn a lot of money, understand money. Like up here we don't. When I say like up here like, in this environment you know, we earn reasonable money, we pay a lot of tax but we don't understand it. You know, like and we were pretty easy bloody targets for them eh, that's my opinion.

On this basis, it seems reasonable to conclude that tax compliance was always unlikely to be wholly effective in the inhospitable climate encountered by the high income earners of the mining communities of Western Australia in the 1990s. As a result of this pent-up demand for their 'products', the promoters of mass-marketed tax avoidance schemes were able to mine a rich seam of potential participants in the Pilbara and similar communities.

APPENDICES

Appendix 'A'

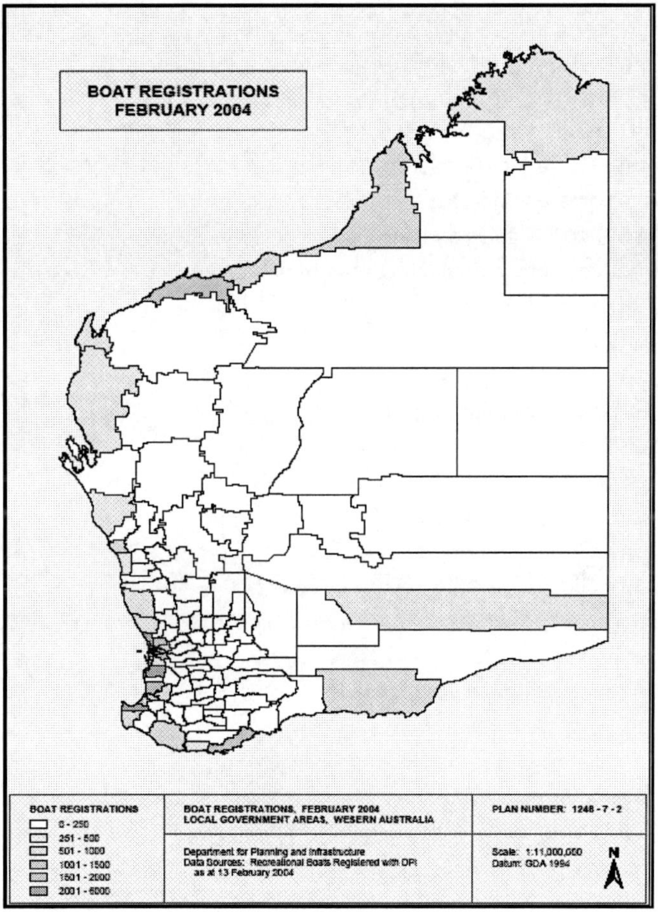

Figure 29 Map – Boat Registrations Western Australia 2004
(Source: Recreation Boats Registered with the
Western Australian Department of Planning and Infrastructure as at 13 February 2004)

Appendix 'B'

Eligible Schemes (2002)

The following schemes were considered to be 'eligible' for the purposes of the Commissioner's response to the Senate Committee inquiry into mass-marketed schemes and investor protection:

3 A Thin Life (Film Investment)
4 ABC Income & Growth Trust Funds Nos 1-9
5 ABC Maxi Earnings Growth Funds
6 Active Cattle Management
7 Amalgamated Publishers
8 Ambridge II Film Partnership
9 Ambridge Film Partnership: Eye of the Beholder
10 Analyze This (Film Investment)
11 Austimber Timber Pty Ltd
12 Austral Timber Pty Ltd
13 Australian Aloe Vera Project
14 Australian Beach Tales Films Project
15 Australian Country Clubs Limited
16 Australian Theatrical Library (Film Investment)
17 Austvin Vineyards Project 1997
18 Avoca Film Partnership: Love Lie Bleeding
19 Banalasta Natural Oils Joint Venture Project No1
20 Banalasta Oil Plantation Project No 1
21 Barkworth Olive Groves Project No 2
22 Barkworth Olives No1
23 Base Metals Exploration & Prospecting Project
24 Blaxland Breeders Trust
25 Bopple Macadamia Plantation Project Prospectus No 2
26 Botanical Books 1 & 2
27 Botanical Script
28 Business & Financial Strategy
29 Cabaret / Amadeus (Theatre Production)
30 Cattle Breeders Nominees Pty Ltd
31 Central Highlands Wine Grape Project No 1

32 Central Highlands Wine Grape Project No 2
33 Central Highlands Wine Grape Project No 3
34 Central Highlands Wine Grape Project No 4
35 Chalice Bridge 1998
36 Clockers (Film Investment)
37 Collective Compositions
38 Connect The World
39 Coonawarra Wine Grape Project 1998
40 CPE TV Series No 1 (Film Investment)
41 Crazy For You
42 Deadly Obsession (Film Investment)
43 Diamond Ridge Wine Grape Project 1998
44 East Kimberley Sandalwood Project No 1 1998
45 Educational Services Project No 1
46 Enviro Systems Renewable Resources
47 Equity Match Franchise 1995
48 Evita (Film Investment)
49 Fallen Angel (Film Investment)
50 First TrackNet Project
51 Fishing Information Line
52 Fortress II Stratoball / Critical Care (Film Investment)
53 Frankland Valley Vineyard Project 1997
54 Freedom Express
55 FX The Series (Film Investment)
56 Golden Triangle Books
57 Golden Vintage 1996 & 1997
58 Grand Hotel (Film Investment)
59 Groucho Film Partnership: A Walk on the Moon
60 Groucho II Film Partnership: Matrix (Production)
61 Groucho III Film Partnership: Deep Blue Sea
62 Harbourside (Film Investment)
63 Harcourt Ridge Estate
64 Harcourt Vines 1997
65 Harper Macrae
66 Heydon Park Tea Tree Project 1998
67 Highway Hero (Film Investment)
68 Hillston Grove Vineyard 1998

69 Hunter Equity Ltd
70 Hunter Valley Investment Scheme
71 HVM Holdings Limited
72 Infomercial Syndicates
73 Insurance Premium Finance (IPF) 1997
74 Insurance Premium Finance (IPF) 1998
75 Interest Recount
76 James Dean (Film Investment)
77 Karri Oak Vineyard 1998
78 Koala Hydroponics Project
79 Kringin Olive Project
80 Kununurra Tropical Forestry Project
81 Les Darcy Story (Film Investment)
82 Liar Liar (Film Investment)
83 Liquid Engineering Industrial
84 Love Until (aka Ugly Dumpling) (Film Investment)
85 Lucky Country (Film Investment)
86 Madison Pacific
87 Main Camp Tea Tree Oil Syndicate Project No 3
88 Main Camp Tea Tree Oil Syndicate Project No 4
89 Main Camp A Series No 1
90 Main Camp Company No 1
91 Main Camp Company No 2
92 Main Camp Company No 3
93 Main Camp Personal No 2
94 Main Camp Personal No 3
95 Main Camp Personal No 4
96 Main Camp Personal No 5
97 Main Camp Personal Syndicate
98 Malaysian Timber Supplies Ltd
99 Man on the Moon (Film Investment)
100 Mandalay Book Publishing "The Royal Cities of Asia"
101 Maranello Film Partnership
102 Matrix—Marketing (Film Investment)
103 Me & My Girl
104 Mean Streets—Blondes in Bikinis (Film Investment)
105 Mean Streets—Bullets For My Baby (Film Investment)

106 Mean Streets—On the Dead Side (Film Investment)
107 Mean Streets—One For a Kiss (Film Investment)
108 Merlin & Son (Film Investment)
109 Michael (Film Investment)
110 Monaro Community Enterprises Ltd
111 Music Scheme 1999
112 Native Foods—Lemon Myrtle Project No 1
113 Native Foods—Lemon Myrtle Project No 3
114 Netlink Hospitality Franchise Project 1997–2000
115 Nixon and The Shadow Conspiracy (Film Investment)
116 No Regrets
117 Northern Rivers Tea Tree Oil Project No1
118 Northern Rivers Tea Tree Oil Project No 2
119 Oil Fields Project No 2
120 Oil Fields Project No3
121 Oils of Nature Limited 1996
122 Oracle 1998
123 Oracle 1999
124 Ord River Sandalwood Project
125 Oz Refunds Franchise System
126 Pacific Drive Film Project
127 Pacific Tea Tree Plantations Project
128 Pay TV Project (Film Investment)
129 Peel Valley Mushrooms Project
130 Peter Pan
131 Pisces Aquaculture Joint Venture
132 Primo Publishing
133 Profound Holstein Breeding Project 1994
134 Profound Holstein Fresian Breeding Project 1992
135 Profound Holstein Fresian Breeding Project 1993
136 Progenitor (Film Investment)
137 QFP Park Pacific Investments
138 QFP Professionals Tomato Project
139 QFP Tomato Project
140 Queensland Essential Oils Limited
141 Rydal Hard Rock Joint Venture
142 *Satcom* Corporate Services Unit Trust

143 *Satcom* Electronic Commerce Services
144 *Satcom* Financial Services Unit Trust
145 Servcom Australia Pty Ltd Franchises
146 Shared Investment Corp Ltd
147 Shared Investment Group Ltd
148 Shattered Image (Film Investment)
149 Simple Simon / Mercury Rising (Film Investment)
150 Southern Highlands Horticultural Co-Operative Ltd
151 Sovereign Enterprise Equity Limited
152 Tarzan and Jane (Film Investment)
153 Tentas
154 Terri's Story (Film Investment)
155 The Boy Who Dared to Dream (Film Investment)
156 The Golden Years (Film Investment)
157 The Pageant (Film Investment)
158 Thin Red Line (Film Investment)
159 Thin Red Line Partnership II
160 Tiger Tiger
161 Towards a Wide World
162 Tradematch Licence
163 Treetop Apples Project
164 Treetop Plum Project
165 Treetop Supersweet Project
166 Wauchope Enterprise Equity
167 Wing Commander (Film Investment)

Appendix 'C'

The opinions of taxpayers relating to perception of fairness of use of tax minimisation schemes by profession

Question 13. How fair is it for individuals to use tax minimisation schemes?	Unfair / Very Unfair	Fair / Very Fair	Neither / Unsure	Total
Accountant / auditor	6 (30%)	11 (55%)	3 (15%)	20
Analyst	8 (47.1%)	5 (29.4%)	4 (23.5%)	17
Architect	1 (100%)	0	0	1
Computer professional	23 (54.8%)	9 (21.4%)	10 (23.8%)	42
Doctor	4 (36.4%)	7 (63.6%)	0	11
Educator / Teacher / Professor	62 (43.7%)	51 (35.9%)	29 (20.4%)	142
Engineer	7 (35.0%)	10 (50%)	3 (15.0%)	20
Health care worker	16 (33.3%)	22 (45.9%)	10 (20.8%)	48
Lawyer / Judge	6 (46.1%)	5 (38.5%)	2 (15.4%)	13
Military officer	0	3 (75.0%)	1 (25.0%)	4
Researcher	16 (57.1%)	4 (14.3%)	8 (28.6%)	28
Scientist	8 (44.4%)	8 (44.4%)	2 (11.2%)	18
Total	**157 (43.1%)**	**135 (37.1%)**	**72 (19.8%)**	**364**

Table 22 The opinions of taxpayers relating to perception of fairness of use of tax min-imisation schemes by profession
(Source: ABC On-line (2007) survey data)

BIBLIOGRAPHY

Articles / Books / Reports

Abercrombie, Nicholas, Hill, Stephen, and Turner, Bryan S, *The Penguin Dictionary of Sociology* (3rd ed, 1994).

Alexander, Craig, and Feinstein, Jonathon S, *A Microeconomic Analysis of Income Tax Evasion* (1987) cited in Erard, Brian, 'Taxation with Representation: An Analysis of the Role of Tax Practitioners in Tax Compliance' (1993) 52(2) *Journal of Public Economics* 163.

Allingham, Michael G, and Sandmo, Agnar, 'Income Tax Evasion: A Theoretical Analysis' (1972) 1 *Journal of Public Economics* 323.

Alm, James, Jackson, Betty and McKee, Michael, 'Institutional Uncertainty and Taxpayer Compliance' (1992) 82 *The American Economic Review* 1018.

Alm, James, Martinez-Vazquez, Jorge, and Wallace, Sally, 'Do Tax Amnesties Work? The Revenue Effects of Tax Amnesties During the Transition in the Russian Federation' (2009) 39(2) *Economic Analysis and Policy* 235.

Andreoni, James, Erard, Brian and Feinstein, Jonathan, 'Tax Compliance' (1998) 36 *Journal of Economic Literature* 818.

Ashby, Julie S, Webley, Paul, and Haslam, Alexander S, 'The Role of Occupational Taxpaying Cultures in Taxpaying Behaviour and Attitudes' (2009) 30 Journal *of Economic Psychology* 216.

Barnett, Kathleen and Grown, Caren, Gender Impacts of Government Revenue Collection: The Case of Taxation (2004).

Becker, Gary S, 'Crime and Punishment: An Economic Approach' (1968) 76 *Journal of Political Economy* 169.

Bernard, John, et al (eds), *Macquarie Concise Dictionary* (4th ed, 2006).

Bosco, Luigi, and Mittone, Luigi, 'Tax Evasion and Moral Constraints: Some Experimental Evidence' (1997) 50 (3) *Kyklos* 297.

Bracewell-Milnes, Barry, 'Is Tax Avoidance / Evasion a Burden on Other Taxpayers?', in Arthur Seldon (ed), *Tax Avoision* (1979) 105.

Braithwaite, John, 'Large Business and the Compliance Model', in Valerie Braithwaite (ed), *Taxing Democracy: Understanding Tax Avoidance and Evasion* (2003) 177.

Braithwaite, John, 'Through the Eyes of the Advisers: A Fresh Look at High Wealth Individuals' in Valerie Braithwaite (ed), *Taxing Democracy: Understanding Tax Avoidance and Evasion* (2003) 245.

Braithwaite, John, Markets in Vice: Markets in Virtue (2005).

Braithwaite, Valerie, 'A New Approach to Tax Compliance' in Valerie Braithwaite (ed), *Taxing Democracy: Understanding Tax Avoidance and Evasion* (2003), 1.

Braithwaite, Valerie, 'Games of Engagement: Postures within the Regulatory Community' (1995) 17 Law and Policy 225.

Brooks, Michael and Head, John, 'Tax Avoidance: in Economics, Law and Public Choice' in Graeme S Cooper (ed), *Tax Avoidance and the Rule of Law* (1997) 53.

Brooks, Neil, 'The Responsibility of Judges in Interpreting Tax Legislation', in Graeme S Cooper (ed), *Tax Avoidance and the Rule of Law* (1997) 93.

Brown, Charles V, Taxation and the Incentive to Work, (2nd ed, 1983).

Browne, Peter, 'Fair Shares' (1985) 52 Legal Services Bulletin as quoted in Ivan Potas, *'Thinking about Tax Avoidance'* (1993) 43 Australian Institute of Criminology: Trends & Issues in Crime and Criminal Justice, 2.

Christopher, Anthony, 'The Law is the Law is the Law' in Arthur Seldon (ed) *Tax Avoision* (1979) 75.

Clotfelter, Charles T, 'Tax Evasion and Tax Rules: An Analysis of Individual Returns' (1983) 65 *The Review of Economics and Statistics*, 363.

Clyne, Peter, The New Techniques of Tax Avoidance (1979).

Coleman, Cynthia, Hart, Geoffrey E and Sekhon, Jas S, *Income Tax Analysis—Cases, Questions and Commercial Applications* (2nd ed, 1997).

Coleman, Cynthia, and Freeman, Lynne, 'Cultural Foundations of Taxpayer Attitudes to Voluntary Compliance' in Simon R James (ed), *Taxation: Critical Perspectives on the World Economy* (2002) 140.

Crane, Stephen E and Nourzad, Farrokh, 'Tax Rates and Tax Evasion: Evidence from California Amnesty Data (1990) 43(2) *National Tax Journal* 189.

Davies, Christie, 'Can High Taxation be Enforced?' in Arthur Seldon (ed), *Tax Avoision* (1979) 59.

Department of Environment and Conservation (Western Australia), Proposed Burrup Peninsula Conservation Reserve Draft Management Plan 2006–2016 (2006).

Deutsch, Robert L et al, *Australian Tax Handbook 2000* (2000).

Deutsch, Robert L, 'Tax Reform: The never-ending saga' (2009) 8 *Atax Matters* 5.

Devos, Ken, 'Penalties and Sanctions for Australian Taxation Crimes and the Implications for Taxpayer Compliance' (2002) 17 *Australian Tax Forum* 257.

Devos, Ken, 'The Attitudes of Tertiary Students on Tax Evasion and the Penalties for Tax Evasion—A Pilot Study and Demographic Analysis' (2005) 3(2) *eJournal of Tax Research* 222.

Erard, Brian, 'Taxation with Representation: An Analysis of the Role of Tax Practitioners in Tax Compliance' (1993) 52(2) *Journal of Public Economics* 163.

Evans, Chris, et al, *A Report into the Taxpayer Costs of Compliance* (1997).

Evans, Chris, 'Studying the Studies: An overview of recent research into taxation operating costs' (2003) 1 (1) *eJournal of Tax Research* 64.

Evans, Chris, 'Taxation Compliance and Administrative Costs: An Overview', in Michael Lang et al (eds), *Tax Compliance Costs for Companies in an Enlarged European Community* (2008) 447.

Evans, Chris, 'The Battle Continues: Recent Australian Experience with Statutory Avoidance and Disclosure Rules' Judith Freedman (ed), *Beyond Boundaries: Developing Approaches to Tax Avoidance and Tax Risk Management* (2008) 37.

Faure, Micharel G and Visser, Marjolein, 'Law and economics of environmental crime' in Hans Sjögren and Göran Skogh (eds), *NewPerspectives on Economic Crime* (2004) 57.

Feldstein, Martin, 'The Effect of Marginal Tax Rates on Taxable Income: A Panel Study of the 1986 Tax Reform Act' (1995) 103(3) *The Journal of Political Economy* 551.

Freedman, Judith, 'Defining Taxpayer Responsibility: In support of a General Anti-Avoidance Principle' (2004) 4 *British Tax Review* 332.

Freedman, Judith, 'Beyond Boundaries: Developing Approaches to Tax Avoidance and Tax Risk Management' in Judith Freedman (ed), *Beyond Boundaries: Developing Approaches to Tax Avoidance and Tax Risk Management* (2008) 1.

Freiberg, Arie, 'Ripples from the Bottom of the Harbour: Some Social Ramifications of Taxation Fraud' (1998) 12 *Criminal Law Journal* 136, 137, as quoted in Braithwaite, John, *Markets in Vice: Markets in Virtue* (2005).

Friedland, Nehemia, Thibaut, John and Walker, Laurens 'Some Determinants of the Violation of Rules' (1973) 3(2) *Journal of Applied Social Psychology* 103.

Gammie, Malcolm, 'Tax Avoidance and the Rule of Law: A Perspective from the United Kingdom', in Graeme S Cooper (ed) *Tax Avoidance and the Rule of Law* (1997) 181.

Glover, John and Tran-Nam, Binh, 'The GST Recurrent Compliance Costs / benefits of Small Business in Australia: A Case Study Approach' (2005) 1(2) *Journal of the Australasian Tax Teachers Association* 237.

Grabosky, Peter, 'The Deputy Crown Solicitor and the bottom of the harbour scheme' in Peter N Grabosky (ed), *Wayward governance: illegality and its control in the public sector* (1989).

Graetz, Michael J, and Wilde, Louis L, 'The Economics of Tax Compliance: Fact and fantasy' (1985) 38(3) *National Tax Journal* 355.

Hasseldine, John, 'Gender Differences in Tax compliance' (1999) 3(2) *Asian-Pacific Tax Journal* 73.

Hayek, Friedrich August, *The Constitution of Liberty,* (1960) 438, in David R Myddelton, 'Tax Avoision—Its Costs and Benefits' in Arthur Seldon (ed), *Tax Avoision* (1979) 41.

Heywood, Andrew, *Political Ideologies—An Introduction* (2nd ed, 1998).

Hite, Peggy A and McGill, Gary A, 'An Examination of Taxpayer Preference for Aggressive Tax Advice' (1992) 45 (04) National Tax Journal 389.

Houston, Jodie and Tran, Alfred, 'A Survey of Tax Evasion Using the Randomized Response Technique' (2001) 13 *Advances in Taxation* 69.

Ilersic, Alfred R, 'The Economics of Avoidance / Evasion' in Arthur Seldon (ed), *Tax Avoision* (1979) 21.

Jary, David and Jary, Julia, *Collins Dictionary of Sociology* (3rd ed, 2000).

Kamleitner, Bernadette, Korunka, Christian, Kirchler, Erich, 'Tax compliance of small business owners: A review' (2012) 18(3) *International Journal of Entrepreneurial Behaviour & Research*, 330.

Kasipillai, Jeyapalan, Aripin, Norhani and Amran, Noor Afza 'The Influence of Education on Tax Avoidance and Tax Evasion' (2003) 1(2) *eJournal of Tax Research* 134.

Kirchler, Erich, The Economic Psychology of Tax Behaviour, (2007).

Krever, Richard, 'Plain English Drafting, Purposive Drafting, Principle Drafting: Does Any of it Matter?' in Judith Freedman (ed), *Beyond Boundaries: Developing Approaches to Tax Avoidance and Tax Risk Management* (2008) 189.

Kornhauser, Marjorie E, 'Normative and Cognitive Aspects of Tax Compliance: Literature Review and Recommendations for the IRS Regarding Individual Taxpayers' (2007) 2 *National Taxpayer Advocate Annual Report to Congress* 138.

Lapidoth, Arye, 'New Legislative Measures in Israel to Counter "Aggressive Tax Planning" ' (2006) 60 (6) *Bulletin for International Taxation* 255.

Levi, Margaret, *Of Rule and Revenue* (1988), as quoted in Braithwaite, John, *Markets in Vice: Markets in Virtue* (2005).

McBarnet, Doreen, 'When Compliance is not the Solution but the Problem: From Changes in Law to Changes in Attitude' in Valerie Braithwaite (ed), *Taxing Democracy* (2003) 229.

McBarnet, Doreen, and Whelan, Christopher, Creative Accounting and the Cross–Eyed Javelin Thrower (1999).

McKerchar, Margaret and Evans, Chris, 'Sustaining Growth in Developing Economies through Improved Taxpayer Compliance: Challenges for Policy Makers and Revenue Authorities' (2009) 7(2) *eJournal of Tax Research* 171.

Milton, Charles R, Entrekin, Lanny, and Stening, Bruce R, *Organizational Behaviour in Australia* (1984)

Moody, J Scott, Warcholik, Wendy P and Hodge, Scott A 'The Rising Cost of Complying with the Federal Income Tax' (2005) 138 *Special Report*.

Murphy, Kristina, 'An Examination of Taxpayers' Attitudes towards the Australian Tax System: Findings from a Survey of Tax Scheme Investors' (2003) 18 *Australian Tax Forum* 209.

Murphy, Kristina, 'Moving Forward Towards a More Effective Model of Regulatory Enforcement in the Australian Tax Office' (2004) 6 *British Tax Review* 603.

Murphy, Kristina, 'Aggressive tax planning: Differentiating those playing the game from those who don't', (2004) 25 *Journal of Economic Psychology'* 307.

Myddelton, David R, 'Tax Avoision—Its Costs and Benefits' in Arthur Seldon (ed), *Tax Avoision* (1979) 41.

Organisation for Economic Co-operation and Development, 'International Tax Avoidance and Evasion' *Issues in International Taxation* (1987, 1).

Organisation for Economic Co-operation and Development, *Study into the Role of Tax Intermediaries*, (2008).

Oxley, Prue and Elwela, Darshana, 'Tax Compliance Costs of New Zealand Small Businesses, 2004: Designing the Survey for its Policy Purpose', in Margaret McKerchar and Michael Walpole (eds), *Further Global Challenges in Tax Administration* (2006) 435.

Parsons, Talcott and Bales, Robert Freed, *Family, Socialization and Interaction Process*, (1955).

Pickup, David, 'In Relation to General Anti-Avoidance Provisions: A Comparative Study of the Legal Frameworks Used by Different Countries to Protect Their Tax Revenues' in Judith Freedman (ed) *Beyond Boundaries: Developing Approaches to Tax Avoidance and Tax Risk Management* (2008) 9.

Potas, Ivan, 'Thinking about Tax Avoidance' (1993) 43 *Trends & Issues in Crime and Criminal Justice*.

Rawlings, Gregory, 'Cultural Narratives of Taxation and Citizenship: Fairness, Groups and Globalisation' (2003) 38(3) *Australian Journal of Social Issues* 269.

Richardson, Sir Ivor, 'Reducing Tax Avoidance by Changing Structures, Processes and Drafting', in Graeme S Cooper (ed) *Tax Avoidance and the Rule of Law* (1997) 327.

Roth, Jeffrey A, Scholz, John T, and Witte, Ann Dryden 'Understanding Taxpayer Compliance: Self-Interest, Social Commitment, and Other Influences' in Jeffrey A Roth, John T Scholz and Ann Dryden Witte (eds), *Taxpayer Compliance Volume 1: An Agenda for Research* (1989) 71.

Seldon, Arthur, 'Avoision: The Moral Blurring of a Legal Distinction without an Economic Difference' in Arthur Seldon(ed), *Tax Avoision* (1979) 1.

Shover, Neal, Job, Jenny, and Carroll, Anne, 'The ATO Compliance Model in Action: A Case Study of Building and Construction', in Valarie Braithwaite (ed), *Taxing Democracy: Understanding Tax Avoidance and Evasion* (2003) 159.

Slemrod, Joel and Yitzhaki, Shlomo, 'Tax Avoidance, Evasion, and Administration' in Alan J Auerbach and Martin Feldstein (eds), *Handbook of Public Economics* (2002) 3, 1423.

Smith, Kent W, and Kinsey, Karyl A, 'Understanding Taxpaying Behaviour: A Conceptual Framework with Implications for Research' (1987) 21 (4) *Law and Society Review* 639.

Stiglitz, Joseph E, 'The Effects of Income, Wealth, and Capital Gains Taxation on Risk-Taking' (1969) 83 *Journal of Public Economics* 263.

Taylor, Natalie, 'Understanding Taxpayer Attitudes Through Understanding Taxpayer Identities' in Valerie Braithwaite (ed), *Taxing Democracy: Understanding Tax Avoidance and Evasion* (2003) 71.

Torgler, Benno, Tax Compliance and Tax Morale: A Theoretical and Empirical Analysis (2007).

Torgler, Benno and Schaltegger, Christopher A, 'Tax amnesties and political participation' in Benno Torgler (ed) *Tax Compliance and Tax Morale: A Theoretical and Empirical Analysis* (2007) 264.

Tutt, Nigel, The Tax Raiders: The Rossminister Affair (1985).

Tyler, Tom R, Why People Obey the Law (2006).

Vanistendael, Frans, 'Judicial Interpretation and the Role of Anti-Abuse Provisions in Tax Law', in Graeme S Cooper (ed) *Tax Avoidance and the Rule of Law* (1997) 131.

Vitenbergs, Anna and Brehaut, Loreen, *Pilbara Journey: Through the Twentieth Century* (2000).

Vogel, Joachim, 'Taxation and Public Opinion in Sweden: An interpretation of recent survey data' (1974) 27(4) *National Tax Journal* 73.

Waincymer, Jeffrey, 'The Australian Tax Avoidance Experience and Responses: A Critical Review' in Graeme S Cooper (ed) *Tax Avoidance and the Rule of Law* (1997) 247.

Wallschutzky, Ian G, 'Possible Causes of Tax Evasion' (1984) 5 *Journal of Economic Psychology* 371.

Wallschutzky, Ian G, Taxpayer Attitudes to Avoidance and Evasion (1985).

Wallschutzky, Ian G, and Gibson, Brian, 'Small Business Cost of Tax Compliance' (1993) 10 *Australian Tax Forum*.

Watts, Duncan J, Everything is Obvious: How Common Sense Fails, (2011).

Webley, Paul, 'Tax compliance by business' in Hans Sjögren and Göran Skogh (eds), *NewPerspectives on Economic Crime* (2004) 95.

Wenzel, Michael, 'Motivation or rationalisation? Causal relations between ethics, norms and tax compliance' (2005) 26 *Journal of Economic Psychology* 491.

Willott, Sara and Griffin, Chris, 'Building your own lifeboat: Working-class male offenders talk about economic crime' (1999) 38 *British Journal of Social Psychology* 445.

Woellner, Robin, et al. *1997 Australian Taxation Law* (7th ed. 1997).

Woellner, Robin, et al, 'Can Simplified Legal Drafting Reduce the Psychological Costs of Tax Compliance? An Australian Perspective' (2007) *British Tax Review* 717.

Worsham, Ronald G, 'The Effect of Tax Authority Behaviour on Taxpayer Compliance: A Procedural Justice Approach' (1996) 18(2) *Journal of American Taxation Association*.

Case Law

Commissioner of Taxation v La Rosa [2003] FCAFC 125.

Curran v Federal Commissioner of Taxation (1974) 74 ATC 4296.

Ensign Tankers (Leasing) Ltd v Stokes [1992] 1 AC 655.

Federal Commissioner of Taxation v Everett (1980) 10 ATR 608.

Federal Commissioner of Taxation v Sleight [2004] FCAFC 94.

Federal Commissioner of Taxation v Spotless Services Ltd (1996) 34 ATR 183.

Howland-Rose and Ors v Federal Commissioner of Taxation [2002] FCA 246.

IR Commrs v Brebner (1967) 43 TC 718.

Jacques v Federal Commissioner of Taxation (1924) 34 CLR 328 at 358.

Krampel Newman Partners Pty Ltd v Federal Commissioner of Taxation [2003] FCA 123.

Meredith v Federal Commissioner of Taxation and Ors [2001] FCA 1135.

Meredith v Federal Commissioner of Taxation [2002] FCAFC 271.

Phillips v Federal Commissioner of Taxation (1978) ATR 783.

Puzey v Federal Commissioner of Taxation [2003] FCAFC 197.

R v Charlton [1996] STC 1418.

Russell v Federal Commissioner of Taxation (2009) FCA 1224.

Ryan v Federal Commissioner of Taxation [2004] ATC 2181.

Tupicoff v Commissioner of Taxation (1984) ATC 4851 and 15 ATR 1262.

Vabu Pty Ltd v Federal Commissioner of Taxation (1996) ATC 4898.

Vincent v Federal Commissioner of Taxation [2002] FCAFC 291.

Legislation

Australia

Acts Interpretation Act 1901 (Cth).

Fringe Benefits Tax Assessment Act 1986 (Cth).

Income Tax Assessment Act 1936 (Cth).

New Business Tax System (Alienation of Personal Services Income) Act 2000 (Cth).

Taxation Administration Act 1953 (Cth).

Tax Agent Services Act 2009 (Cth).

Singapore

Income Tax Act 1948 (Singapore).

Other Sources

ABC Television, 'The Crackdown', *Four Corners,* 18 June 2001 <http://www.abc.net.au/4corners/stories/s312807.htm> at 17 August 2013,

ABC On-line (2007) survey <http://www.onlineopinion.com.au>.

Agell, Jonas, and Persson, Mats, 'Tax Arbitrage and Labour Supply' (Working Paper No 6708, National Bureau of Economic Research, 1998).

Apps, Patricia and Rees, Ray, 'Household Production, Full Consumption and the Costs of Children' (Discussion Paper No 157, The Institute for the Study of Labor (IZA), 2000.

The Auditor-General of Australia Audit Report No.23 2003-04 Performance Audit The Australian Taxation Office's Management of Aggressive Tax Planning <http://www.anao.gov.au/WebSite.nsf/Publications/87DA23D16D5A18B2CA256E290003B3A6> at 31 March 2005.

Australia State of the Environment Report 2001 (Theme Report) Prepared by: Ann Hamblin, Bureau of Rural SciencesCSIRO Publishing on behalf of the Department of the Environment and Heritage <http://www.deh.gov.au/soe/2001/land/land01-10.html> at 3 September 2005.

Australian Bureau of Statistics, 1220.0—Australian Standard of Classification of Occupations (2nd ed 1997).

Australian Bureau of Statistics, Census Data <http://www.abs.gov.au/AUSSTATS/abs@.nsf//web+pages/Census+Data> at 1 April 2008.

Australian Bureau of Statistics, Details Page <http://www.abs.gov.au/ausstats/abs@.nsf/DetailsPage> at 22 September 2007.

Australian Bureau of Statistics, 1367.5 Western Australian Statistical Indicators Labour Feature Article—Regional wage and salary earners in Western Australia (2004).

Australian Bureau of Statistics, 2020.0 Basic Community Profile—Australia: 1996 Census of Population and Housing (2000).

Australian Bureau of Statistics, 2020.5 Basic Community Profile—Western Australia—Pilbara: 1996 Census of Population and Housing (2000).

Australian Bureau of Statistics, 2020.5 Basic Community Profile—Western Australia: 1996 Census of Population and Housing (2000).

Australian Bureau of Statistics, 2710.0 Census Characteristic of Australia: 1991Census of Population and Housing (1993).

Australian Bureau of Statistics, 2730.5 Census Counts for Small Areas: Western Australia 1991 Census of Population and Housing (1993).

Australian Bureau of Statistics, 3228.0.55.001 – Population Estimates: Concepts, Sources and Methods, (2009).

Australian Bureau of Statistics, 6101.0 – Labour Statistics Australia (1985).

Australian Bureau of Statistics, 6306.0 – Employee Earnings and Hours, Australia Aug 2008, (2009).

Australian Bureau of Statistics, 1991 Census of Population—Regional Profile, State Library of Western Australia, (2010).

Australian Bureau of Statistics, 1996 Census of Population and Housing—Basic Community Profile (2000).

Australian Bureau of Statistics, 2001.0 2001a, Basic Community Profile for Pilbara—Community Profile (2002).

Australian Bureau of Statistics, Census of Population and Housing Selected Social and Housing Characteristics Australia 2001 (2003).

Australian Bureau of Statistics, 2001 Census QuickStats : Pannawonica (L) (Urban Centre/Locality) <http://www.censusdata.abs.gov.au/> at 30 August 2010.

Australian Bureau of Statistics, Basic Community Profile—Australia: 2006 Census of Population and Housing, (Catalogue 2001.0, 2007).

Australian Bureau of Statistics, Basic Community Profile—Western Australia: 2006 Census of Population and Housing, (Catalogue 2001.0, 2007).

Australian Bureau of Statistics, Basic Community Profile—Western Australia: Pilbara (Statistical Division) 2006 Census of Population and Housing, (Catalogue 2001.0, 2007).

Australian Bureau of Statistics, Basic Community Profile—Pilbara: 2011 Census of Population and Housing, (Catalogue 2001.0, 2012).

Australian Bureau of Statistics, 2001g, A profile of the Region, Development Commission Region of Pilbara, Western Australia, <http://www.istp.murdoch.edu.au/Susty_case_studies/Pilbara/socio-cultural/Demographics.htm> at 3 September 2005.

Australian Bureau of Statistics, Australian National Accounts: National Income, Expenditure and Product, (Catalogue 5206.0, Table 7, 2012).

Australian Government Bureau of Meteorology <http://www.bom.gov.au/climate/map/temperature/IDCJCM0005 temperature.shtml> at 19 July 2007.

Australian Securities and Investments Commission database at <http://wwww.search.asic.gov.au/cgi-bin/gns030c> at 22 December 2005.

Australian Securities and Investments Commission's database <http://wwww.search.asic.gov.au/cgi-bin/gns030c> at 8 July 2008.

Australian Taxation Office, Taxation Ruling TR 2006/2, <http://law.ato.gov.au/atolaw/view.htm?docid=TXR/TR20062/NAT/ATO/00001> at 15 June 2008.

Australian Taxation Office, Taxation Statistics 1994-95 (1997), provided on compact disc by ATO.

Australian Taxation Office, Taxation Statistics 1995-96 (1998), provided on compact disc by ATO.

Australian Taxation Office, Taxation Statistics 1996-97 (1999), provided on compact disc by ATO.

Australian Taxation Office, Taxation Statistics 1997-98 (2000), provided on compact disc by ATO.

Australian Taxation Office, Taxation Statistics 1998-99 (2001), provided on compact disc by ATO.

Australian Taxation Office, Taxation Statistics 1999-2000 to 2005-06 available from, ATO, Home > Corporate> General Accountability Information> Taxation statistics>Personal Tax (2008) Australian Taxation Office <http://www.ato.gov.au/corporate/content.asp?doc=/content/00117625.htm&page=33> at 23 June 2008.

Australian Taxation Office, Taxation Statistics 2009-10 (2012).

Australian Taxation Office, The Commissioner of Taxation—Annual Report 2009–2010.

Australian Taxation Office, 'Tax Office on target' (media release 97/50, 30 October 1997).

Australian Taxation Office, 'New warning for tax scheme investors' (media release 2000/101, 30 October 2000).

Australian Taxation Office, 'Most mass marketed scheme investors set to benefit from interest reduction' (media release 2001/58 23 July 2001).

Australian Taxation Office, 'Tax Office announces settlement offer for mass marketed scheme investors' (media release 2002/07, 14 February 2002).

Australian Taxation Office, 'Practical guide to Part IVA' (media release 2005/70, 13 December 2005).

Australian Taxation Office, 'Test Case Litigation Program', <http://www.ato.gov.au/taxprofessionals/content.asp?doc=/content/57395.htm> at 12 July 2008.

Australian Taxation Office, Miscellaneous Tax Ruling MT 2012/3, 4 June 2010.

Australian Taxation Office, 'Cooperative Compliance Model' <http://www.ato.gov.au/Businesses/content.aspx?menuid=0&doc=/content/22630.htm&page=13&H13> at 9 September 2011.

Australian Taxation Office, Taxation Ruling TR 94/8.

Australian Taxation Office, 'Individual Tax Return Instructions 2013' <http://www.ato.gov.au/Individuals/Tax-return/2013/In-detail/Publications/Tax-return-for-individuals-2012-13/> at 17 August 2013.

Baume, Michael, Member for Macarthur, (Speech delivered in the Commonwealth House of Representatives, Canberra, 5 May 1978) as quoted in Woellner, Robin, et al. 1997 Australian Taxation Law (7th ed. 1997).

Bouris, Mark, 'Blue-collar workers keen to invest', The West Australian (Perth) 2 September 2006, Real Estate 3.

Chand, Satish, 'International tax arbitrage via corporate income splitting' (Working Paper No 02-1, Australian National University Asia Pacific School of Economics and Government, 2002).

Charles Sturt University Australian Emergency Management Forum Hazards Disasters and Survival <http://www.csu.edu.au/faculty/arts/sslib/aemf/HDS/chapter_7.htm> at 13 March 2008.

Commonwealth of Australia and Victoria, Royal Commission on the Activities of the Federated Ship Painters and Dockers Union, Final Report (1984) vol 1 (Costigan Report).

Commonwealth of Australia, Official Committee Hansard; Senate Inquiry Reference: Mass marketed tax effective schemes and investor protection, Canberra, 26 July 2001, E 736.

D'Ascenzo, Michael, 'In Defence of the Rule of Law' (Speech delivered at the Taxation Law Workshop, Aitken Hill, Victoria, 26–28 October 2001).

Daude, Christian, Gutiérrez, Hamlet and Melguizo, Ángel, 'What Drives Tax Morale?' (Working Paper No 315, Organisation for Economic Co-operation and Development Development Centre, 2012).

Department of Land Administration (Western Australia), History of Country Town Names (2006) <http://www.dli.wa.gov.au/corporate.nsf/web/History+of+country+town+names> at 19 February 2006.

Devos, Ken, Penalties and Sanctions for Australian Taxation Crimes and Their Effect on Taxpayer Compliance' (Paper presented at the 5th International Conference on Tax Administration, Atax UNSW, Sydney, 4 April 2002).

Devos, Ken, An Investigation of the Factors which influence and Deter the Compliance Behaviour of Australian Individual Taxpayers, (Unpublished PhD thesis, Monash University, Australia, 2011).

Devos, Ken, 'An Assessment of the Influence of Sanctions and other Factors upon International Taxpayer Compliance', (Paper presented at the Tax Governance, Vienna, 20-21 September 2012), 56.

Email from Kristina Murphy to Alexander Fullarton, 20 September 2007.

Email from John Craig to Alexander Fullarton, 4 April 2011.

Emerging Industries on the Burrup: Skill Needs and Strategies <http://www.training.wa.gov.au/resources/docs/Burruppercent20Taskforcepercent20Report.pdf> at 11 June 2006.

Facsimile from Peter Marshall, General Manager Main Camp Tea Tree Oil Limited, to Alexander R Fullarton, 10 April 2002.

Fjeldstad, Odd-Heige and Semboja, Joseph, 'Why people pay taxes: The case of the development levy in Tanzania' (Working Paper No 1998:5, Chr. Michelsen Institute, 1998).

Ginting, Edimon, 'Can Tax Reform Work in an Economy Where Tax Avoidance and Evasion are Endemic?' (Paper presented at the Ph.D Conference in Economics and Business, University of Western Australia, November 1997).

Gruen, Nicholas, 'Tax Cuts to Compete: The influence of Corporate Taxation on Australia's Economic Growth', (Information Paper No 85, Committee for Economic Development of Australia, 2006).

Gupta, Ranjana, 'How the Perceptions of Tax Evasion as a Crime mirror the Penalties' (Paper presented at the Australasian Tax Teachers' Association Conference, Brisbane Qld, 23 January 2007).

Hobson, Kersty, 'Say No to the ATO': The Cultural Politics of Protest against the Australian Tax Office' (Working Paper No 37, Centre for Tax System Integrity, 2002).

House Standing Committee on Regional Australia, Parliament of Australia, Inquiry into the use of 'fly-in, fly-out' (FIFO) workforce practices in regional Australia (2011).

Interview with Lindsay Gibson, Principal Ray White Karratha (Karratha, 7 June 2006).

Interview with Glen Jennings, Manager College Information Systems, Pilbara TAFE Karratha Campus (Karratha, 8 June 2006).

Interviews with respondents to research.

Karlinsky, Stewart and Bankman, Joseph, 'Developing a Theory of Cash Businesses Tax Evasion Behaviour and the Role of Their Tax Preparers' (Paper presented at the 5th International Conference on Tax Administration, Atax Faculty of Law, University of New South Wales, Sydney, 4-5 April 2002), 136.

Lampathakis, Paul, 'Justice Scandal: Brokers let off', The Sunday Times (Perth WA) 30 November 2008, 28.

Legislative Assembly of the Australian Capital Territory, Report on 2003 National Conference of Public Works and Environment Committees 'The Sustainability of Regional Development Addressing The Triple Bottom Line' Vicki Dunne MLA Chair 8 August 2003. <http://www.legassembly.act.gov.au/committees/reports/pe22conference.pdf> at 3 September 2005.

Letter from Michael Carmody, Australian Commissioner of Taxation, to Thomas Anderson, 28 March 2002 (held by the author).

Letter from the Director Aggressive Tax Planning Australian Taxation Office to Alexander R Fullarton, 16 December 2008 (held by the author).

Letter from Malcolm McLean to Maxwell K Young, 18 June 1998 (held by the author).

Letter from Mr Robert K O'Connor to Messrs Clayton Utz, 28 August 1997, in Satcom Electronic Services Franchise Business Opportunity Disclosure Document August 1997 (held by author).

Letter from Serra and Company to Maxwell K Young, 20 May 1998 (held by author).

Letter from Serra & Company to a scheme participant, 27 May 1997 (held by author).

Loo, Ern Chen, McKerchar, Margaret and Hansford, Ann, 'Tax Compliance Behaviour: Findings Derived from a Mixed Method Design' (Paper presented at the 8th International Tax Administration Conference, Sydney, 28 March 2008).

Marriott, Lisa, Randall, John and Holmes, Kevin, 'Influences on Tax Evasion Behaviour: Insights from a behavioural simulation experiment' (Paper presented at the Australasian Tax Teachers' Association Conference, Sydney NSW, 21 January 2010).

McKerchar, Margaret Anne, The Impact of Complexity Upon Unintentional Non-compliance for Australian Personal Income Taxpayers (PhD Thesis, University of New South Wales, 2002).

Meriküll, Jaanika and Staehr, Karsten, 'Unreported employment and tax evasion in mid-transition: Comparing developments and causes in the Baltic States' (Working Paper No 6/2008, Bank of Estonia, 2008).

Murphy, Kristina, 'The Role of Trust in Nurturing Compliance: A Study of Tax Scheme Investors' (Paper presented at the Current Issues in Regulation: Enforcement Compliance Conference, Melbourne 2-3 September 2002).

Murphy, Kristina, Mass Marketed tax schemes: Findings from a survey of investors (2003) <http://ctsi.anu.edu.au/UP.Murphy.taxschemes.html> at 10 May 2005.

Murphy, Kristina and Byng, Karen, 'A User's Guide to 'The Australian Tax System Survey of Tax Scheme Investors' ' (Working Paper No 39, Centre for Tax System Integrity, 2002).

Myers, Allan J, 'Tax Avoidance and the High Court since Sir Garfield Barwick' (Lecture delivered at the Melbourne Law School, University of Melbourne, 12 April 2005.

North West Shelf LNG Pty Ltd, 'A Brief History of the North West Shelf', (Press release, June 2003) <http://www.australialng.com.au/downloads/NWSALNG_brochure.pdf> at 15 February 2006.

Parker, Gareth, 'It's $1000 a week or rent a tent in Karratha', *The West Australian* (Perth, Western Australia) 17 June 2006, News 7.

Prebble, Zoë and Prebble, John, 'The morality of Tax Avoidance: Why the Legal Difference Between Evasion and Avoidance is Insufficient to Ground a Moral Distinction' (Paper presented at the Australasian Tax Teachers Association Annual Conference University of Tasmania, January 2008).

Satcom Electronic Services Pty Ltd, Business Opportunity Disclosure Document, (August 1997).

Scadding, Garry, Non-Indigenous History of the Pilbara (undated) <http://www.istp.murdoch.edu.au/Susty_case_studies/Pilbara/socio-cultural/Non-Indigenous_History.htm#mining> at 3 September 2005.

Senate Economics References Committee, Parliament of the Commonwealth of Australia, Inquiry into Mass Marketed Tax Effective Schemes and Investor Protection Interim Report (2001).

Shoebridge, Joanne, 'Tea tree growers confident better times are just around the corner', Landline, 11 April 2004 <http://www.abc.net.au/landline/content/2004/s1081381.htm> at 4 May 2010.

Sydenstricker-Neto, John, Research Design and Mixed-Method Approach; A Hands-on Experience (1997) <http://www.socialresearchmethods.net/tutorial/Sydenstricker/bolsa.html#Research> at 4 August 2010.

Tanzi, Vito L, 'Globalization, Technological Developments, and the Work of Fiscal Termites' (Working Paper No. 00/181International Monetary Fund, November 2000).

Wadhawan, Satish C. and Gray, Clive, 'Enhancing Transparency in Tax Administration: A Survey' (Discussion Paper No 3, United States Agency for International Development Bureau for Africa Office of Sustainable Development, 1998).

Webley, Paul, Adams, Caroline, and Elffers, Henk, 'VAT Compliance in the United Kingdom'(Working Paper No 41, Centre for Tax System Integrity, 2002).

Western Australian Electoral Commission, State Elections, <http://www.waec.wa.gov.au/elections/> at 3 February 2013.

Witte, Ann Dryden, 'What Factors Affect Voluntary Compliance? The Impact of Tax Laws, Tax Administration and Taxpayer Attitudes on Taxpayer Behaviour' (Paper presented at the Tax Compliance Intensive Weekend Workshop, Bowral NSW Australia, 25-27 August 1989).

***ibidem*-Verlag**
Melchiorstr. 15
D-70439 Stuttgart
info@ibidem-verlag.de

www.ibidem-verlag.de
www.ibidem.eu
www.edition-noema.de
www.autorenbetreuung.de